RED CROWN
& DRAGON

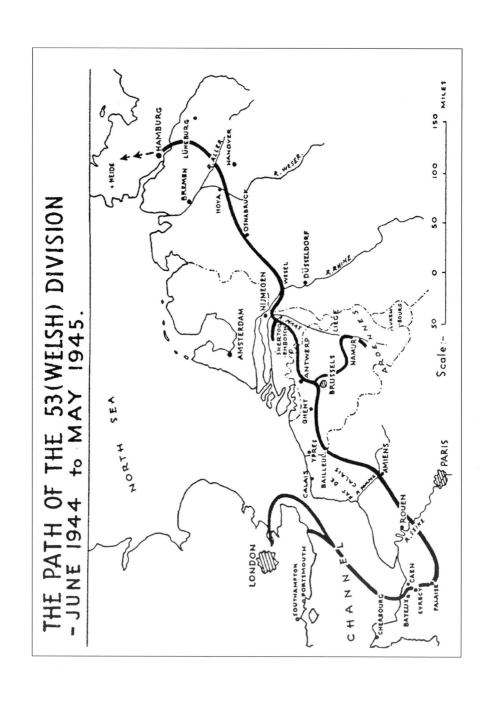

THE PATH OF THE 53 (WELSH) DIVISION — JUNE 1944 to MAY 1945.

RED CROWN & DRAGON

53rd Welsh Division in North-West Europe 1944–1945

PATRICK DELAFORCE

AMBERLEY

First published 1996 by Tom Donovan Publishing
This paperback edition first published 2009

Amberley Publishing
Cirencester Road, Chalford,
Stroud, Gloucestershire, GL6 8PE

www.amberley-books.com

Copyright © Patrick Delaforce, 2009

The right of Patrick Delaforce to be identified as
the Author of this work has been asserted in
accordance with the Copyrights, Designs and
Patents Act 1988.

ISBN 978 1 84868 817 9

British Library Cataloguing in
Publication Data.

A catalogue record for this book is available
from the British Library.

Typeset in 10pt on 13.5pt Sabon.
Typeset by FonthillMedia.
Printed in the UK.

CONTENTS

Introduction

Amongst the half dozen British divisions who trained and exercised for nearly four and a half years in WWII, before being flung into the cauldron of the Normandy beachhead battles — was 53rd Welsh Division.

When Field Marshal Sir Bernard Montgomery was presented with the Freedom of the Borough of Newport shortly after the end of hostilities he declared '53 Welsh Division has been and is, one of my best divisions'. And General Dempsey, the British Second Army Commander, said of the Division after the Reichwald and Rethem battles 'You fought like tigers against the best German troops on the whole front'.

Under their GOC Major General 'Bobby' Ross CB, DSO, MC they fought almost non-stop for ten months, suffered 10,000 battle casualties and gained a fine Victoria Cross in Normandy. At the outbreak of war the three Brigades were of course embodied in Wales. 158 (North Wales) Brigade at Wrexham, 160 (South Wales) Brigade at Cardiff and 159 (Welsh Borders) Brigade at Hereford. The latter subsequently became the infantry brigade of the author's 11th Armoured Division.

The Royal Welch Fusiliers had three battalions in 158 Brigade, (4th, 6th and 7th), but also formed the 71st Anti-tank Regt RA (RWF) and the 116th (RWF) Light AA Regt RA. The Welch Regt had two battalions (4th and 1/5th) in 160 Brigade, with 2nd Battalion the Monmouthshire Regt as their third formation.

In late 1943 71st Brigade joined the Division, nicknamed the 'Foreign' or 'International' Brigade with 1st Battalion Highland Light Infantry (from Glasgow), 1st Battalion Oxfordshire & Buckinghamshire Light Infantry and 1st Battalion East Lancashire Regt.

The medium machine guns and heavy mortars of the 1st Manchesters, the three Field Regiments RA (81st, 83rd and 133rd) provided an awesome artillery support.

On their way to Hamburg, the 'Red Crown and Dragon' Division gained many battle honours including Evrecy, 's-Hertogenbosch, the Ardennes, the Reichwald and the several German river battles.

This book is dedicated to the memory of the many young soldiers of the Division who fell in battle in France, Belgium, Holland and Germany in the final campaign of WWII.

Acknowledgements

'Bud' Abbot, Donald Arnott, David Bolland OBE, MBE (diary & letters home), Wallace Brereton, Ted Cheetham, Alistair Carmichael, A. Christianson FCA, William Clowes & Sons Ltd, Jim Cooper, J. D. Cuthbertson, Lt Col P. A. Crocker (Curator Royal Welch Fusiliers Museum, Caernarfon), Robert H. Chapman, Major R. N. Deane, Major T. C. C. Dumas, Sydney Griffiths, Luc Van Gent MBE, Michael Hannon, Colonel J. M. Grundy (Curator Royal Regt of Wales Museum, Brecon), General Sir Charles Harington GCB, CBE, DSO, MC, Norman Havard, David Henderson, Lt Col R. E. H. Hudson, H. C. Kenway, R. J. H. Lloyd, Major A. J. Lewis MC, Ron Ludgater, Harry Martin, Lt Col B. E. W. McCall MC, John Moore, Desmond P. B. Milligan, David Morgan, Eric Morgan, John Ogle, Bryn Owen FMA (Curator Welch Regt Museum, Cardiff), John A. Ottewell, William Tudor Owen, A. D. Payne, Lt Col Graham Povey, Irfon Roberts, John H. Roberts, Brigadier M. H. ap Rhys Pryce, Lt Col R. J. M. Sinnett, MEW Slade, Fred Smerdon, Richard Trevor, Peter Utley FRSA, Percy Upton, Laurie Woolard, Lt Col A. H. Williams DSO.

I

The Great War & The Limbo Years

The role of the 53rd Division in the First World War is admirably chronicled in Major C. H. Dudley Ward's History published in 1927. From 1915 to 31 October 1918, the Welshmen fought, not the Germans, but their tough rugged Turkish allies (often officered by the Germans). They fought in the savage doomed campaign known as the 'Immortal Gamble' at Gallipoli, Suvla Bay and Mudros. Small pitched battles were fought at Lala Baba, Chocolate Hill, Anafarta, Scimitar Hill and Kisla Dagh. In 1916 they re-formed in Egypt and for the next two years fought in Palestine. They marched across the Sinai Desert from Kantara on the canal to Gaza. Two pitched battles fought in March and April were unsuccessful. General Allenby then took command of the Egyptian Expeditionary Force. When 158 Brigade stormed the heights of Khuweilfeh on 5 November 52 Lowland and 54 East Anglia Divisions finally captured Gaza. Then the Welshmen helped capture Jerusalem on 9 December 1917. The following year they eventually seized Chipp Hill, a key height in Judea and then crossed the river Jordan. Throughout 1918 they fought in the Jordan valley. When the Turkish Armistice was signed on 31 October they returned to Kantara and Alexandria. The campaigns in Palestine were fought in intense heat and the dreaded scorching wind — the Khamsin — forced the temperature up to 130 degrees in the shade. J. N. More's 'Dug-out Doggerel':

> Yes! Such is the Khamsin, dreaded breeze
> With the heat of Hell as its brother
> O! Merciful God, we would rather freeze
> Than pant in the throes of another!

Water was scarce, often brackish, and was rationed to half a gallon per man per day. The Turks, commanded by skilled German generals, often with defensive lines of prickly pear cactus, were a formidable foe.

THE LIMBO YEARS: 1939

The unusual divisional sign was devised by Major General B. N. Wilson CB, DSO, who commanded on mobilisation in 1939. It took the form of a red W, the base of the letter resting on a horizontal bar. On transport the W was shown on a green background but on uniform it was on a khaki background. Brigades were allocated one (158) two (159) or three bars (160 Brigade). The badge not only stood for Wales but was symbolic of a Bardic Crown. Major General Wilson said, 'That is a Welsh Crown'. 'Bobby' Ross who took the Division to Normandy in 1944 promised that he would never alter the sign. Once it came under fire in France its retention was certain.

*   *   *

Shortly after the outbreak of war the 2nd Battalion Monmouthshires were in Caerphilly and 200 other ranks from the mining valleys went back to work in the mines as part of the national industrial needs. They were replaced by a huge draft of London Cockneys.

By 20 September, the Division was providing a thousand harvesters per day throughout Wales and on 9 October, 83rd Field Regt was deployed to seek and destroy a German U-boat reputedly ashore near Barry — which it wasn't!

Wallace Brereton did his basic training late in 1939 at Oswestry and later recalled:

> Gorseinon is a small industrial town in South Wales. I had never heard of it before. Now based there was the 81st (Welsh) Field Regt RA an old established formation originally known as the Glamorgan Yeomanry. For many years it had provided comradeship, fresh air and paid holidays for the young miners from the valleys. Now it had to be modernised and brought up to strength for the given task ahead. This was to be my unit for the next six years. The billets were atrocious. We slept on the floor of a very dirty and neglected church hall. But the Welsh boys were extremely friendly and gave us a genuine warm welcome, sharing their food parcels, mainly of Welsh cakes. Many of the boys were related. It was amusing to see a sergeant major giving a gunner a hard time, then to find out that they were brothers. Many of them had only to hop on the local bus to reach home and then get back in time for evening roll-call.

Ned Petty joined the army in October 1939. In Brampton barracks at Chatham:

> ... we found hundreds of chaps like us there, just in our civilian clothes. It was a collecting point — most of them were tradesmen. After breakfast we all queued

up and were given a slip of paper. All that was on my slip was the number 53. Some chaps said that they had 51, 50 or 49. We were afterwards told that that was the number of the Division we were going to. We didn't know what a division was… sixty or seventy of us went to Narbeth in South Wales posted to 244 Field Coy Royal Engineers, 53rd Welsh Division. There were four Engineer companies to a division. A Field Coy consisted of four sections, approximately 40 men to a section. I was posted to No. 2 Section. After two or three days we were issued with an overcoat, a rifle and a steel helmet. At least this was a start. We still wore our suits and our own shoes, of course! After Christmas we moved to Nayland, Nr Pembroke Dock. My section was again in the crypt of a chapel on a hill.

Ned's mates were Ted, a bricklayer from Blackburn with very long arms and short cut hair with a fringe. Teddy Rees from Swansea tried to teach him 'Land of my Fathers' in *Welsh*. Another Welshman called 'Rog' sang 'Sweetheart' and the 'Indian Love Call'. The MT corporal was called 'sort em out, Sid'. Sapper 'Pukka' Roberts was the ablutions cleaner and 'Blanco' Owens, a smart, short figure was Ned's company sergeant major. His OC, Major Heseltine (father of Michael) was tall, smart, a fatherly figure, quietly spoken and very much respected by the Territorial Army. He owned a Scotty dog who in cold weather wore a canine version of an army greatcoat, i.e. a small horse blanket, adorned with sergeant's stripes and the RE 'bomb' insignia.

On 22 October the Division was ordered to garrison Northern Ireland and to ensure that IRA activities were not disruptive. Nothing changes.

The train sped northwards, the sun set, darkness fell and on we rushed. Even the singing stopped. We looked for clues but all the station names had been obliterated. We stopped for a meal at what turned out to be Carlisle. The train came to its final halt at the small Scottish port of Stranraer… then we made the sea crossing to Larne in Ireland. Ballymoney is a small country town in Antrim. It was not the best town we were to stay in, but it certainly was not the worst. We [Wallace Brereton and the gunners of 81st Field Regt RA] began to get more vehicles, so we often went to play out war games in the beautiful countryside. We sometimes stayed out for two or three days sleeping rough. As more trains poured into Ulster, the whole province became one big training area. The Mountains of Mourne and Sperrin thundered with the sound of live shells.

The regiment moved south to Kilkeel, County Down close to the border. 'This seaside town was fascinating. This period was the "high water mark" of my youth. We spent hard raw days in the mountains, then descended to the little town that had the enchanted atmosphere of a real-life Brigadoon.' Wally joined a new battery — the 459th. 'By this time I had qualified as a signaller as well as a specialist, fiddling with radios, telephones, reels of cable etc with my fellow signallers. We had long sessions practising the Morse Code. We were never bored. There was a cinema, a dance hall and even a bingo hall. The town was full of sweet, unsophisticated girls and there were beautiful places to take them.'

The Royal Welch Fusiliers (158) Brigade arrived in Northern Ireland ahead of the Division, 4 RWF at Lisburn, 6 RWF at Lurgan and 7 RWF at Portadown. In November 1939, 4 RWF moved into Belfast barracks, 6 RWF to Lisburn and 7 RWF to Londonderry. In April two IRA members were executed and that caused much local trouble. There were strikes at Belfast docks, an IRA raid on Ballykinler camp and tear-gas bombs thrown into Londonderry cinemas. Two 4 RWF fusiliers were attacked and roadblocks and observation posts were set up and manned. But by the end of 1940 another threat was perceived. 158 Brigade were digging and wiring a defence line at Newry against a possible invasion from the South.

Lt Col W. G. Hewett, CO 1/5 Welch Regiment, decided that the battalion should have a goat mascot. Unfortunately all local Ulster goats were either black or brown. So the Ulster Constabulary were asked to track down a *white* goat. They found one on a farm near Londonderry which was duly purchased and when the regiment finally went overseas, it was posted to the depot. The 1/5 Welch were proud of their band and drums and their ceremonial drill — for which presumably the white goat was a vital component. Major R. B. S. Davies, their 2 i/c, wrote:

When 7 RWF left for Northern Ireland in mid-October it was duly announced by Lord Haw-Haw on German radio. We were the first British troops to arrive at Portadown, Co. Armagh and received a great welcome. The wearing of the Flash* created additional interest. The Royal Welch fusiliers served at Carrickfergus nearly 250 years ago when they came over to support the cause of William the Orange. I had to decide which of the many local bands should escort us to our Sunday morning service. In April 1940 we moved to Newtownards to take over the Belfast docks in case of an airborne attack. Training increased in intensity with a three day scheme with two nights sleeping in the open. A divisional 3-day exercise took place every month in the Mountains of Mourne with the crossroads of Hilltown as a dominant feature. The 'enemy' held a line from Banbridge to Castlewellan, our supporting troops held at Ballynawhinch, recalls memories of smoky tea and cold nights. Those were the days that prepared us for the Normandy Beaches"

---

* [The Black Flash worn by the Royal Welch Fusiliers as an attachment to the tunic collar, a reminder that RWF were the last regiment in the British Army to have long hair, then waxed and plaited in a black cover to prevent the wax from soiling the tunic.]

160 Brigade were next to arrive. By Christmas 1939 1/5 Welch were in Portadown, 4 Welch in Banbridge. The band of 2 Mons played at the opening of the Northern Ireland Parliament. Their battalion magazine called 'The Toomonar' enhanced their morale.

'The powers that be', wrote Sgt Pat Cullen, 4 Welch, 'decided to build a defence line across Northern Ireland which followed the line of the Upper and Lower Bann river, from north of Lough Neagh to the sea and east to reach the sea below the Mourne mountains. A series of trenches and weapon pits were constructed called the Bann Line. Every unit of 53rd Div had to supply men to work in four-hour shifts in all weather conditions. My area was near Portadown. We had to dig through a cemetery and re-enter the lines behind the church!'

THE LIMBO YEARS: 1940

After the withdrawal of the BEF from Dunkirk, the threat grew of a possible invasion of Northern Ireland, so 61st Division took over the northern area and 53rd Welsh, the southern area and the border with Eire.

Tim Dumas was a 2/Lt with 4 RWF:

I was given 9 Pl. in 'A' Coy. Thankfully I inherited the best Platoon Sgt in the Bn, i.e. Sgt Ellis from Wrexham. In December 1940 the GOC Major General BJ Wilson visited us. I was lecturing my platoon on map reading when in he came, asked a few questions, went 'hmm'. We all met again at lunch at Killyleagh Castle. About a week later our CO Lt Col JAM Rice-Evans sent for me to say that the GOC had asked for me to be his ADC. I had no idea what this entailed but felt honoured to be selected. I took over from David Cuthbertson RA who showed me the ropes. Div HQ was then in Belfast with the Div spread all around County Down. I lived in 'A' Mess along with the CRA Brigadier Christie, the GI Lt Col Jasper Frere; the DAQMG Col Stephenson; the ADMS, the CRE Lt Col Dynes and Captain Joe Grimond who was the Div IO. All the seniors lived outside the mess so most evenings Joe and I were alone there.

One of Joe Grimond's stories ran:

On an exercise early in the war in hot weather I was given a bicycle to represent a tank and sent along a dusty road. Feeling it was time for a snooze, I lent the bicycle against a wall, lay down and fell asleep in the shade. I was awakened by a long blackthorn stick being prodded in my ribs by General Wilson who asked me what I thought I was doing? 'Hiding from you, Sir' was my reply.

Tim Dumas again:

> Another member of 'A' Mess was Lieut. Toby Watkin RWF who ran the Divisional
> Mobile Bath Unit. He was an amusing, unfit, shortsighted, musical non-soldier
> who also ran some sort of Divisional entertainment party. At that time 158
> the Royal Welch Brigade was commanded by Brigadier Trustram Eve, 159 by
> Brigadier Bruxner Randall and 160 by Brigadier Ross, when the General went
> to visit and inspect a unit my job was to telephone the adjutant to check exact
> location, who would meet us and to get the name of Company Commander in
> the order of inspection. Once I got it wrong. As we approached the next major, I
> told the General this was Major Jones and he said 'Morning Jones, What is your
> name?' The General earned a nickname of 'Swill-Tubs' as he always made a point
> of visiting these and the Cook House. He would lift the lid from the tub with his
> blackthorn stick and stir around looking for waste food. If he found any, there
> would be hell to pay. The QM, RQMS, Cook Sgt all came in for a rollicking. Word
> of this however quickly got known and swill tubs were always passable thereafter.
> As we drove round Co. Down I would sit in front with the driver, while a Brigade
> Commander, ADMS, CRA or CRE would be in the back with the General.

The GOC reckoned he always knew exactly where he was going — but
didn't. 'On one occasion we got lost due to the General's cry of "We are lost".
After this I stuck to my guns and we always got to our destination. He was a
fearsome old boy and most people were frightened of him.' (Tim Dumas)

A NORWEGIAN EXCURSION

When the Germans invaded Norway on 9 April 1940 a number of 'guerilla'
companies were formed and called Independent Companies. Each Brigade
produced a platoon of volunteers and each battalion a section. The 53rd
Division No. 2 Independent Company thus totalled 21 officers and 168
other ranks which Major H. C. Stockwell (RWF) commanded. The unit
sailed for Scotland on 5 May, embarked five days later at Leith on MV *Royal
Ulsterman* and landed at Bodö, south of Narvik on 14 May. Major Stockwell
soon commanded a group of companies called 'Stockforce' and skirmished
with the Germans, including seaborn raids by fjord steamer and fishing
boats. 2/Lt N. J. M. Anderson, 4 RWF won the MC when, commanding
three Bren gun carriers, he helped a successful withdrawal of the Scots
Guards. The Welsh No. 2 Independent Company re-embarked on 31 May
having suffered twenty-three casualties. Major Stockwell earned the DSO
but the majority of the Welshmen obviously so enjoyed the cut and thrust in
Norway that they joined the newly formed No. 1 Commando.

The rest of 1940 passed peacefully. Internal security duties and anti-invasion roles blended with training. Many troops lived under canvas, the food was good, and much sport took place including football and boxing competitions against the Royal Ulster Constabulary. Leave was never more than seven days every six months, but dances and concert parties were encouraged. In May Brigadier R. K. Ross DSO MC took command of 160 Brigade and in October, Brigadier Trustram Eve MC of 158 Brigade.

THE LIMBO YEARS: 1941

Every two or three weeks Brigade, Division and Corps level exercises took place as well as field firing exercises in the mountains of Mourne. Jamex (14 January), Cuckoo (10 June), Rudolf (23 June), Summit (4-8 August), Greenland (2-6 September) and Harvest (6-9 October). In March a third division arrived, the 5th Division and on 29 July a new GOC arrived, Major General G. C. Bucknall MC.

Tim Dumas, ADC to the GOC recalls:

Once the Duke of Gloucester (April 1941) came to watch a demonstration of firepower by the MMGs of the Cheshires. However the Duke was bored and his ADC told me that what he really wanted was some whiskey. I told my General this and suggested I borrow his DRs motorbike and rush ahead to the hotel in Newcastle and warn them to be ready earlier than expected. This worked beautifully and the Duke was drinking his whiskey on entering the hotel. On that occasion the GOC said, 'Well done, Dumas!'

The Reconnaissance Regiment was officially formed on 1 January 1941 in Belfast under Lt Col G. M. F. Prynne. They marched in February to the extended camp on the north side of Dundrum Bay near Downpatrick. Philip Cowburn, their historian recalls in *Welsh Spearhead* how the new mechanised cavalry (but not tanks) were initially to be formed of anti-tank companies each of four officers and eighty men whose original mundane task was that of defending their three brigade headquarters. 158 Anti-Tank Coy was made up from men of 4, 6 and 7 Royal Welch Fusiliers, 159 Anti-Tank Coy from the lst Herefords, 4 KSLI and 3rd Monmouthshires. Finally 160 Anti-Tank Coy came from 4 and 1/5 Welch Regt and 2nd Monmouthshires. Initially fierce rivalry and jealousy hampered integration but by March regimental training took place along the winding coast roads by Tyreha to Ardglass. The establishment consisted of 49 Bren gun carriers and 30 Bedford 'Ironside' AFVs. When Peter Utley recently commissioned joined the Reconnaissance Regt he:

… was assigned to command No. 1 Troop of 'B' Sqn with five 'standard' armoured cars and five Bren gun carriers, and two 'sgt Jones'. The cars on a standard 'standard' car chassis were unwieldy and slow. I was relieved when they were replaced by Humber LACs and later two Humber HACs replaced two of the LACs. In exercise Wrekin (February 1941) 53rd Div represented the Germans opposed to the Belgian, Czech and Dutch Brigades, supported by the Home Guard.

Peter plotted his route using 'green roads and on the first day captured the "enemy" Command HQ effectively ending the exercise several days early!'

On 6 May six Standard Beaverettes appeared, then in July, 23 Recce cars 'standard'; known as 'inkpots' and finally in October, 32 Humber light Recce cars MkII. Philip Cowburn wrote:

> It was not always easy to get home even if one wanted to. The carriers seemed to have bogiewheels made of marzipan. After all exercises all roads to Ballykinder were littered with vehicles, mostly carriers, incapacitated by broken tracks and half demolished bogies. But necessity taught lessons!

In mid-November the Division moved back to the Welsh border counties with their HQ at Whitchurch, Lichfield, Comberbach and Hereford. For the next four months training and exercises continued — Victory, Pottery, Victory II and Wrekin. The 'enemy' were frequently the Free Czech and Belgian Brigades backed up by the local Home Guard.

Standard Beaverette of 53rd Recce Regt

Carriers of 53rd Recce Regt

Nick Cutcliffe served with 4 RWF from early 1940 until he was wounded at Falaise in August 1944, and wrote:

> I was sent off to the new School of Infantry at Barnard Castle — later to become known as the Battle School — a tactical school for junior officers. It also set out to toughen the students by physical demands greater than any we young men — already fit as fleas — had ever experienced.
>
> The keynote was realism. All firing was with live ammunition — rifles, machine guns, mortars, artillery, the lot. Obstacle courses tackled in full kit, with rifle — saw us plunging through barbed wire, crawling through ditches, crossing water on high wires, jumping through flames and over various other sadistically designed hazards, to the continuous accompaniment of ear-shattering explosive charges, before we stumbled up the final hill and fired off our ten rounds at cut out targets of fierce looking German soldiers who had us in their sights. Everything we did was at the double, even going to lectures or to meals.

Nick Cutcliffe became an instructor at the Divisional Battle School from its first course at Penmaenmawr in March 1942 through to its move to Tonbridge in May, until November. He went back again in April 1943 as Chief Instructor and stayed there until the end of May 1944 when the school closed in anticipation of Overlord. In addition to Battle Drill taught in the Rifle Wing, or Carrier Wing or Mortar wing, short courses were held for REME for all

Horrors Ahead! Capt Nick Cutliffe's sketch of the Divisional Battle School

LADs in the Division, a Night Recce Course with tanks, a Camouflage Course, an Aircraft Recognition Course, a Stretcher Bearers Course and a Snipers Course. Besides the Commandant (Lt Col Ted Ripley), the Chief Instructor, there were fourteen officer instructors and an average number of forty officers and twenty NCOs attended at any one time.

Towards the end of March, the Division was moved a little closer to the 'sharp' end in Kent as part of 12 Corps, entrusted with the defence of the area most likely to be invaded. The HQs were at Harrietsham, Sturry, Bearsted and Norton Faversham. A wholesale shuffle took place in May when 159 Brigade joined 11th Armoured Division and were replaced by 31st Tank Brigade with their slow ponderous Churchill infantry tanks. Their units were 9 RTR, 10 RTR and 141 RAC. Two large exercises followed, 'Tiger' 19-31 May with 12 Corps battling with the Canadian Corps and 'Raree 3' in July.

By May 1942 Sapper Ned Petty had earned his first stripe:

> In Maidstone my company was now a real mixture. To begin with all Welsh, then about 50, but a new intake were nearly all London men, all aged about 21, a very happy crowd. Their attitude was 'well, we're here, whether we like it or not, so we may as well make the best of it!'

Monty visited the Division on several occasions usually checking on their fitness and in September Major General 'Bobby' Ross became the new GOC.

The *Sunday Pictorial* chaperoned by 12 Corps Public Relations visited the Division 18-22 September 1942. The Recce Regiment hit the centre pages. 'B' Sqn carriers crashing *into each other* in Eastwell Park! Sgt Hill in action behind his Bren and Sgt Jones poised in mid-air vaulting out of his carrier in best battle school fashion. Corporal Davies was shown marching grimly with his stengun at the ready, his denims clinging to him after his swim in the river Beult. Their reporter, Harry Ashbrook wrote, 'I saw war streaming over the quiet soil of Kent. An army was on the move. The squat dun-coloured armoured cars thundered on at 50mph. Behind them Bren-gun carriers, lorry drawn anti-tank guns and motorcycles. The weapons were old — but the tactics were new.'

PROFILE OF A GENERAL

Robert Knox came from a military family. His father was Brigadier General R. J. Ross CB CMG. 'Bobby' as he was usually known was born on 23 August 1893, educated at Cheltenham and then the Royal Military College, Sandhurst. He was commissioned into the Queens Royal Regiment in February 1913 and served with the 2nd Battalion in Bermuda and South Africa. Serving with the BEF in France and Belgium he was promoted to lieutenant in September 1914. By October 1915 he was a captain having been awarded the MC. The following year he became GSO3 with 30 Division in the BEF, then Brigade Major with 22 Infantry Brigade. That year he was awarded the DSO and went as GSO2 to 60 Division with the Egyptian Expeditionary Force. He was a contemporary of Monty who during WWII 'often dropped in for cups of tea!' After WWI he became adjutant of 2nd Battalion Queens Royal Regiment and then spent 1920-21 in Waziristan. Next was a nine-year attachment to the Egyptian Army and Sudan Defence Force until 1932. He returned to the Queens, and married Kathleen Ogden in 1933. He was promoted to Lt Colonel in 1937 and took the Queens to Palestine where he was awarded various medals, including his fourth mention in despatches. In 1940 at the age of forty-seven he was promoted to command 160 Brigade in 53rd Welsh Division. Two years later he became GOC and led the 'Red Crown and Dragon' through the rest of the war including nearly a year of bitter fighting in North-West Europe.

A few vignettes of General 'Bobby' Ross. Sir Charles Harington (now General with DSO, MC) was initially CO of lst Bn Manchesters, then GSO1:

General 'Bobby' was popular with everyone — very gregarious, sense of humour
— a Father figure to the troops. He knew Monty well, who was often dropping

Major General 'Bobby' Ross

in to see Bobby in his caravan for a cup of tea. They must have known each other in the Great War or perhaps later in Palestine with 3 Division. He was a good delegater, did not bypass his Brigadiers such as Coleman (the most popular) or 'Fish' Elrington who went up on a mine. 'Bobby' never got on with Horrocks as a Corps Commander — did not like each other, but got on terribly well with that red-faced Scotsman [Lt General] Neil Ritchie. Curious but 'Bobby' was a very keen poker player.

HC (Bud) Kenway knew the GOC well. He was commissioned into 6 Royal Welch Fusiliers in early 1942 and was posted to HQ 158 Brigade as Liaison Officer, and then to HQ 53 Division in late 1943:

In addition to normal LO duties I found myself from the start acting as a sort of operational ADC to Bobby Ross when he went forward visiting brigades and units. I explain later why his ADC did not do this. The pattern was that we would travel in two armoured scout cars; I would lead in the first with a radio on the divisional net and Bobby Ross would follow in the second.

It was on these visits that I came closer to Bobby Ross but even then it was rather impersonal and confined to operational matters with no small talk or thinking aloud. Of course there was a wide gulf of experience between us; he was a very senior regular officer with a DSO and MC from the First World War and I was the youngest, most junior and probably least experienced officer on his staff at the time. However, I believe that other more senior members of his staff did not really get close to him. Although he was confident and impressive and greatly respected as a commander he was not charismatic like many other generals and was rather reserved and introspective by nature. In my experience he was always courteous, never overbearing and never tried to impress as a great 'character' like a Monty, a Patton or a Horrocks. He was ruthless when necessary, as all successful commanders need to be at times, but I do not think he was ever unfair.

He certainly liked his creature comforts in the way of food, wine and accommodation and I am sure that is why his ADC Geoff Saunders was selected for the job. It was certainly not for his military prowess and that is why Bobby Ross did not use him on the full range of ADC duties.

One of the difficulties in getting close to Bobby Ross was his mess arrangements. He lived in 'A' Mess with nobody below the rank of Lt Col except for his ADC. Thus there were no informal contacts with anybody else. Bobby Ross must have been highly thought of by his superiors as a divisional commander. He took the Division to Normandy as an untried formation comprised almost entirely of territorial and conscripted personnel. He remained in command throughout the campaign during which the Division had developed into an efficient, highly respected and successful formation. He was then awarded the CB for what he and the Division had achieved.

'I was GSO 1 of the Div from May 1943 to September 1944,' writes [Brigadier] M. H. ap Rhys Pryce:

I joined HQ 53 Division at Bearsted near Maidstone and became a member of 'A' Mess consisting of the GOC, the CRA Brigadier JC Friedberger; the A/Q Lt Col R Neilson; the CRE Lt Col GS Clarke; Colonel WH Marsden RAMC, the Rev LJB Snell RAChD, the Senior Chaplain and the ADC. He was a wealthy young man and he kept us very well fed (eg driving to Dover to get fresh fish) and the chef had previously been at the Savoy Hotel. 'Bobby' Ross was a very nice man and a first class commander. If there was any real action going on at the front, he would get into his Armoured Car and go up to see it. I heard that in the 1914-18 war he once walked back through an enemy barrage to get more ammunition and returned with it through the barrage. We were once visiting some troops behind the line when some enemy shells came over. The paper I held was spattered in the mud. 'Bobby' took absolutely no notice. He might have been in somebody's drawing room!

The General liked to live well and to seek entertainment for himself — and for his troops. Lt Jim Cooper joined the Division at Bearsted to take over and amalgamate the Divisional Concert party with that of the disbanded 42 Armoured Division:

There was no war establishment for a Concert Party, but by the end of the war it had risen to 39 (which includes our own cinema operator and driver, and we were given by the CRE our own cook to look after our food arrangements on our own). [Before Overlord] We produced a new show to tour round the division every two months. Bobby Ross always came to see our production and was most interested in our activities. Very little of progress in the CP could happen without his agreement. Once our clown (he was one in civilian life and very funny) received a posting order. I went in to see the General in 'A' Mess to tell him. He simply replied 'Leave it with me we must not let Tich leave the Division' and he didn't!

Jim Cooper was awarded 'passionate' leave to see his girlfriend by the GOC who also insisted that the Concert Party did not travel *together* in the *same* ship to Normandy — just in case!

As a military commander General Ross used his artillery to great effect to support his infantry battalions, he rotated his brigades ably so that their heavy losses were just bearable. He was very keen on immediate mobility and every battalion had to have a bicycle company, although in the event they were rarely used and were soon discarded.

THE LIMBO YEARS: AUTUMN 1942-43

On 20 November Prime Minister Winston Churchill visited the Division. He inspected 4 Welch Regt and 2 Mons and visited other units. Just before Christmas, Exercise Ghost took place, to be followed by Hammer One and Hammer Two.

In January 1943 the 'D' Rifle Companies in battalions of the Division were disbanded and a new 's' (Support) Company formed of Mortar, Carrier and Pioneer platoons, plus a HQ Coy of Admin and signals platoons. Six months later the 158 Brigade were taken to Salisbury Plain to watch the biggest bombardment by guns and mortars yet staged. The Russian generals invited as observers remarked 'Better if you had been firing at the Germans!'

'In Sheerness' wrote Gunner Wally Brereton 81 Field Regt 'we were issued with a new type of hat. Since 1939 we had been wearing the traditional forage cap. The new one was a cross between a Tam O'shanter and a beret. We were never told how to wear it. The jokers of the regiment wore it in the most bizarre way that they could concoct.'

The most important exercise yet followed, for two weeks in March — Exercise Spartan took place when 12 Corps 'invaded' and pushed inland against 8 Corps. In the Autumn of 1943 another crucial change occurred. The

Division once again returned to a three brigade formation when 71st Brigade joined on 18 October with three 'foreign' battalions, 1st East Lancashire, 1st Highland Light Infantry and 1st Oxfordshire and Buckinghamshire Light Infantry.

Three weeks later they arrived in Stanmer Camp to train with 31st Tank Brigade Churchills. It was a cheerless spot, cold at night in tents and no shower baths, but they soon returned to Faversham. 'When we were not on exercise route marches or training schemes' wrote Donald Arnott 'A' Coy, 1st Battalion Oxfordshire & Bucks, 'time was taken up in a multitude of ways. Marching into Faversham each Saturday morning for the RSM's drill parade, trips there for a bath, church parade or a football match at the recreation ground, and off duty visits to the Argosy Cinema and Salmon's Café. The TOC H Canteen was a favourite meeting place, as well as the Roman Catholic Canteen which was so quiet and pleasant.' 'D' Company under Major Pierce had their parade ground in the Shepheard Neames Brewery loading-bay; 'Inspection and drill by C. S. M. "Trotter" Mitchell took place to a background of good humoured banter from the brewery female workers!'

Yet more exercises followed — Fortescue 23 June, Harlequin 25 August, Paul 25 September, Canute II 8 November and Canute III 2 December. Lt General Neil Ritchie CBE DSO MC had just taken over command of 12 Corps and visited the Division on 26-27 November. For the next vital eighteen months, 53rd Welsh would be under his command.

Second Lieutenant GCRL Pender joined 1st Battalion Highland Light Infantry as a young subaltern in August 1943:

> On arrival I reported to the Adjutant, a very smart officer — his awesome presence dressed in tartan breeches, service dress, jacket and puttees. My batman Private John Ward quickly put me at ease, a typical Glaswegian, tough, kind, humorous with an understanding for crushed 2nd lieutenants. The next year was spent in training, including a hundred mile march in three days. Food was short in the country and even bread was rationed. It was unbearable for the Jocks who had tremendous appetites. There were great shouts down the column of 'Ony bread, Missis?' It was touching to see the locals come to their garden gates and hand out bread, cakes, beer and lemonade to the columns. The pipes and raucous singing of the Jocks became louder and louder. In the gaps between the companies one heard the pipes, the beat of the drum and the left, right, left, right of the CSM.

The 116 (RWF) LAA Regt spent nearly two years off and on the Davis Estate outside Chatham having been reinforced by a large draft of Scots from disbanded Searchlight regiments. 380 Battery was diverted to defending Budleigh Salterton in South Devon for a while and 382 Battery visited Elstree to make a training film. The 1st Battalion East Lancashires who had fought with the

BEF on joining the Division spent six months in the Milstead area. In October 1943 they perfected their vehicle waterproofing and scramble net drill from erected towers representing ships from which mesh was draped. The following month in Exercise Dyke, around Hove, they had two weeks of tank/infantry co-operation: troop with platoon; squadron with company and regiment with the tank Battalion 141 RAC (the Buffs). All ranks rode on and in tanks, and some even drove them! In December Exercise Canute was aptly named with a 'dry' practice for an assault landing. Major Lane's 'D' Coy became *the* Bicycle Company. 'Probably many of those Army bicycles, so well known for their weight and strength, are still in use somewhere in France and Belgium!'

'In October 1943 I was G1 and 160 Bde under Brigadier Dorman Smith was carrying out a week long exercise on the Downs north of Brighton,' wrote Lt Col ap Rhys Pryce:

We had a small advance Div HQ at Plumpton. One evening I walked along the country roads in late evening. Suddenly the beam of a searchlight about two miles away shone above me, I noted that the adjoining fields were at once illuminated so as to make it easy for Infantry to move and to recognise each other at 50 yards or more. I suggested to 'Bobby' Ross the GOC, that we should recommend to 12 Corps the use of searchlights to ease movement at night. 'Alright' he said 'You write a letter to Corps' I did so. Back came a reply telling us to carry out trials — which we did. There came a final trial on the Downs in the presence of General Dempsey, the Commander 2nd British Army and 'Artificial moonlight' was accepted. It was found that while the light greatly helped the attackers, it gave no particular help to the defenders. In Normandy we arranged for the searchlight beams to shine above the admin area and the Corps Superintendent of Signals told me the time for his DRs was cut in half and MT did not need to use lights. For a big raid on 23rd July near Le Bon Repos, one SL behind the front shone vertically into the air and the tanks used it as a guiding beacon for the return journey.

Where however were the Luftwaffe? And 'Monty's Moonlight — the popular title for this nightime venture — should have been called 'ap Rhys Pryce's moonlight'!

Lt Col R. E. H. Hudson, CO 83rd Field Regt RA, recalled:

Firstly Canterbury. The [Baedeker] raids and the work we had to do in the town. Later the great Divisional Service we held in the sand-bagged Cathedral [May 1942]. Then Westbere, the '43' inn sign, the school cricket ground, the rector and the visit of the Archbishop of Canterbury, Alfriston. We knew it hot and cold, wet and fine, foggy and clear. Shades of Wagon, Flagon, Dragon and 'Q' Brecknocks' petrol pumps. Not only Alfriston, but 'Blocks 1-8' including one visit to Bognor and our sight of the Dieppe raiding fleet. Summer [1943] in Herne Bay. A few warlike noises and the sight of convoys in the estuary — little did we think then, that we should be sitting out there in a year's time. Suffolk and baronial halls came next. A very pleasant interlude including one visit to Norfolk all very new ground to most of us. Back to Kent again via Herne Bay to Sutton Valence, where we just missed the strawberry season. Many exercises we survived — Tiger, Highdown, Raree, Hammer, Spartan and Gallop for instance. Senny Bridge, Larkhill and Redesdale were well known health resorts — but good fun while they lasted. Then there was our state visit to Newport [May 1943] and the great welcome they gave us. This was one of the best memories I have.

THE LIMBO YEARS: 1944, PRELUDE TO OVERLORD

Early in January General Montgomery returned from Italy and assumed command of 21st Army Camp. His first visit was on 2 February, in the morning, at Mote Park, Maidstone and in the afternoon at Sittingbourne. Nearly nine thousand officers and men listened to him explain some of his plans for 'Overlord'. Four weeks later King George VI visited the Division. And still the tempo of exercises was stepped up with Shudder I in February, Shudder II in March, Henry in April, Sky and Bud in May. Vehicle waterproofing, exercises with the 'Funnies' of 79th Armoured Division (Crocodiles, AVREs, Buffaloes, Flails etc). In February the East Lancs trained for street fighting in the bombed ruined areas of Eastbourne. Their CO, Lt Col G. W. P. N. Burden, wanted his men to be 100% qualified as swimmers (courtesy of Sittingbourne Public Baths), for watermanship (for river and canal crossing in assault boats), how to handle a boat, and as a *last* resort to swim across. They achieved 93%! Sgt Bate was i/c snipers since experience had shown in the last war that the Germans took sniping more seriously than the British. The CO insisted on *barefoot* drill at Milstead to harden feet before the invasion. And eleven members of the US Army were attached to the battalion to compare equipment, training and tactics. Every battalion now had a small quota of young, tough Canloan officers from Canada who fought (and often died) leading their Welshmen into battle. And also in February the Recce Regiment were allowed to wear *black* RAC berets!

'For 7 RWF April and May 1944 were months of expectancy,' wrote Lt Col A. H. Williams:

But although the Battalion's thoughts were centered upon the coming assault on Fortress Europe, training went on very much as before. Exercise 'MUG' involved a 70-mile march to Sonning-on-Thames where day and night crossings were practised. All ranks underwent a 'night inoculation for battle' at Wouldham Quarry; platoons battled for the inter-platoon tactical championship, the Medway was crossed by rope and landing trials went on incessantly.

On 23 May, the 2nd Army commander, Lt General Dempsey visited the Division and a week later Monty gave a pre-invasion lecture to all senior officers at HQ 12 Corps. The concentration of the Division was now ordered, in preparation for the invasion, to be completed by 6 June.

Shortly before D-Day Herbert Isherwood's unit, 13th Field Dressing Station RAMC, was stationed at Herne Bay:

> My CO Major Alastair McClaren told me the unit would shortly be going on to the Continent, and to keep that information to myself. My instructions were to keep the unit supplied with rations and mail throughout the campaign — at least once every 24 hours — I had 'carte blanche' as to how I did it. 13 FDS moved on 19th June to the Guards Depot at Pirbright, enclosed by a 12-foot high steel fence, patrolled outside by armed police. Obvious that the authorities were making sure that no one went AWOL.

A poet in the Ox and Bucks wrote 'salute the Soldier' published in Regimental Orders.

> Hail, soldier, huddled in the rain
> Hail, soldier, squelching through the mud,
> Hail, soldier, sick of dirt and pain,
> The sight of death, the smell of blood
> New men, new weapons bear the brunt
> New slogans gild the ancient game
> The infantry are still in front

Cpl Bert Isherwood, 13 FDS (Forward Dressing Station)

> And mud and dust are much the same
> Hail humble footman poised to fly
> Across the West, or any Wall,
> Proud plodding, peerless PBI
> The foulest finest job of all

It was known that the Division would not land with the first waves of attack but would follow in behind 3rd British and 50th Tyne Tees Divisions.

Rev H. E. W. Slade, Chaplain 83 Field Regiment RA:

From Sutton Valence we went out during those eight months on frequent exercises, sometimes no further away than Alfriston, sometimes as far afield as Scotland. There were trying exercises in the rain, exasperating exercises of what seemed purposeless digging and we exercised in the invigorating frost and snow of January, later on to be almost literally reproduced when the regiment went into action in the Ardennes. It was in the happy atmosphere of friendship [at Sutton Valence] that the gradual sealing-off of the regiment in preparation for action took place. Mail began to be censored, leave was stopped, the first V-1s made their way noisily over the parks towards London and then with 6th June we were ready to move, leaving Sutton Valence a few days afterwards.

83 Field Regt embarked on SS *Port McPherson*, *Frank Lever* and *Samark* and arrived off Arromanches beach on 24 June.

Fusilier (and poet) John Ottewell, D Coy 7 RWF described their journey to the invasion fleet:

> Bedford three tonners, all bumper to bumper
> 'White-starred' and camouflaged, bound for the shore
> Heavily laden with men and materials
> All off to Normandy, ready for War
>
> Streets thronged with Londoners cheering and waving
> Tossing our pennies and 'bobs' to the kids
> Spitfires high above knocking off Doodlebugs
> Pensioner's walking sticks tapping our 'lids.'
>
> Soon aboard transports and landing craft, Infantry
> Packed in like sardines, above and below
> Spewbags and vomiting, still on the harbour swell
> Poor bloody infantry, waiting to go

Captain Nick Cutcliffe 4 RWF, 2 i/c D Coy:

On 6th June the officers of 4 RWF were on a Tewt [Tactical Exercise Without Troops], studying the problems of taking up an anti-panzer locality in the bridgehead preparatory to the break-out. The CO then said 'I expect you'd like to know that the invasion is on. We landed in Normandy and airborne forces have been dropped too.' We looked at each other and smiled and muttered 'Good Show' with studied phlegm! I thought how typically British was our attitude. Here was the event for which we had been working for years; which meant life or death for us, which meant we had committed ourselves to win the war or perish. There was no Gallic hysteria, nor American boisterous enthusiasm — just a barely-expressed feeling of satisfaction. We were given a little blue leaflet in a cellophane cover of useful words and phrases in four languages, for use if one escaped after being captured. Officers were also given a hacksaw blade and a small and ingenious compass shaped either like a sixpence or a collarstud or magnetised fountain pen clip, or one made of metal battledress buttons.

Most of 4 RWF sailed aboard the liberty ship *Cotton Mather*:

Our sleeping quarters reminded me of the Black Hole of Calcutta in the after hold, fitted out with canvas bunks in tiers of four. All was very dark and congested. We fed on 'Compo' rations, tinned food in boxes, sufficient for 14 men for one day. We stayed off Southend for several days, so we unearthed a powerful wireless, fixed the set up on deck for hours and hours of 'swing'. The radio, games of 'brag', daily rifle inspections, company PT taken by the officers on one of the hatches helped to keep boredom at bay. Many of the men acquired a 'combat crop' by having their heads shaved. I decided to grow a moustache! (Captain Nick Cutcliffe)

There were forty-nine ships in the convoy, each about 5000 tons, escorted by two destroyers and two corvettes, with two US fighter planes above.

Captain David Bolland was Staff Captain RA at Division HQ. After the campaign he wrote *Team Spirit*, an excellent account (illustrated by John Ogle) of the logistics and back up support within the Division. He also kept a very interesting diary of which excerpts appear in this book:

June 1944, Monday, 5th, first indication that Second Front would begin on 6th June when we received the magic code word 'Adoration 0200 hrs' This meant wireless silence until ordered to be broken. Very heavy aerial activity from midnight onward. Tuesday, 6th. At last the doors of that locked room in Div HQ at Woodcut House opened. Out of it came special orders of the day from Gen Eisenhower and Gen Montgomery, hundreds of maps of France, 'Invade

Mecum', Michelin tourist guides to France etc. At last D-Day had come and all was agog. Wednesday 14th, Major General RK Ross GOC 53 Div spoke to us at Tudor House, Bearsted of the shape of things to come. An excellent straightforward talk. Friday, 16th, Brigadier JC Friedberger, our CRA and TAC HQ 53 Div left for marshalling area at 8am. Several mysterious flying bombs appeared — looking like miniature aeroplanes. Seemed to explode on the ground after circling around for some time. Saturday 17th. At 1am 116 Light AA Regt and 279 A/Tk Bty moved to marshalling area, followed by 81 and 83 Field Regiments who moved at 4am. Sunday 18th. At last the day had come to move from Bearstead. It was obvious to everyone in the area that we were about to go because our waterproofed vehicles stacked with kit were 'fair proof'. Went off in advance to Marshalling Area 's' near Romford crossing the Thames by the Greenwich Ferry. The main body went through London and had a marvellous reception from the people of the East End, bringing out cigarettes, showering tea and cakes. It made one feel rather like a Crusader going out to fight the foe in a distant land.

David Bolland eventually sailed on Sunday 25th on the 10,000 ton Victory ship built in Canada called *Fort Crevecour*:

Life on the ship was hard for the men who had to sleep between decks about 300 in each hold. Two concerts were held without any musical instruments. The leading lights were 'spud' Riley GSO3 and Ronnie Urquhart, Field Security Officer. On Saturday 24th I listened to an impromptu choir of Welsh Boys from Div Signals singing songs until the sun went down at 10.45pm. It was grand

Divisional A&Q team for 'Overlord'

to hear their magnificent voices floating across the water. They ended up with 'Eternal Father' 'Cwm Rhondda', 'Abide with me' and 'Home of my Fathers'. Tuesday, 27th. As dawn broke we could see the vast armada lying off the beach [Asnelles-Sur-Mer]. As far as the eye could see there were ships — battleships, cruisers, destroyers, MT ships, coasters, hospital ships with landing craft buzzing in and out getting on with the job. Sappers of the Docks Operating Coy boarded our ship, using the ships machinery they removed the hatch covers and unloaded the hundred of vehicles into the loading craft personnel following, leaving the ship by scrambling nets.

To his mother he wrote home, 'The journey by LC was about one mile dodging in and out of various other craft all unloading personnel, stores, vehicles, petrol. We had to wade the last 50 yards to dry land. This was where the waterproofing came in, as the vehicles were covered to about 5 feet in water — a weird experience.' Bolland joined Division HQ at St Amatol on the Bayeux — St Lo road late on Wednesday 28th. The next day: 'Monty visited Div HQ today and looked very fit and quite regardless of the fact that there was a war on.'

Divisional HQ Staff May 1944. Front row, l-r: Lt Col F. M Hext, CREME; Lt Col G. G. S. Clarke, CRE; Lt Col G. R. Kerr, ADOS; Lt Col M. H. A. P. ap Rhys Price, GSO1; Col W. H. Marston, ADMS; Brig J. C. Friedberger, CRA; Maj Gen R. K. Ross, GOC; unknown; Lt Col R. Neilson, AA&QMG; Lt Col D. E. Harrison, CRSigs; Lt Col J. E. Bridge, CRASC; Capt G. L. Saunders, ADC. Middle Row, l-r: Capt R. Urquhart, FSO; Lt Riley, LO; Capt J. C. Suffolk, Div IO; Capt E. L. Williams, GSO3 (Ops); unknown; Lt Col Rev L. J. B. Snell, SCF; Maj J. Grimond, DAAG; Maj K. Goodacre, GSO2; Maj N. Pascall, APM; Capt D Phelps, GSO3 (Int); Capt P. C. Batterbury, Staff Capt Q; unknown, Camp Comdt. Top Row, l-r Lt M. J. Cooper, Ent Offr; Capt E. J. Oldham, OC APIS, LT H. C. Kenway, LO; Lt H. Clunies-Ross, LO; Lt J. Reid, LO; Capt R. Thompson, SO Edn; Capt H. Smith-Daye, Catering Advisor; unknown; Lt F. Bullock, Asst Camp Comdt; unknown

2

Arrival: 'smell of putrefaction'

On 23 June Lt J. E. Reynolds in his Troop HQ Carrier drove off 'B' Squadron Recce Regt LCT into 3½ feet of water at Le Hamel beach. Philip Cowburn their historian wrote: 'The sea journey was more like a good holiday.' And one member of the squadron: 'Our first impression of France was one of desolation. The beach defences had been smashed a fortnight earlier by the assault troops and naval guns. They certainly did look a mess. There was smashed concrete everywhere and a light railway line torn to shreds.' The squadron moved inland to the de-waterproofing area. 'Here we stopped for quite a while joining the hundreds of trucks, tanks, artillery pieces, "Ducks", Bulldozers, etc. which were crammed into this area with their drivers feverishly ripping off the asbestos compound from their engines.' The irrepressible Corporal Dunsmore was caught brewing up a little char by the cooks' 3-tonner. The portly cook's favourite shout was (freely translated) 'Fizz Off'. For the next few weeks the 53rd Recce Regiment acted as traffic control and carried mines forward to the infantry at Secqueville-en-Bessin, Le Haut du Bosq, Les Saullets and Le Mesnil Patry. The rest of the regiment arrived on 24 July on the *Vancouver City* and *John E. Ward*.

'We moved into the detritus of the assault' recalls Lt Peter Utley, B Sqn:

> The smell of putrefaction was all about us, but the worst smell was from the incinerated bodies of tank crews in their burnt out vehicles. I tried as best I could to keep my troopers away from such sights. In their thin-skinned vehicles unfortunate comparisons were bound to come to mind.

However, the most dramatic 'non-arrival' was that of Brigadier 'Bolo' Whistler who had taken command of 160 Brigade on 14 January 1944. He was taken off the invasion ship and flown to Normandy to command with great skill and dash, 3rd British (Monty's Iron Sides) Division. He was succeeded by Brigadier C. F. C. Coleman (4 Welch). By 28 June the Division was concentrated around Soubles (near Bayeux), Beny-sur-Mer and St André, now part of Lt General

Richard O'Connor's 8 Corps. The young virgin Welshmen plus their 'foreign' brigade were to be pushed deep into the cauldron.

Lt Col A. H. Williams, CO of 7 RWF recorded that they:

> ... embarked on the 10,000 ton liberty ship *Lee S. Overman*, a veteran of the African landings. The convoy waited for seven whole days at Thames Gate, a delay which puzzled everyone at the time, while all ranks lounged in the sunshine, boxed and practised for the Eisteddfod, which so impressed the American crew that they donated six pounds towards prizes. The convoy sailed on 24th June. After avoiding several salvoes of shells from the big guns of Cap Gris Nez, the ships anchored off Ouistreham. The beaches were littered with wrecked landing craft driven ashore by the great storm. Soon 7 RWF took over from 1st Battalion Welsh Guards at Brettville-sur-Orgueilleuse.

7 RWF found Brettville in ruins. Burnt out tanks, equipment, steel helmets, arms and ammunition littered the area. Their position was soon called 'suicide Wood' because of the efficient German snipers. Two patrols were sent across the river to 'explore' Gavrus, Bougie and Monceaux under Sgt Morgan and Major Wennink. Sharp encounters with the Hitler Jugend took place and 7 RWF suffered sixteen wounded in the first twenty-four hours. The RWF Brigade then took over a sector of the line at Rauray, south of Fontenay. Corporal Mostyn Thomas of 'D' Coy 1/5 Welch Regiment kept a journal. When he finally went to war his battledress pockets were full of sweets, chocolate, cigarettes, matches and two .36 grenades:

Normandy Coast: Courseulles-sur-Mer

26th June. HMS *Canterbury* was steaming westwards at a cracking pace flying a Red Dragon at the masthead, escorted by three frigates. One dropped depth charges either to subdue submarines or to impress us with their big bangs! Our ship arrived off Juno Beach at mid-day. HMS *Warspite* a mile or so to the west let off a broadside and a huge belch of smoke spurted from the barrels. 'DON' Coy scaled down the nets into an American tank landing craft. The sea was choppy but a dry landing on JIG Beach, NE of Asnelles. 27th June. The tommy cooker and chocolate drink in self heating cans were of great use and comfort. The final briefings consisted of disarming and treatment of PW; to be positive, no handing out of food, chocolate or cigarettes or water. PW to be escorted to the IO as soon as possible for interrogation. The evacuation of wounded and British dead by

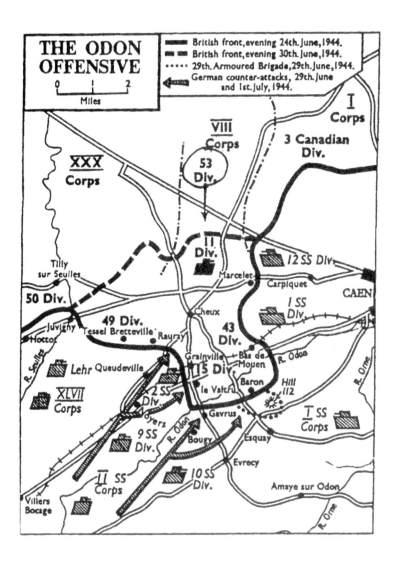

stretcher bearers. No one to be retained with obvious wound dressings, all to be
sent to the RAP. German dead to be left in place and removed when convenient.

The Royal Welch Fusiliers Brigade (158) had sailed partly from Tilbury, partly
from Newhaven. On landing the three battalions marched through Ver to Crepon,
two miles inland. It was their first taste of continental dust. At Crepon there was a
sign 'only two miles to Assembly Area — keep going — keep smiling.' Later that
night TCVs (Troop Carrying Vehicles) arrived and drove the brigade in heavy
rain through Bayeux to a concentration area near Noron, five miles to the south-
west. Soon they relieved a Scottish brigade in the Tourville-Mond Rainville area.
'My company commander and friend, Major Peter Owen, calling his first action
'O' Group beneath some trees (on 1st July),' wrote Capt Tim Dumas, now of
'C' Coy 4 RWF, 'together with a platoon commander [Lt Hughes] and a platoon
sergeant were all killed by a mortar bomb. Two days later we lost another Pl
Cmdr killed [Lt Morris] and one wounded [Lt Harley] so that by 4th July, I
was the sole officer left in 'C' Coy, with a slight hand wound, while virtually no
other casualties had been suffered in the Bn. I was quite a junior captain so quite
rightly Capt Nick Cutcliffe took command and we were patched up with some
re-enforcement platoon commanders. Not a very good start.'

Here we saw our first dead Germans. One sniper in camouflage smock was
already turning green, his lips beginning to recede from his teeth. Near the
forward platoon were several others and a couple of dead Tommies were lying in

the open. I went to look at them. I had to get used to the sight sooner or later and the sooner the better. (Nick Cutcliffe 'D' Coy on outskirts of Rauray)

Cutcliffe took command of 'C' Coy which had lost four officers and three NCOs, and whose morale was low:

We were all busy [4th July] improving our trenches, digging deeper, erecting head cover, making communication trenches and camouflaging. The defence mentality was creeping in, that a slit was a funk-hole rather than a place from which to shoot Germans. Some troops built miniature underground fortresses with two small loopholes, through which it was difficult to see, let alone fight!

Corporal Sidney Griffiths was part of 'A' Coy — the bicycle company of 4 RWF:

We landed on the right of Gold Beach carrying our cycles on our shoulders. Lt Dick Ireland was first off, myself behind him, Mulberry harbour off to our left. Later we rode on bikes through Bayeux. I remember riding over the cobbles past the Cathedral, the square being full of people of all ages cheering and waving. 18th June. In the farm a country girl dressed all in black came to milk the cows with her stool and pail. She was plump and had a fresh complexion and the lads pulled her leg. 24th June. We went into the back garden of a wine merchants premises. I noticed that Fusilier George Reynolds was missing. He appeared carrying two large bottles of wine. I told him he was looting and to return the wine otherwise he would carry the Mortar bombs. He soon fell in! We spent a wet night in the vicinity of Carpiquet airport. Our men raided a supply dump for food in the darkness. We had a few extras that night.

On 25 June Corporal Griffiths had been ordered to search a chateau near Cheux. He took Fusilier George Reynolds with him who found a wine vat: 'There was George on the floor, pack off and opened with his mug in his hand drinking wine...' On their return to 'A' Coy Fusilier Lane shot himself in the foot: 'as he was cleaning his rifle'. When 4 RWF occupied a defensive position near Rauray, Corporal Griffiths saw a dead body of a sergeant of Lancashire regiment of 49 Polar Bear Division. 'He had fallen on his back, half his face shot away, but now covered with a cheese cloth. His BD blouse was open revealing a tattoo of an Indian chief's head, with feathered headdress. It was Brierly who had served with me in 70th Royal Warwicks Regt. I said a quiet farewell to an old comrade.'

The adjutant of 6 RWF, Capt Hugh Roberts wrote:

At St André we dug in earnest for the first time, round the hedgerows very careful of our track discipline and insisting on all small points of training. The countryside was unlike anything over which we had trained in England. Tewts (Tactical Exercises without Troops) therefore were run to work out new tactics.

It is perhaps curious that the Army high command had known for a long time that Normandy with its 'bocage' countryside was the heart of Overlord and that suitable areas in the UK had *not* been specifically selected for training. Hugh Roberts describes the 'bocage':

Thick high hedges surrounded leafy orchards or small fields deep with hay and corn, each hedge was lined with tall trees (bushy topped or poplar) which obscured all observation and were themselves a paradise for snipers. The villages were built of stone, haphazardly with deep lanes leading through them. There were many dairy cattle and horses in the fields near the farmhouses where milk, eggs or calvados could be obtained.

The bocage countryside came as rude shock to most of the British Army.

Lt Col 'Jimmy' Rice Evans CO 4 RWF, Ken Saunders his IO and Irfon Roberts, Signals officer had worked out that the Germans held the hedgerow junctions at the small field corners with a couple of LMGs. The LMG positions were interconnecting by a communication trench through the hedge. Dotted about singly amongst the hedges were well camouflaged tanks which would fire rapidly for a short time and then quickly change position. All this meant a new drill and we put our heads together to worry one out.

A platoon would be responsible for one field, and a company would take a frontage of two fields leaving one platoon in reserve. The platoon would deal with one hedgerow corner at a time, neutralising the other at the same time, two sections would keep up covering fire *diagonally* across the field whilst the third section sneaked up the side of the hedge directly towards the first target LMG. The 2" mortar would be the only HE support and for A/Tk defence the PIAT would have to be got forward as quickly as possible. No. 77 grenades would be carried by the sections. A/Tk guns would be difficult to get through the steep, difficult thick hedgerows. (Captain Nick Cutcliffe, 4 RWF)

Capt Hugh Roberts of 6 RWF also described the 'killing fields' of the bocage:

Three days before 49 Div [the Polar Bears] had fought a bitter battle at Rauray. Unburied German dead lay in the hedges and in great numbers in the cornfield in front. There were many knocked out tanks. [The Polar Bears and 24 Lancers had destroyed 33 Panthers.] British dead were still lying in the exposed slit trenches. The whole area was pitted with shell holes and each day the mortar fire stripped more branches from the trees. We learned the meaning of life in a slit trench, the feeling of sitting like an Aunt Sally being potted at by an enemy who knew where we were and whom the weapons in the rifle companies could not reach. All our slit trenches especially near trees had to be roofed against air bursts, any movement brought down fire. One CSM was hit in a most awkward place whilst performing a delicate operation in an exposed position! There was no fixed front. It was a series of platoon positions, *not* connected up by crawl trenches but mutually supporting. It was always necessary for runners, commanders or men distributing food to walk *above* the ground. There was no continuous wire in front. At night especially one could always imagine the enemy creeping up in the deep corn or working his way round behind. None of the small patrol operations were completed without loss. Our artillery gave back much more than we received, directed by aerial OPs and FOOs. These artillery officers did very gallant work with our forward troops.

Capt N. Squire was FOO of 83 Field Regt RA, supporting 6 RWF near Rauray. Late on 2 July he went forward with two signallers laying a line as they went:

> We got into position and connected the telephone, to be greeted by a violent ringing of the bell of the phone, loud enough it seemed to raise the 'Bosch' for miles around. We hastily disconnected the line and to calm our nerves, I brought out my hipflask to comfort the Coy CO and my signallers. Having passed it around, I nudged the chap on my left to give him a sip. As he didn't respond, I nudged him harder and he toppled over. This chap was a dead German! Not a pleasant night.

160 BRIGADE: 'HURTLING DEATH AND DESTRUCTION'

Ordered to relieve a brigade of the 15th Scottish Division, near Grainville-sur-Odon and Le Valtru the three battalions of 160 Brigade were soon in considerable trouble. Major A. J. Lewis 4 Welch:

> We relieved 9th Cameronians in bocage country. It was an inferno into which we had moved. Multibarrelled mortars with their loud screech, phosphorous shells, heavy guns, light guns, airbursts, mortars and Spandau MG — all were hurtling death and destruction into the area, ceaselessly as it seemed. The first 12 hours saw a full scale attack by the Germans, with tanks against one company. A 6 pdr A/Tk gun knocked out a tank with its first three rounds, but German infantry penetrated into one of the forward company positions, but were eventually driven out.

The new CO, Lt Col J. W. C. Williams (Lt Col Coleman had been promoted to brigadier) was greeted on 1 July by a direct hit on his command post within five minutes of his arrival. He, the 2 i/c and adjutant were buried in the debris but unhurt. 'At the Colleville railway crossing,' Major Lewis continued:

> in front of us, we saw the results of a particularly vicious period of shelling which without warning had landed in the midst of a company of our sister Bn (1/5 Welch). It was their bicycle coy. Hampered by those encumbrances it had been quickly transformed into a struggling mass of wounded, dead and dying.

1/5 Welch under Lt Col E. R. G. Ripley (Their third CO in a year) went into their first action on 1 July. Capt Bill Tudor Owen, IO of 1/5 Welch:

> Colonel Ripley, a giant of a man resembling a Viking went on a recce, with me, in a jeep towards the hamlet of Le Valtru. After passing Cheux, he became restless. It was getting dark and approaching the crossroads, he leaped off the jeep and strode down the road towards the buildings. He was challenged by a sentry, failed to respond (he had a hearing defect) and was shot. A dreadful blow at a time when we hadn't been bloodied.

Sgt Machin, the Intelligence Sergeant of 1/5 Welch:

> At midnight in single file through those shell-blasted ghostly relics of Le Mesnil-Patry, Cheux, Colville and Mondrainville, we passed over the railway line. Suddenly the silence was torn asunder in the rending explosion of exploding bombs. The Bosch mortars were laying down harassing fire. Those mortars had been sighted and corrected perfectly. The very earth shook as amidst the inferno we dived into ditches, behind walls or whatever cover happened to be to hand. Before the Battalion reached Le Valtru we had suffered 40-50 casualties. Our Major Jack [Morrison-Jones the 2 i/c] with cool deliberation commanded and directed the takeover from the Seaforth Highlanders. I proudly remember the magnificent composure of everyone through those first dark and dreadful hours. We remained at Le Valtru for 48 hours and suffered about 150 casualties before being relieved by 4 Welch on the evening of 2/3 July.

Corporal Mostyn Thomas was a LMG Group NCO with 18 Platoon 'D' Coy and wrote in his diary:

> ... leading into Tourville, 'C' Coy to the SW, 'D' Coy to the NW — an artillery barrage struck both companies and continued for some minutes. It was a fierce bombardment, the screaming shells, explosions and the smell of cordite was our introduction to the lethal side of war. Projectiles struck banks of the road where I lay hard against the SW side, splinters of stone and shrapnel whirred past. Men were whirling around from blast or making for cover. At the bend were some

Edward Lewis, Fred Storr & Mostyn Thomas, 1/5 Welch Regt

occupied slits. I saw the face of Sullivan but there was no movement. Then we went through the tangle of bicycles, the wounded and the dead of 'C' Coy. Smoke shells had been used. Some bodies were on fire. Most of the men must have been killed. There was little noise except for one man calling 'Mam, Mam, Mam'.

Around Mondrainville, 2 Mons took their share in the 160 Brigade defensive locality. On 29 June they lost eight casualties including two officers to 105 mm shelling and two days later battalion HQ was shelled, wounding another three officers and nine signallers. Their 2 i/c Major John Price, a notable rugger player, was one of the casualties.

71ST BRIGADE: 'CAMEMBERT CHEESE AND CALVADOS' — AND PATROLS

71st Brigade's defensive area was Cheux — Le Haut du Bosque with 1st East Lancs in front down to the railway at Grainville-sur-Odon, 1st Ox and Bucks forward of Le Haut du Bosque with 1 HLT behind them at Cheux. Patrols and experience of heavy nebelwerfer mortaring were to be their lot for the next two weeks. The 1st East Lancs were commanded by Lt Col Burden who, aged forty-seven, was debarred from going overseas. But General Dempsey said: 'You have one of the finest battalions in my Army Group and that being so, you shall come with us whatever they say.' So he did, and he and thirty-six officers and 804 other ranks set sail in LSI SS *Longford* and SS *Ben-McCree* for Juno beach. In the marshalling area, Camp J10 near Newhaven, their three Canloan officers Lieutenants Day, Phelps and Ellis became temporary baseball instructors. None of them ever returned to Canada. Unusual in 53rd Division, no less than 200 men including ten officers had served with the BEF from Tournais to Dunkirk. On arrival Major Lake led a number of successful patrols. Lt G C. R. L. Pender 1st HLI recalled:

> We dug a Battalion defensive position expecting massive counter-attacks. We were also introduced to camembert cheese and calvados. My Company Commander Major Bowie made a point of shooting at every barrel of stuff [spoilsport!]. We all remained sober. Major Dick Kindersley OC 'A' Coy put his HQ in a chateau near Cheux and discovered the owner's family silver buried in the garden. It was all returned to its rightful owner who was delighted to have it back!

And Lt Mackinlay of the HLI proved to be a splendid patrol leader. The Ox and Bucks under Lt Col James Hare sent out many probing patrols and raids led by Lt Arthur Morley, Lt Tim Rylands and Lt P. J. Badman towards Queudeville. On one occasion a patrol under Lt E. A. Yates was fired on by the 6 RWF by mortars and small arms — but they missed! The IO, Capt D. R. Ashe, pieced together the jigsaw of information gained from the patrols usually carried out with several casualties.

*   *   *

When Sapper Ned Petty arrived in the bridgehead he found: 'Everything was quiet but it was obvious that bitter fighting had been going on there very recently. There were several newly dug graves dotted about, obviously very shallow and temporary. I found it particularly saddening because quite a lot of them had steel helmets with our Welsh "W" Sign on them. I wasn't sorry to get away.' His first tasks (RE Coy with 71st Brigade) were blowing craters in fields to bury dead bloated cow carcasses, then attaching each dead cow by rope to a Bren gun carrier to tow the body into the hole — a rotten job. The RE bulldozers were busy roadmaking and road repairing. Ned helped prepare a water point with round canvas tanks each holding 1500 gallons. Bricks were needed for hardcore on roads so cottage walls were duly knocked down! 'In 20 minutes Sapper Damsell the latrine expert could produce an efficient 'product': dig a suitable hole, with a roll of hessian 5' high, on five poles with a square screen round the hole and 2 compo boxes to form a seat. Easy!'

Alistair (Mac) Carmichael from the Royal Signals Section attached to 71st Brigade drove Brigadier Bloomfield's 'International' half track used as the Brigade TAC HQ. L/Corporal McDonald drove the Brigadier's Humber staff car. Capt Meinertzhager was GSO3. The wireless generator was Eddie Davies, a Yorkshireman and Corporal Ingle was a Lancastrian. 'The Brigadier and myself developed a great understanding, a great officer. I cannot remember him raising his voice to me at any time and respected my ability. As time went on I respected him as a Father and I am sure [he regarded me] as if I were his son.' Eventually 'Mac' was to drive two more brigadiers and a colonel, acting Brigade commander. There did seem to be a high rate of red-tabbed officer turnover!

Most of the British Army watched the RAF destroy the city of Caen on the night of 7 July when 450 heavy bombers unleashed thousands of tons of high explosive on the unlucky city. Lt Peter Utley, Recce Regt wrote:

Normandy Scenes

My studies of architecture made me anxious to get into Caen to see the churches
of William the Conqueror and his Queen. As it was I sat on the turret of my
armoured car and watched wave after wave of Allied bombers reduce the place
to rubble. Recce was forced into an infantry role and we learned how to dig fox
holes and live in intimate proximity with the creatures of the soil.

Corporal Mostyn Thomas, 1/5 Welch described how the snipers on their front
were dealt with:

> From the high trees across the Grainville-Gavrus road, their fire was so heavy
> that two Vickers MG of the Manchesters were brought in. They fired for about
> 20 minutes from the garden facing west, packed up their guns and went off.
> Their technique was to fire laterally from left to right, then vertically up and
> down the trees followed by an extended burst. The sniper fire ceased for a while
> — to be replaced by enemy artillery fire. After Le Valtru, 'D' Coy officers usually
> carried rifles... 'C' Coy must have lost 80 men since last night. 8th July. LOB
> back 10 kms to Loucelles to 'A' Echelon in a field. The platoon truck was nearby.
> Our field packs had been looted. This was quite common. The excuse was that
> underwear had to be laundered. The Coy cooks came up to the mark with food.
> Hot piled up mess tins, eaten in the open, mugs of tea and duff to follow. Then
> disaster, *new* uniforms and clothes. We looked like *Rookies*!

The pipers of the Highland units were great morale-boosters. Mostyn Thomas
again:

> 15th July. In the early evening 1 HLI marched past down the hill, round the bend
> towards Tourmauville. In front was their Piper in his kilt and tam. He played a
> stirring march and the valley echoed with the sound of his pipes. A magnificent
> sight. I wished them well.

Corporal Bert Isherwood of 13 Field Dressing Station under Captain
Rowlands boarded the liberty ship SS *John E. Ward* (6000 tons) at St Georges
Dock and went ashore at Port-en-Bessin on the top of a loaded Scammel on
a LCV manned by Canadian sailors. On 1 July 13 FDS took over from 15th
Scottish Forward Dressing Station, which Bert described:

> Ambulances were coming and going to the entrance and from the exit of the
> 'Big Top', a huge trench dug out by bulldozers, some 6 feet deep, 40 feet wide
> and the length of four 3-ton Bedford trucks. Tarpaulin sheeting stretches across
> the space between the trucks and over the extra trench. Completely under cover,
> protected from the weather, the inside of the trench is divided into sections
> — operating theatres, dental theatre, pre-op station, dressing stations, post-

op station, rest station with an office at the entrance to record all casualties coming in for treatment. The whole is illuminated by electric lighting generated by our mobile generating unit driven by a motor run on white spirit — the responsibility of L/Corp Martin Ellis RASC. The top and sides of the tarpaulin cover on the outside sported large red crosses on white circular backgrounds. Casualties arrive at the entrance by ambulance, by stretcher and walking wounded and battle fatigue cases come under their own steam. All are operated on or otherwise treated and despatched to Casualty Receiving Station, or to a Field General Hospital or back to their own units. Casualties arrive from Regimental Aid Posts, or Field Ambulance Units or even direct from the line.

Every British casualty had nothing but praise for the efficient and usually compassionate evacuation and treatment of their wounds.

An infantry division with its nine 'teeth' battalions is supported by no less than five artillery regiments — three field 25 pdrs, an anti-tank and a light Ack-Ack Regt. Lt Col W. L. C. Phillips wrote:

Battery Commanders and FOOs spent most of their time with their infantry and saw little of the guns. In this campaign, artillery was used in such masses that the chances of a BC or TC shorting his own battery or troop were few and far between. Being with the infantry they could alter a fire plan in case things went wrong. Their presence was undoubtedly good for the morale of the infantry. He knew the guns were on call. Wireless was all important on the regimental 'net', all FOOs were in touch with each other and with the guns and could get fire in about two minutes. If the infantry wireless 'collapsed' a battalion CO could talk to his brigadier on the gunner wireless network.

The 71st Anti-tank Regt (RWF) took up defensive preparations west of Caen at St Mauvieu, Le Bon Repos, Evrecy, Grainville, Mondrainville, Hill 112, Maltot and Cheux. With guns in forward position, in many cases unapproachable except under cover of darkness, the regiment suffered many casualties. Yet there can be little doubt that the sight and proximity of the guns did much to keep up the spirit of the infantry they were supporting. The 116 RWF LAA had some good and interesting shooting at the Luftwaffe in the early days in Normandy. They also formed the Divisional Counter-mortar organisation in which Lt de Carteret played a leading role.

Captain David Bolland, Staff Capt RA at Division HQ continues his diary/ letters home for the first half of July — up until the first major offensive actions mounted by 53 Welsh Division:

Saturday, 1st July. The bombing last night of (enemy) tanks concentrated near Villers-Bocage was a wonderful sight. Tomorrow we relieve 15 Scottish Div. First time in this campaign, OPs are deployed operationally. Sunday, 2nd. Div HQ moved to Putout-en-Bessin. First time division is fully committed in the line. We all live in holes in the ground just big enough to take a valise. Infantry takeover in areas Grainville-sur-Odon, and Mondrainville. Monday, 3rd. Enemy attacked 158 Bde in area of Baron. Jack Knight of 133 Field Regt, Dick Bradford of 71 A/Tank Regt killed in action. Tuesday, 4th. Local cheese, Camembert is very good costs about 19 francs (1/-), milk at 5 francs a litre, and butter 4/- per lb. Eggs very scarce costs 6d each! Enemy put in heavy attack at Brettevillette which was beaten off chiefly through large fire plan. Wednesday, 5th. Every day we have an A/Q conference at Rear Div HQ. AA and QMG, Robert Neilson. Daag Joe Grimond. DAQMG Frank Wilson; APM Nick Pascall; CRASC Joe Bridge; ADOS Gordon Kerr: CREME Lt Col F. M. Hext. SC 71 Bde Len Marsh; SC185 Bde Bob Lemon; SC160 Bde Tubby Milton; and many others. These A/Q conferences are always good fun, treated with a reasonable amount of levity, not apparent on the 'G' side! Thursday, 6th. The Division have been staunchly holding a line just south of Cheux. The guns were deployed just north of Tilly-Caen road. A sight fit for sore eyes — everywhere a mass of artillery field, medium and heavy. Average expenditure of 25 pdr ammo was 200 rds per gun per day. Friday, 7th. Rear Div at Brouay. Here we started our Div Cemetery now unfortunately filling up rather rapidly. [Bolland watched the huge aerial bombardment of Caen]. Saturday, 8th. I go out to the Regiments daily (we now have 6 Field, 151 Field, 4RHA, 59 Medium and Heavy Battery under command as well as all five gunner regiments). Sunday, 9th. Mobile cinema showed at 332 Battery Command post. Of course it broke down. I also had a court-martial to arrange for tomorrow. Mobile Baths are now very popular. People used to scoff at them on exercises, and how glad they are to get them now! The battle is pretty static, very disheartening for our infantry. There they are taking all that the Hun can give them, mortaring small arms fire. We are giving them all we can in the way of fire support. Fired 250 rounds per gun today. Tuesday, 11th. [David Bolland noted the names of Div HQ. Major General RK Ross; his ADC Geoff Sanders; GI Lt Col Ap Rhys Price; A/Q Robert Neilson. G2 Kenneth Goodacre; G3's Les Williams, Dennis Ellis and Ian Simpson. G3 (INT) Donald Phelps. IO John Suffolk, also Padre Snell (the Bishop), Dick Thomson, Education Officer, etc] Thursday, 13th. Went with CRA (Friedberger) and BM to CCRA's conference at HQ 12 Corps at Bretteville L'Orgueilleuse attended by CCRA Second Army and Six CRAs and planning of an operation which I felt would never come off — and it didn't. Friday, 14th. A rocket firing Typhoon attacked our lines. One rocket landed in RHQ 116 Light AA Regt and another on the 25 pdr Ammunition Point. 6 lorryloads went up — it was a magnificent fireworks display but must have been dreadful on the spot. All praise to Ian Andrews OC 50 Coy RASC and Bill Ling his 2 i/c. They get up ammunition at all hours of the day or night.

Bert Isherwood, 13 FDS, recorded a bizarre incident in the 'Big Top' Hospital tent on 6 July: a young wounded German SS Panzer soldier on a stretcher was being examined by a MO and Pte Mandlebaum: 'As the MO bent over him, the German spat up into his face. The MO (Jewish as of course was the Private) exhibited surprise but no anger. I think the Nazi would rather die, and if it had been left to me, I would have let him.' But two days later Bert and mate, Fred Nappi had found a large round drinking trough in a farmyard near Cheux. Filled with water and heated by a fire below it produced a very passable hot bath. 'We had almost completed our ablutions when a Messerschmitt 109 peeled from their formation. A hail of bullets spewed right through the trough. Fred and I, naked and wet and caked all over with Norman soil had escaped, running for our slits.' Another strange event took place on 9 July. A four stretcher Austin ambulance driven by 'Broad' Garrett and 'sandy' Sandford with Sgt Jim Mason in the back drove towards Tilly-Sur-Seulles to find the Ox and Bucks. They missed the left fork at Fontenay-le-Pesnil and drove to the crossroads at Juvigny — of course without a map. They came across a tank man in black overalls with a large spanner beside his tank. They asked the way to Tilly. One German tanker then said to another German tanker 'was ist los Heinz?' Although in the ensuing fracas Sgt Mason was wounded in the leg and the ambulance wrecked, the three of them rather surprisingly, survived to tell their tale. 'They lay in the ditch all night keeping an ear open for the enemy while the sounds of war went on all around them!' On 12 July Bert noted: 'The Luftwaffe had complained that they had seen war supplies getting carried in army truck(s) with red cross emblems.' Bert had in fact carried up petrol for 212 Field Ambulance and 13 FDS.

A tank bulldozer smashing through *bocage*, thick high hedgerow

A crab flail tank for clearing a path through minefields — noisy but effective

3
Operation Greenline:
'attack on Cahier'

12 Corps had been ordered to capture the high ground Bougy-Evrecy-Maizet, south of the river Odon and two miles south-west of the small bridgehead at Baron. The unfortunate 43rd Division — the 'Fighting Wessex Wyverns' — had lost two thousand casualties in the two day Operation Jupiter on 10/11 July to try to take the bitterly contested high ground of Hill 112 and Maltot. The initial task now fell to 71 Brigade and specifically to 1st Battalion Oxford & Buckinghamshire LI to take on the northern/right flank, the hamlet of Cahier, two woods code-named 'Jumbo' and 'Tiny' and a mill on the river Odon at Gavrus. The start line was protected by 2nd Monmouthshires and the objectives were defended by 272 and 277 Infantry Divisional troops. They

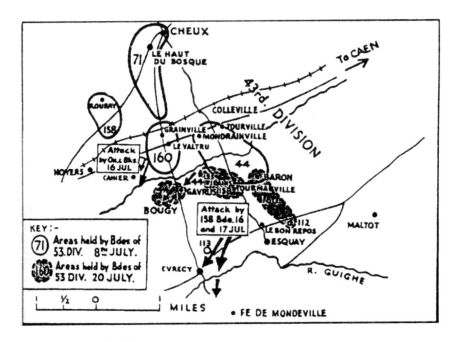

Operations along the Rivers Odon & Guighe, July 1944

were well dug in and hidden in typical 'bocage' country. The attack started at 03.00 hrs still in darkness on 15 July. Lt Col James Hare directed 'C' Coy on 'Tiny' Copse. 'D' Coy towards the mill and 'A' Coy to positions south-east of 'Tiny' Copse, with 'B' Coy in reserve for 'Jumbo'. Lt Colonel Tyler's 81st Field Regt and twelve of the Manchesters' 4.2-inch mortars were to support the attack. Very fierce close fighting followed, as 'C' Coy were involved in hand to hand fighting in the woods and by 06.15 hrs had to withdraw. 'B' Coy actually got into Cahier, captured twenty prisoners, but all their officers became casualties from heavy mortar fire. 'D' Coy dominated the bridges over the river Odon on the road to Gavrus. The situation was critical as the companies directed on 'Tiny' and Cahier were forced to yield their gains to counter-attacks. But at 14.00 hrs Major A Livingstone's 'A' Coy backed by the fire of three Divisional gunner regiments launched a second attack and by 16.00 hrs Cahier was occupied and found to be empty of German troops.

Those were the bare bones of a savage day's fighting. The Ox and Bucks lost eight officer casualties, 55 other ranks killed, 93 other ranks wounded and 18 missing, a total of 175. But they had taken 138 prisoners and killed or wounded another 145 enemy, all from 277 Wehrmacht Infantry Division. They also captured eighteen machine guns. The dead were buried in Brovay churchyard. There were many heroes that awful day. Private Frank Short of 17 Platoon took two German officers prisoner and shot a German who threw a stick grenade and killed Captain John Cooper. During the attack on the Cahier mill Frank Short 'was suddenly confronted by a German already in a firing position to my left. The first shot hit the top of my right leg, but he panicked, dropped his rifle and ran. I hit the ground with excruciating pain but I was determined to get my attacker.' And he did. 'Major Pierce (the Coy CO), yelled for us to keep our heads down.' But Frank was hit a second time by a Spandau as was Major Pierce, and Frank feeling the worse for wear sought shelter in the river Odon, in mid-summer a mere stream. 'The water was now running with my blood as a lone German sniper tried to finish me off.' Frank survived and was taken back by carrier to the RAP.

Sgt Roland 'Nobby' Clarke was awarded the DCM. He tracked down a Spandau team in the woods pinning 'C' Coy down and emerged with the LMG over his shoulder and the German machine gunner, now a prisoner. Private 'sandy' Sandford of 13 Platoon was less fortunate. Trapped in the open by heavy MG fire the platoon took shelter in long grass. A little later: 'It was a hopeless situation, no ammunition, nothing to fight with and a lot of wounded infantrymen needing attention.' As the Germans came near, brandishing their Schneissers, 13 Platoon including the walking wounded got to their feet with their arms above their heads, to be marched off to the German lines. 'Moments later a massive British barrage fell on captors and captured. 'Nobby' was hit in the legs, Dick Scroggs in the hand; Sgt Jefferies was seriously wounded and removed in a wheelbarrow.' Eventually 'sandy' ended up in Rennes POW hospital where he was liberated by Patton's 3rd US Army.

The Ox and Bucks moved out of the line for a rest and back to Mouen where they were dive bombed by screaming Stukas.

THE BATTLES FOR EVRECY

15th Scottish Division, who had taken a terrible beating in Operation Epsom, were given a major role in Operation Greenline. Their objectives were Gavrus and Bougy, two villages south-east of Cahier, south of the river Odon. Their third objective were the hills north of Esquay around Le Bon Repos and the dreaded Hill 112. In bitter fighting they had succeeded at a cost but had failed to capture Evrecy a mile or so south-east of Bougy, south-west of Esquay. The Royal Welch Fusilier Brigade (158th) were given this difficult task under Brigadier Silas Jones.

Brigade HQ made a large sand model dug in a cleared patch of corn and briefing took place on 15 July. The initial attack was to be by 7 RWF to take the high ground south of the Esquay-Evrecy road. The next stage would be to descend the slope beyond, cross the little river Guighe east of Evrecy, climb the next hill and assault and capture the Ferme de Mondeville. 'A' Coy 6 RWF under Major Hughes was to come under command.

The start line for 7 RWF was on Hill 113 and the artillery barrage opened at 23.30 hrs on the night of 16th/17th. In the lead were 'B' and 'A' Coys on the right, 'A' Coy 6 RWF on the left followed by 'C' and 'D' 7 RWF and 'C' 6 RWF with 'C' Coy 4 RWF on their right as flank protection. The heavy mist which came down suddenly was thickened up by German smoke bombs, but the leading companies reached the main road — the first report line. By 02.00 hrs they had crossed the little river Guighe and were advancing up the slope towards the farmhouse. But the supporting tanks and anti-tank guns could not be got across. Nevertheless the GOC ordered Brigadier Silas Jones to clear the river valley to the east of Evrecy and hold it. Communication between units was ineffective. Eventually 7 RWF were ordered to withdraw for fear they would be cut off.

Lt Col A. H. Williams DSO, CO of 7 RWF wrote:

The battalion attacked the hill on the night of 16/17th. This involved an advance of over 2500 yards and at first all went according to plan. Soon however a heavy fog came down and it was this that finally decided the issue. Cohesion became more and more difficult and when the small river at the foot of the hill was reached companies had become unavoidably but seriously disorganised. By this time enemy opposition had become intense and though sporadic fighting continued all night, only one platoon succeeded in obtaining a lodgement at the foot of the hill itself.

As dawn was approaching, the order came to retire and very shortly afterwards the fog which had so greatly aided the enemy during the night, lifted quite suddenly, leaving the battalion completely exposed on a long slope. Enemy fire now became very heavy and severe casualties were suffered from mortar and artillery fire as well as from sniping. During this withdrawal I was severely wounded, saved by Lts DC Jones and Capt. Dryland.

Captain D. M. Evans records: 'After the evacuation of the CO the 2 i/c Major Dickson took command of a battalion reduced to three rifle companies of two weak platoons each.' 7 RWF had indeed suffered grievously. Officer casualties included Major E. D. K. Menzies, OC 'B' Coy, Lts Mackney and Joynt both missing, 100 other ranks killed or wounded and another 98 missing. The heart had been torn out of the battalion — for the time being. It was a brutal and savage introduction and a warning of the struggle to come.

Fusilier John Ottewell, 'D' Coy 7 RWF wrote in his journal 'A Cry from the Heart',: 'We, the Signals Dugout, the TCV (Communications truck) and close defence platoon were also taking hell. From 11.30 pm until well after 3 am the next morning, impact, Moaning Minny mortars and 88 mm shells along with airburst rained on our position without respite. Of course this always happens to forward TAC HQ's up with the Battalions. Knock out your 'communication links' between Division Brigade and Battalion and nobody knows 'what in the hell's going on'. No co-ordination. No command and control. No Sitreps, Mobrebs, ASTU calling for airstrikes. Yes the 16/17 July was a bad night for the RWF Battalions. Our casualties at TAC were significant. Our TCV had been hit, nearly all the cables on our ten line exchange were cut. Quite a number of the 2nd Battalion Monmouths dug in around our orchard had been killed or wounded. One 88 mm shell hit a Bren Carrier with reserve ammo. The phosphorous mortar shells exploded and soldiers in a nearby slit trench were badly burnt.'

Captain Hugh Roberts MC, the Adjutant 6 RWF described their first night attack:

It was now completely dark when we moved forward. A fog came up, growing thicker every moment. Churchill tanks without lights were groping their way forward along the same road as we marched, hugging the verges. Propaganda leaflets dropped by enemy planes fell eerily about us; they told us we were 'caught like foxes in a trap.' There were houses still burning by the road as we crossed the little river. The shelling increased and the fog thickened till one could only see a few feet.

'A' Coy were attached to 7 RWF to help capture Ferme de Mondeville; 'C' Coy followed, their task of left flank protection. They were followed by 'D' Coy, Brigade HQ and 's' Coy.

It was after midnight when we neared the start line on the open ridge between Hills 112 and 113. Both leading companies were soon engaged in close fighting against seasoned troops inc. SS. Despite the opposition, the darkness and the appalling fog 'A' Coy reached their objective. Major OEH Hughes was awarded the Croix de Guerre afterwards. 'C' Coy on the left met enemy in strength, but the mist, darkness and fields of standing corn made control and co-ordination impossible. So they dug in to await daylight and suffered many casualties inc. Major GE Gristly who was wounded, was missing and never found. 'B' Coy under Capt Hill protected two Sapper platoons making a recce for vehicles to cross the little river. (Captain Roberts)

'We were to seal off the eastern end of Evrecy and stop any penetration from the SW coming in from the direction of the village,' wrote Nick Cutcliffe, now Major OC 'C' Coy 4 RWF. He attended the 'O' Group at 7th RWF Battalion HQ by Lt Col Williams:

He arrived very late, gave his orders rapidly, obviously harassed by the lack of time... All this for a night attack of considerable complication. I had not seen the ground not even the start line. *The situation was manifestly absurd.* I gave my orders with a certain amount of trepidation.

Evrecy after the battle

Initially all went well despite the fog, mist and mortaring.

> It was the first time we had been mortared in the open. Some of the chaps found
> it rather unnerving. I didn't have time to worry — I was so pleased that I was still
> alive that I began to develop a sensation approaching that of exhilaration. One
> bomb behind me felt particularly close, it fell amongst Rear HQ killed one man,
> wounding several others. Some rather wild Spandau fire, so too much readiness
> to go to ground. One jittery fellow with 'trigger itch' let off a burst of sten and
> most of *his* platoon went to ground mistaking it for a Schneisser's sound. These
> men were all well trained and knew exactly what to do.

In the mist 14 Platoon became separated so Nick closed up the remainder. Tim
Dumas, walking on a compass bearing towards a Calvary on the Evrecy — Le
Bon Repos road duly arrived there with the rest of 'C' Coy. They disposed of a
German patrol and opened fire at first light on another which turned out to be
Nick Cutcliffe and company! Later they were ordered to withdraw to the start
line. The rest of the battalion had attacked at the same time as 6 RWF with 'D'
Coy on the left, 'A' Coy on the right. They met strong opposition, withdrew
behind the hill and dug in east of Gavrus.

Nick Cutcliffe described the perilous withdrawal of his 4 RWF Company.
When the mist cleared he could see two Tiger tanks in a cornfield two hundred
yards away north of Evrecy. There were no anti-tank guns available and only
two Piat bombs 'so stalking them was out of the question'. Linas Evans with
'A' Coy 6 RWF 'came through us clearing the area along the stream. He was
later wounded and captured, taken to hospital in Rennes and fed on bread
green with mould.' Next visitor was Peter Dryland, IO of 7 RWF who brought
orders to withdraw:

> We felt that reinforcements were needed rather than withdrawal. We followed
> 7 RWF Battalion HQ along the road towards Le Bon Repos. A vicious burst
> of mortar fire fell on them. I saw Colonel Williams lying in the ditch with his
> arm half off. Jerry was now very much aware of our withdrawal. In addition to
> mortar stonks he swept the road with MG fire from the other side of the valley.

Nick called over the air for smoke to cover their withdrawal. Soon fire was
coming in from in front:

> I lined up the Coy in the ditch. On the word 'GO' we jumped out and ran hell for
> leather, widely dispersed up the forward slope. Jerry opened up with all the MGs
> he could lay his hands on… we got to the top and over it.

Jimmy Rice Evans, his CO, 'welcomed me with some emotion; I think he'd given us up for lost'. 'C' Coy had five killed, twenty-two wounded and four missing that long night.

Corporal Sidney Griffiths, 'A' Coy who was wounded that day and evacuated:

> We were in the cornfield and darkness was falling. We passed many knocked out and burning [Churchill] tanks, one tank commander hanging out of the turret. He was dead. We got our seriously wounded on a Bren Carrier including Sgt Owen and Fusiliers Bowler and Berry. Later in the Field Hospital in Bayeux I looked in on Lt Judd and Lt Morgan who had been wounded that day.

Major Macindoe BC of 330 Bty, 133 Field Regt RA supported 4 RWF with his FOO Capt Winder. They too got separated from Battalion HQ in the thick mist.

> Dick and I went too far forward. It was a still night and every rattle of Spandau fire seemed to be within 100 yards of us. It was an ill-starred attack that night when 4 RWF lost so many men so quickly. I was with Col Rice-Evans dug in on the reverse slope. We received the heaviest artillery and mortar bombardment that I recollect in the whole war. He succumbed to shell-shock and had to withdraw. Two OP signallers, Bde Rose and Gnr Blackley were killed and Dick Winder received a serious wound in his leg and we saw no more of him.

THE SECOND BATTLE OF EVRECY

During the 17th the Brigade spent a difficult day under heavy shelling. Captain Hugh Roberts, Adjutant 6 RWF wrote:

> When dawn came and the mist lifted we discovered with much consternation that most of our Bn position was completely overlooked by the enemy on the high ground to the south. Any movement brought down fire and no food or water could be brought up. Two carriers bringing up ammo. received direct hits. Fusilier Pyrah, one of the drivers was killed. Our ridge was open fields with no fences, arable, deep in crops. The enemy knew the ground, crept up, fired with LMG and sniped. Our losses were serious inc. Capt Griffith the IO and Sgt Scott, both killed.

And so it went on during the day. But the orders came down from Corps to Division to Brigade that Evrecy *had* to be taken. A second attack had to be mounted that evening with 4 RWF and 7 RWF leading and 6 RWF in support along the track Gavrus to Evrecy supported by Churchill tanks and barrage. Nick Cutcliffe and his company of 4 RWF were LOB (left out of battle) but wrote in his journal: 'The attack went in at 21.15 hrs. Soon our worst fears were confirmed. Men started to come back. The attack had been a complete failure.' ('A' and 'D' Coys led into intense fire. Spandau teams dotted about in the cornfields took heavy toll as 4 RWF moved down the bare slope. All the officers of 'A' Coy were killed or wounded. CSM Jones rallied the company but Majors St Clair Ford and Ken Ellis were killed, and Lt Philip Morgan commanding 'B' Coy severely wounded. Of the twelve in the company officers involved only two came back unhurt. 'A' and 'D' Coys had been reduced to a third of their fighting strength, and 'B' had lost half its strength. The MO Capt W. J. Cameron and his RAP staff worked for thirty-six hours without rest and treated 150 casualties.)

> The opposition had been much heavier than anticipated. Tanks and 17-pdr A/Tk guns were unable to get their pieces in action and suffered heavy casualties. No one had reached the objective. This news had a very bad effect on the morale of those left behind. That night several of our vehicles were hit including the ambulance which went up in a blaze of flame. The Doc and his stretcher bearers did valiant work. Afterwards 'Doc' Cameron told me it wasn't *he* who kept going but God that sustained him. We were so dazed and apathetic that we left the bodies of our dead untouched where they were! [Nick Cutliffe]

There were many heroes that day. L/Corporal Redfern and Fusiliers Ellis and Butler went out five times in their carrier under heavy fire to bring back wounded men from the cornfields. 6 RWF crossed their starting line at 21.20 hrs with 'B' Coy leading. The enemy had been reinforced during the day but were well dug in on the reverse slope in standing barley with dug in tanks. Some fierce hand-to-hand fighting took place. In bitter fighting over 200 prisoners mainly of 276 Wehrmacht Infantry Division were taken and many more killed, but at a cost. Captain F. E. Hill and twenty-eight unwounded men came back out of the action from the two leading companies — 'B' and 'D'. Lts Peter Jeffs and Sam Kirk were killed as was Major McWhor and CSM Pritchard. The CO Lt Col E H Cadogan personally carrying a Bren gun and leading a platoon attack was badly wounded in the neck. Capt Hugh Roberts:

> The light started to fail. Our tanks could no longer give support. Our ammunition was almost exhausted. Although we had over-run the enemy's FDLs we could not dig in on a forward slope and had no option but to withdraw over Hill 113 for a reverse slope position.

Panther and Tiger tanks and SPs, some dug-in, some mobile raked all the attacking RWF battalions. There seemed to be no answer to the six-barrelled Nebelwerfers. In the dark the enemy infantry counter-attacked and followed up closely as the RWF Brigade withdrew. In the dark, fighting became ever more confused as the RWF passed through the lines of two Scottish battalions of the Gordon Highlanders and KOSB of 15th Scottish Division. Friendly troops fired on each other. All three commanding offices were casualties. Twenty-five officers were killed and wounded and there were several hundred other rank casualties.

The supporting arms had tried their best — Churchill tanks, the Manchesters with their 4.2-inch mortars and MMG and the gunners — 133 Field Regt RA had fired 20,000 rounds in six days of attacks and counter-attacks. Captain David Bolland, Staff Captain RA wrote in his diary:

> Monday, 17th. Today will probably go down as one of the blackest days in the history of 53 Div. In the early morning 158 Brigade put in their attack on Evrecy. The attack failed owing to difficulties in crossing the river with supporting arms and due to heavy mist causing considerable disorganisation. The Brigade withdrew and re-organised having suffered fairly high casualties including the loss of 'A' Tp, 71 A/Tk. Regt Denis Whaley of 83 Field Regt has been killed by a direct hit on his OP. All planes of B Flight 653 AIR OP SQN were damaged in one attack on their ALG. Tuesday, 18th. At 3am 158 Bde make another attack on Evrecy. Went well at the start and large numbers of PW taken. One Bn reached objective but subsequent heavy mortar and MG fire prevented them from holding their objective. They were ordered to withdraw by GOC 15 Scottish Division. Diversionary attack by 53 Div particularly 158 Bde probably misled enemy as to the place of the main attack [of Goodwood when three Armoured Divisions attacked south-east of Caen]. So the losses of last few days have not been in vain.

Well, Goodwood was an expensive failure. Certainly operation Greenline was a disaster.

Lt Colonel M. H. ap Rhys Pryce was GSO1 at the time of the Evrecy battles and wrote:

> [a] The German position was an excellent defensive one.
>
> [b] It was manned by first class troops.
>
> [c] We could not get our AFVs across the water obstacle.
>
> [d] FOG
>
> [e] But of course it fulfilled Monty's main plan which was to keep the best German troops and most of their armour in front of us, while the Americans swept round.

In the period 12-26 July the Division lost 290 killed in action, and 405 additional battle casualties. Corporal Bert Isherwood 13 FDS wrote in his journal:

> Thursday, 20th July. A constant never ending stream of wounded passing into our FDS. There must be one hell of a battle raging in the area of Evrecy. The stretcher cases tell me of a maze of concrete and guns and remorseless enemy counter-attacks with Tiger tanks, with well thought out patterns of crossfire from heavy MG, nebelwerfers mortars and 88s coming down on road junctions and other keypoints.

Greenline was over.

Evrecy July, 1944 by Fusilier John A. Ottewell

> Men of the 'Black Flash', 'sospan' and 'Dragon',
> Wading through 'bayonet' wheat, knee-high and wet,
> Mortars and 'eighty-eights' playing their 'overtures'
> Spandaus and Schmeissers are waiting and set.
>
> Up to the hill enshrouded in mortar smoke,
> Tellermines, 's' mines, a mushroom the slope,
> Tiger tanks, panzerfausts blasting our carriers,
> Air burst exploding like 'bubbles of soap'.
>
> Now cross the singing Guighe into the alder wood,
> Remnants of companies merged to platoon,
> Screams for the stretchers with 'Mother' and 'Jesus'
> 'steady old son.... we'll have you out soon.'
>
> Men of the 'Black Flash', 'sospan' and 'Dragon'.
> Limping it back.... all haggard and pale,
> Two hundred dead for handful of prisoners,
> Just one consolation, 'They've brought up the mail.'

Note: 'Black Flash' — Royal Welch Fusiliers; 'sospan' — 4th Welch (Llanelli); 'Dragon' — 2nd Monmouthshire.

4
Bridgehead:
July – Raids and Patrols

For the next few days after Greenline and the tragic failure to take Evrecy, the Division took up defensive positions. In 71 Brigade, 1st East Lancs dug in around Bougy, 1st Ox and Bucks around Gavrus and 1st HLI on the reverse slope to the east with a company to watch Evrecy, known to be held by the Germans in strength.

The East Lancs relieved 8 Royal Scots in a position under constant mortaring. Major Lake led a battle patrol of twenty-four men from 'A' Coy to seize a prisoner, as did Lt Carroll and Lt Harper. The latter led a 'five minute raid' backed by 81st Field Regt support and tanks. A ten man charge, one minute through the cornfield, three minutes to kill everything in sight and one minute to scarper just as fast back home. They surprised an enemy post

The Ridge near Evrecy

of 991 Grenadier Regt and took one or two prisoners. On 31 July they took over from the HLI at Gavrus, largely destroyed with wrecked tanks nearly all British plus some burnt out 88 mm. After their tribulations at Cahier, the Ox and Bucks moved back to Mouen and were bombed both by Stukas and by an RAF Typhoon. The following day the pilot and his wing commander turned up to apologise. Then to Bougy to relieve the East Lancs on 27 July.

Bud Abbot with 'C' Sqn Recce Regt recalls:

> We relieved the Ox and Bucks infantry after their attack on Cahier in positions around Point 112/113 better known to the lads as 'Sausage Hill'. Our troop officer explained we were to repel an expected enemy counter-attack. We were to let their armour roll over us and deal with any following infantry. The thought of a 'Panther' or 'Tiger' rolling over the little slit trench [not deep enough to stand in] was not to be relished. One Piat was discharged at a suspicious noise. A voice from the turret in the darkness shouted out 'What the bloody hell is going on?', from a lost Churchill tank.

Major Crozier's diary mentioned some of the 1st Manchesters' activities in late July:

> 15th, 'B' Coy go with 158 Bde under command 15 Div on their attack on the line Noyers-Monceux-Evrecy-Maizet. 16th. Attack went in but only partly successful. Bosch used artificial fog and heavy bombing which caused some confusion and loss of direction. Attack to go in tonight. 17th. Attack again held with fairly heavy casualties in 158 Bde. All CO's casualties. Our HQ bombed again last night and fire nearly got the LAD.

The 4 RWF sent out strong patrols on the 19th towards Esquay under Lts Davies, Walker and Suttie. Each of them met strong resistance from mortaring or SP guns, and Walker and fifteen men were killed in these engagements. All that they proved was that the enemy had decided to retain Evrecy in considerable strength.

By 20 July a series of complicated moves and reliefs had taken place: 71st Brigade holding Gavrus and Bougy; 158 Brigade recovering from Greenline around Les Vilains and Tourmauville and 160 Brigade holding Baron and the area near Le Bon Repos crossroads.

However, the next unpleasant engagement came the next day. 1/5 Welch were holding a defensive position about Baron on the 21st, with two companies out on the high ground towards Le Bon Repos.

> At 1600hrs 'A' Coy 1/5 Welch commanded by Major Northcott reported being attacked by four tanks. The enemy — SS troops — had attacked our right

forward company at Le Bon Repos with the intention of over running it and then turning right to roll up the whole of our forward defences.

Sgt J. Machin, 1/5 Welch Intelligence continues:

These are the unforgettable moments when the whole front leaps into violent life. These are moments of agony, of drama, of heroic deeds, which nothing will ever erase from living memory. At 1800hrs, a platoon of 'B' Coy holding a left

Right: View near Baron

Below: Le Bon Repos crossroads

forward position was over run by enemy tanks and infantry. At 1930 hrs two squadrons of our tanks opened up with their Besas in the general direction of Le Bon Repos church. Despite urgent DF tasks fired by the divisional artillery the SS troops pressed on. They killed two stretcher bearers with a four foot square Red Cross flag, trying to save a wounded tankman. At 2000hrs 'A' Coy reported tanks 50 yards away from their positions. The last communication came at 2130hrs by which time 'A' Coy had been totally swamped and were entirely lost. As night fell the battered forward line contracted into the area of 'C' Coy under Major JH Morgan. Permission to withdraw to the top of Baron Hill was denied until 0600hrs in the morning when the remnants of 1/5 Welch retired under cover of smoke. Private George won the DCM for knocking out an enemy tank. The new CO Lt Col Gibson had arrived a few days before this tragic battle of Le Bon Repos.

Mostyn Thomas, with 18 Platoon 'D' Coy:

Rain fell in the late afternoon. 'D' Coy were subjected to uninterrupted artillery and mortar fire for about six hours ending in a frenzied nebelwerfer bombardment at about 2000hrs in which I was blown cleanly out of my slit-trench, pulled back by Eddie Burnell. The next crescendo was around the top of the hill at the crossroads, then it moved to the extreme right at Le Bon Repos Xds, then to our right around 'C' Coy. Observation became poor due to the smoke and debris. LMG fire cracked over us and thudded into the ground. Tanks could be seen and our artillery response was heavy. It was bedlam. Jerry rolled up the front, 'A' Coy went down in the late evening.

We were submerged in German mortar and artillery fire when their infantry advanced. Ianto Evans voice came over 'Get your heads up' repeated many times, loud and clear weapons came out, heads came up. My head was up but I was caught by the nebelwerfer which exploded to my right. The blast came at my right shoulder and head. I was thrown out of the trench completely concussed. Stretcher bearers carried me away to the RAP where I was labelled and sent off to CCS at Div Hospital. The accommodation was primitive. Stretchers with one blanket, were on the ground in a marquee. Our only interest was sleep. We were in an awful state. Uniforms soaked from the rain, stiff with mud, dirty with beards.

Nevertheless Mostyn Thomas was back with the battalion on 26 July. The SS had been supported by six Tiger tanks and their third attack was successful. They retained the important crossroads at Le Bon Repos and dug in. The action cost 1/5 Welch 25 casualties plus 3 officers and 115 other ranks missing and probably dead. It was a bad day for the Welch Regt.

Most of the battalions kept up the pressure by sending out patrols and raids. 7 RWF down to three rifle companies sent out two patrols on 20th, and the Divisional Commander 'chose' Lt Edwards, with Fusiliers Lacey and Guilier to check on the Ferme de Mondeville — their original objective in Greenline. The first two were taken prisoner. After their horrendous losses, 158 Brigade was now reinforced by officers and men from the 8th, 9th and 13th RWF. Lt Col H. J. Tedder became CO of 4 RWF and Major R. J. Stead-Cox was promoted to command 6 RWF. The Brigade took over from 43rd Division and stayed for ten days at Chateau de Fontaine, Maltot and Eterville — most of the time being shelled by nebelwerfers.

Capt Hugh Roberts, 6 RWF:

Our defensive positions at Maltot [21st July] had been the scene of two very bitter battles for the village by 43 Wessex Wyverns. There were many unburied dead, much of our own. So a plague of flies... We were shelled for all eleven days we spent there, artillery and Nebelwerfer, beat down on us like the roll of a drum. Our mortars fired smokeshells into cornfields where enemy was dug in, set fire to corn and when they upsticks and ran, our 3" mortars plastered the Bosch with HE. Our mortar officer was rebuked for using smoke bombs except for specific smoke screens. Anyway not considered 'cricket' to use such tactics. Our officers now dressed exactly like the men with badges of rank hidden, and to carry rifles to mislead snipers. Later German PW told us they could always pick out our officers by their moustaches. A batch of German deserters came in with 'leaflets' claiming they had murdered their own officers. Three Russian deserters blew themselves up on boobytraps laid by our Pioneers. At breakfast one morning a German m/cycle and sidecar entered Maltot at speed. The indignant NCO had taken the wrong turning. We captured their breakfast, blackbread, sausages and coffee. 'S' Coy got the M/C. Bn HQ got the German cigars.

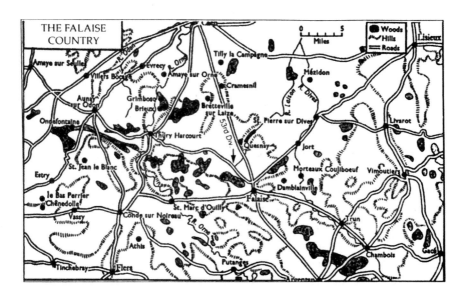

Corporal Richard Trevor drove a Bren gun carrier of 6 RWF; he was later wounded in the chest with shrapnel near Thury Harcourt:

> Near Maltot in a daylight raid into an orchard one of our men was shot through the head by a sniper — they were everywhere. Shells coming in from all sides. My carrier went over a dead cow. Fusilier Stevens was mortally wounded and died, but Sgt L Fox and myself survived. One of our platoon was trapped by the legs and we saw the rest of his body blown away. The orchard was a death trap. On our first raid on Hill 112, Fusilier J Pyrah said if he was to die, he did not wish to be burnt. A shell went through the side of the carrier, hit the petrol tank. I could see him in flames and his screams stayed with me. There was never much time to bury the dead, but it was always the Carrier Platoon's task to do it. The smell was terrible. Some bodies had been looted and some were booby-trapped. On another raid Sgt B Maxwell was telling everyone to get down but was himself killed.

Private Laurie Woolard, originally DLI of 50 Division joined 1/5 Welch with eleven other Durhams, as a re-reinforcement:

> Rumour had it that they had lost its cycle Co and the CO had been sent back to Beach duties. [Not true — he had been killed in action]. We dug in with the Welsh lads, constantly under air bursts. Our OP post on Hill 112 was a desperate place under a Box Barrage from Jerry. Our anti tank guns used to have a go at German tanks every day. I shared a trench with a Welsh Corporal who exposed his head over the trench at stand to. I saw a flash from a nearby tree and the Corporal's teeth and nose shot all over me. I lost my head and let fly at the tree with a Thompson S/M gun, with every bullet in that gun. Medics and an officer crept over to me, took away the corporal. He gave me some whiskey. I crawled over to the tree, cut the dead sniper down. I was drenched in blood and I had them clothes on 2 weeks before I got back to B Echelon… I had lots of skirmishes with that bunch of lads. My DLI mate Willets, a Brengun driver and I [a 3" Mortar man] were transferred to 2 Bn Mons.

4 RWF were holding an area around Chateau de Fontaine just west of Hill 112. Major Nick Cutcliffe found a sentry asleep:

> … and told him I would take him to the CO. Some men don't seem to realise how important a job it was. Punishment is difficult in the field. Any detention or imprisonment *out of the line* is infinitely preferable to line service, apart from the disgrace which doesn't seem to worry some people! And is in fact no punishment but a reward. The enemy were referred to as Jerry, Bosch, Germans, Enemy, Hun in approximately that order of popularity!

One night when the 4 RWF were on the move towards the river Orne, Nick Cutcliffe 'slept in a beautifully dug, but unpleasant smelling German trench. This characteristic smell persuaded everything German — trenches, discarded clothing, prisoners. It was half sweet, half sour, not a "dirty" smell, perhaps due to their sausages, their garlic, their tobacco or their hair oil.'

Cutcliffe's company had been responsible for the well-planned daylight raid on the large triangular field on the slopes of Hill 112. The battalion then had four days in a 'rest' area close to the ill-fated Evrecy battle area:

We passed on the way to Baron the place where old 'Bishop' Northcote's Coy of the 1/5 Welch disappeared — to a man. He gave a running commentary over the air. His last message was: 'There are Huns in the orchard about 50 yards from me.' It was a genuine rest period — no shelling — Mobile bath, company barber unearthed his clippers, weapons were stripped. G1098, kit and clothing inspections were made. Hundreds of letters home were censored — a fairly useless chore, as no vital military secrets could be known to the senders. The Div concert party found itself a barn and NAAFI vans distributed cigarettes, beer, soap, sweets etc. An officers shop set up in Tainville. The only problems were horseflies, mosquitoes and the necessity for route marches to harden up the RWF feet for the future pursuit! The worst problem was the need to send out burial parties to locate Fusiliers dead from the recent battles and raids.

Divisional management now decided on some revenge for the Welch Regt disaster. Two days later, on 23rd, 4 Welch were entrusted with a reprisal raid to retake Le Bon Repos crossroads and penetrate as far as Esquay. No less than five Field Regiments, one Medium Regt and all the firepower of 1st Manchesters would provide a rolling barrage of HE and smoke. Major AJ Lewis recounts what happened:

At the Battalion Orders Group volunteers were called for from the Company Commanders for this dangerous operation. Needless to say four hands immediately shot up, so a coin was tossed, and Bill (Major Clements) and I were the lucky ones. A troop of 'Crocodiles', Churchill tanks fitted with flame throwers were allotted to each company. We were to advance behind an artillery barrage, moving on a timed programme, and during the final stage the 'Crocs' were to move in under the barrage while the tanks supported them with fire.

The advance started with the artillery fire lifting two hundred yards every two minutes and the infantry following up two hundred yards behind it, while the tanks shot us in from both flanks. Very soon we ran into fixed line fire from enemy machine guns and what seemed like a miracle happened. The whole company ['A'] just walked through it without a single casualty. On our left the leading platoon of 'C' Company seemed to be in trouble. They had walked into a heavy concentration of Artillery fire and suffered heavy casualties. By this time the Germans were throwing everything they had at us, shell, mortar fire, moaning minnies and machine gun fire. We were starting to have casualties ourselves, and my faithful batman who had been with me for nearly three years fell at my side killed by an enemy bullet through his throat. He was operating my 38 wireless set, and that was put out of action by the same bullet, and from then on I had to rely on runners for my communication. There was no sign of the Crocs when the barrage lifted on the objective. We could not wait being so close to the enemy, so as the last shell landed we charged in with fixed bayonets. God! How those Germans must have hated it. The Company turned the Germans out of their trenches shooting them down if they showed any sign of resistance.

The 'Crocs' arrive and fire large squirts of flame at one of *my* platoons. The Germans and my own troops run away from those hellish flames. The 'Crocs' then turn their attention to a house on the corner where some twenty Germans letting out agonising screams are sizzled to death. My lads appear to have dodged the flames, but God knows how. Our infantry continue to knock hell out of the enemy and they are soon on the run. The raid is a success. The code word for withdrawal is received and the sections leap frog back covering each other as they move. The Carriers take back our wounded.

Major Clements (a Welsh Rugby International) of 'C' Company was wounded early in the attack, but carried on. He was awarded the MC for his services. Captain David Bolland's diary entry:

Sunday 23rd, 4 Welch put in an attack on Esquay preceded by smoke screens along the whole front at 3, 5 and 7pm At 10.45pm the 4 Welch returned having killed approximately 80 enemy with loss of 10 KIA and 60 wounded [many only slightly]. Prisoners captured testified as to accuracy and devastating effect of our artillery fire.

Ron Ludgater was the Cockney platoon comedian, regarded by some as a bit 'bolshie'. He joined 1st Manchesters from the Rifle Brigade and spent his twentieth birthday in a slit-trench:

As Epsom operation went wrong and tailed off, we moved our Vickers MMG up to a line on the Hill 112/Evrecy road. One evening we were told to load up and move left about ¾ miles for a big shoot. We settled near the edge of 8th Bn Rifle Brigade (11th Armoured). One of their blokes scowled at me when our Vickers started. As soon as the firing finished, everything was chucked into the carriers and away we scuttled back to our holes and positions. We left under much abuse because the inevitable mortar and 88mm fire came down on them! A common practice but most unpopular!

Wally Brereton, 81st Welch Field Regt RA, with his FOO Capt Green, the driver of the OP carrier, Frankie Silva, and the radio ack Peter Bonnington occupied a semi-static OP on Hill 113 overlooking Evrecy: 'A few yards away was a huge dugout, Bn HQ for 1st HLI. A javelin with a pennant indicated that the CO Lt Col Torquil Macleod was in residence. Inside it was just like a scene from "Journey's End". At the far end was a pile of straw held in place by a plank chalked on it "CO's Roost!"' Several officers of the HLI and our Capt Green talked whilst I sat in my carrier with my D MKV field telephone, message pad at the ready.

Lt GCRL Pender with 'D' Coy 1 HLI wrote:

20-21st July. Found us at Le Bon Repos area still in defence. All this time we were active and receiving a steady flow of casualties. The next day we moved to Hill 112 a much fought over mini-hill. It was a high cornfield and the corn came up to the average Jock's shoulders or head. It stretched for miles in each direction. It smelt of death from the fallen of both sides. The mess was absolutely awful. 'D' Coy was on a forward slope in full view of the enemy. One could not get out of one's slit trench during daylight without being mortared or machine-gunned.

Sapper Ned Petty, 244 Field Coy RE observed the condition of 1 HLI towards the end of July:

The first thing we saw in that orchard was just blankets obviously covering men dotted about. They had arrived about 2 o'clock in the morning. Now it was 4 o'clock in the afternoon, so they had had about 14 hours sleep. When they got up, I thought there was something wrong with them. They just stood still, staring. They were all very dirty and stood as though they were still asleep. We were told they had been holding this place for three weeks. No proper sleep, just getting an hour or two in their little trenches when they could. Eventually they stood in three ranks staring blankly in front of them. They numbered off and there were 85 of them. I understood they were around 600 strong to start with when I looked at them. I wondered how they could be expected to fight again.

Friday, 28 July. 'The new radio provided by a charity back in the UK', wrote Corporal Bert Isherwood 13 FDS, 'has Steve Madden the AFN disc jockey at SHAEF belting out his signature tune, Charlie Barnett's "Skyliner", Glenn Miller, and on BFN The Squadronaires, The Skyrockets, Harry Roy, Joe Loss, Ambrose et al to entertain the troops.'

L/Corporal Alistair 'Mac' Carmichael, driver of Brigadier Bloomfield's half-track was encouraged by Brigade HQ Sgt Major to display his culinary talent. 'A spot of butchering of (recently) killed Normandy cattle I found quite an experience, retrieving undercut steak, liver and suet round the kidneys along with potatoes from the nearby farm, turned into chips. Many of the lads were very suspicious until the good smells came their way.'

The last big raid carried out in July was by 2 Mons from Hill 112, a mile north-east of Esquay. It was a typical 'Monty' style operation. 'D' Coy under Major G. F. K. Morgan were to attack an enemy platoon area of thirty men, under a seventy-two gun barrage, plus the Manchester MMGS, six 'wasps' (carrier flame throwers) borrowed from 1 HLI. It was reasonably successful. They killed thirteen and took fifteen prisoners from 10 SS Panzer and 271 Infantry Divisions but lost sixteen casualties to DF by mortars. L/Sgt Staddon received the MM. The raid started at 21.30 hrs and took only eighteen minutes. In their first month in action 2 Mons had two officers and nineteen other ranks killed and seven officers and 125 other ranks wounded.

5

August and breakout

Captain David Bolland's diary reports the raids and fighting patrols at the beginning of August:

Wednesday, 2nd. At 0545 4 RWF put in their attack on the Triangle wood [near the Eterville-Evrecy road] which they reached at 0615 and began withdrawal at 0635. Raid successful. 36 Jerries killed and 3 PW taken. We had 3 killed and 22 wounded. Patrols reported enemy movement on all fronts but no sign of withdrawal. In the evening 4 Welch raid Esquay making useful identification about 10 SS PZ Div and 271 Infantry Div.

Thursday, 3rd. Another day of raids along the whole Div front. Things are looking like a real breakthrough on the American front. Wish we could get a move on here, but I suppose our day will come.

Friday, 4th. Patrols pushing on this morning reported that Le Locheur, Evrecy, Le Bon Repos Crossroads and Le Hamel were all clear but set heavy immense booby traps. Fired propaganda shells at Amaye-Sur-Orne and Clinchamps. 83 and 133 Field Regts moved to new areas at Gavrus and Bougy in late afternoon. The 20mm and 40mm troops of 116 LAA Regt went home to UK to train as infantry. George Formby entertained the Div today in a hanger at Carpiquet, gave excellent show with his wife Beryl and Company.

The new brigade organisation had come into effect on 2 August although Corporal Bert Isherwood with 13 FDS wrote as early as 22 July: 'Talking to NCOs at the Supply points, I gather there are going to be changes in the constitution of the brigades since 158 Brigade has heavy casualties, one RWF Bn is going in each of the Brigades.'

Lt Col GWPN Burden CO 1 East Lancs:

5th August. We leave 71 to join 158 Bde. This was most unwelcome news. We had great comradeship in the 'Independent' Brigade. No longer would we operate with same gunners, same Field Ambulance etc. Now we had to get to know new Brigade staff, RA Regt, Services in the midst of a battle. The quite natural protests were registered as was quite natural. As expected refusals to alter anything were received. On the 6th the Bn marched to Le Homme and the next day Brigadier Sugden took over from Brigadier Silas Jones.

The Divsional Recce Regiment now started to act in their traditional role, Sgt Roach of 'A' Sqn took an armoured car patrol down to Le Bon Repos crossroads on the 4th, as Corporal May recounts:

The troop Sgt was to be in command. With Tpr Crosier, my driver, we crept over the brow of the hill at zero hour to see a large open expanse of shell-potted ground with many knocked-out tanks and vehicles scattered about. My first thought was whether my car would add to this collection. I had never felt quite so frightened before. Our progress was slow but we edged down the narrow road, dodging a demolished carrier and bumping over shell holes. There was a road barrier 300 yds ahead which I kept well covered with my Bren. Despite mines, cleared by the Assault troop, 'A' Sqn got into the shell-torn village of Esquay where enemy light tanks and half-tracks deterred further advance. And 'C' Sqn advanced on the right and reached the River Orne at Pont de Coudray after an amazing advance of 5-6 miles in the wake of *retreating* enemy!

The advance of 12 Corps started with 59th Pithead Division on the right, 53rd Welsh on the left. By 6 August the advance had reached the Orne between Amaye and Feuguerolles. Operation 'Bluecoat' with 11th Armoured Division and 15th Scottish had made deep penetrations further south through Beny-Bocage towards Vire. Most of the British Army after the months of bitter additional fighting were now on the move.

Lt G. C. R. L. Pender 1 HLI recalls:

We watched the RAF thousand bomber raid on Caen and heard about the assassination attempt on Hitler's life. 4th August. There were no enemy to be seen in front of us. 16 Platoon was sent off, by ourselves on an advance on Le Locheur about four miles eastwards. We advanced through mine fields, which were cunningly sown with anti-personnel mines. It took a long time to clear them. It was a job to keep awake. We reached Le Locheur which was empty. My platoon was exhausted. We were so out of touch in our 38 set, which was no surprise.

On the same day 2nd Mons moved forward to Amaye where Lt H. G. Smith led a brave patrol over the blown bridge to recce the far side. Two days later the Division had a bridgehead at Grimbosq, two miles to the south.

Gunner Wally Brereton and his 81st Welch Field Regt OP Carrier 'Roger Fox':

We took our place among the HLI Bren gun carriers in a particularly nasty battle one wet night. The leading carrier hit a mine and blew up. The HLI Pioneers had a laborious task of mine lifting. Two of the men were killed lifting mines connected in pairs. The infantry advanced through the woods to capture the village as the enemy had retreated eastwards. We settled down to a hot meal. One soldier produced a football which they started to kick round a field. A lone piper played a dirge in the corner.

After the Brigade reorganisation took place, the gunner regiments were re-aligned as follows:

158 Brigade still was supported by 83 Field: 1/5 Welch by 329 Bty; 1 East Lancs by 330 Bty and 7 RWF by 460 Bty. 160 Brigade still supported by 133 Field: 4 Welch by 331 Bty; 6 RWF by 332 Bty and 2 Mons by 497 Bty.

They were in action every day and particularly in the dramatic bridgehead battle on the 7th. Hitler had ordered Field Marshal Von Runstedt, *not* to fall back to the river Seine but continue to fight. 59 Division had forced a bridgehead over the Orne when a powerful counter-attack came in. Lt F. S. Hayes 460 Bty, a GPO, had reported to RHQ of 83 Field Regt preparatory to a 'recce' across the river:

> The CRA Brigadier JC Friedberger, and the Infantry Brigadiers were at an OP which commanded the bridgehead. German artillery was shelling all round this ridge as a preliminary to an attack. Then it came; the enemy broke out of wood in full view. Suddenly 'Victor Target DF 273' was called for over the wireless net by the CRA. This meant a concentration of fire upon a known point by all guns.

Hayes could hear troops promptly reporting 'Ready', including his own. A minute later came the order 'Fire'.

> The Germans were about 200 yards from our FDLs when the devastating effect of 72 25-pounders burst upon the attackers. [As the effect of the blast settled, someone counted 14 in grey uniforms still alive out of what must have been 500]. The next moment, out of a smoke screen on the right flank, appeared the enemy's Panzers and Tigers. The CRA ordered 'One Troop fire red smoke' and gave a map reference. Soon brilliant bursts hung above the attacking tanks as a distress signal to Typhoons patrolling overhead. Screaming down, firing armour-piercing shot, they delivered rocket bombs on their quarry. The effect was decisive; hardly a tank emerged from this holocaust without black smoke pouring out of it.

So the bridgehead was saved and the dismayed remnants surrendered to that terrific display of might. The Manchesters of course had been involved in all the battles so far. Major Crozier recorded:

I had a look over some captured equipment, took a couple of Bosch 81mm mortars out and fired them back at the Bosch. Wonder how he likes his own stuff coming back at him! 4th August. Evrecy and Esquay are in a terrible mess, just heaps of rubble, an example of what modern artillery can do. 5th August. Made a strong complaint to Division over the failure to bury our bodies which in some cases have been left for days.

On the 8th, 116 LAA had unusual targets as David Bolland noted: 'Near 83rd Field, two US Flying fortresses came over and bombed our chaps. This was forgiven but two hours later two Thunderbolts came roaring over and dive-bombed gun positions of the 6 Field Regt and a Field Ambulance. It was just too bad so our LAA boys opened up — quite right too!' 6 RWF, now part of 160 Brigade, also had a very bad day. Advancing towards Leffard the battalion and their supporting 4 CLY tanks were heavily shelled and several officers were wounded but 'C' and 'D' Coys compelled the enemy to withdraw and reduced the shelling. Major the Lord Davies, bravely but rashly volunteered to rescue some wounded French civilians in the village of Les Loges-Saulces. Their vehicles flying a Red Cross entered the village and loaded the stretchers with the wounded. They were fired upon and captured, only Fusilier Elverstone escaped. A search party set off at dusk with tanks and carriers under Captain Owen and the 2 i/c Major Prichard. They were ambushed, the leading tank was hit by a bazooka, and the 2 i/c was never seen again.

Later Lord Davies and the survivors who had been taken prisoners by an Austrian division, persuaded fifty of their captors to 'linger behind' and be themselves taken prisoner by the Recce Regt. It may have helped that the Austrian IO had been a master at Lord Davies' school! Several battalions were temporarily loaned to 59 Pithead Division; 4 and 7 RWF had reconnoitred the rivers Guigne and Orne. The latter described by Captain Hugh Roberts: 'flows in a deep broad valley, slopes broken by gullies, completely wooded and we had to fight to clear wooded ground overlooking the Orne.' The 7th Battalion Royal Norfolks of 59 Division had seized and held for three days against violent enemy counter-attacks, a bridgehead at Grimbosq, over the Orne. When they were relieved on the 9th by 7 RWF the enemy had been so mauled that they had been forced to withdraw. The 12th SS Panzer Division was withdrawing eastwards from the Forêt du Grimbosq which was cleared on the 10th.

Unfortunately Lt Col Dickson, 7 RWF, was informed that the village of Fresney-le-Vieux, four miles east of the river Orne just south of the forest was clear of enemy. The preparatory gunner support was called off. In confused fighting on the evening of the 11th in the orchards and buildings of the village, 7 RWF had three officers wounded (including two company commanders), eight other ranks killed, twenty-five wounded and twelve missing. So 7 RWF

were withdrawn and the next day 1/5 Welch put in a set piece attack supported
by Corps artillery. The enemy company defending Fresney put up considerable
resistance aided by fire from Hill 182 on the right. After five hours of furious
fighting aided by flamethrowers, tanks and carriers the village was taken.
But 1/5 Welch had suffered badly with three officer casualties, thirty other
ranks killed and sixty wounded. The dead were buried near Bn TAC HQ in a
shrubbery near Fresney.

Corporal Mostyn Thomas:

> We found in Fresney in one room were two Germans about my age. One with a
> right thorax wound lying flat on his back on the table. The other with a gunshot
> wound through the shinbone, who could speak English. He was telling the
> stretcher bearer that they understood the British would not take any prisoners
> unless they were wounded. So they shot each other.

Amongst the 280 prisoners of *3rd Bn 978 Grenadier Regt* (who lost forty-five
killed that day) were many Russians, Poles and Sudeten Germans.

Just a mile or so to the south was the village of Bois-Halbout known now as
'Boiled Halibut'. So as Fresney was being so painfully stormed, Lt Col Burden's
1 East Lancs were given the task of taking 'B-H' supported by a regiment
of Churchill tanks, large artillery support, and the Manchesters MMG and
mortars. Lt Sharlot, OC Pioneers, led to find the FUP with Capt Carter, the IO.
Just after 08.45 Sharlot suddenly came upon two German soldiers who fled.
He, Pt White and another gave chase, shot one and followed the other into an
outpost in a small wood. There they found eighteen more Germans (plus six
Spandaus). All were asleep and all were made prisoner. A good start but heavy
mortaring on the start line caused losses. Up came 'D' Coy on their bikes and
the CO told them to drop them. They were neatly stacked two by two. The
attack went well but fighting in the village became confused. The six Panthers
found in the main street knocked out two Churchills. Sgt Hatton of 'C' Coy
knocked one out with a Piat.

Major Griffin's 'A' Coy:

> I heard our Churchill tanks in the village behind me. The comforting crack
> of their MGs amused me for I could see no enemy behind us. A moment later
> we were horror-stricken to find ourselves standing in the way of two German
> MK IVs coming down the road with machine guns blazing! With no apparent
> movement 8 Platoon and myself were in the ditch bordering the road.

Major Griffin's Piats were unfortunately in a carrier some way back. The
tanks then destroyed Sgt Crossley's platoon which had pushed on beyond
its objective. But Sgt French brought up a 6-pdr anti-tank gun into action,

60 yards from the well-defended town hall. Pte Eastwood and his stretcher bearers impressed both friend and foe evacuating wounded of both sides. Lt Wildgoose was hit and Lt Col Burden offered him his jeep to take him back to the RAP. He declined saying, 'Oh I'm alright, Sir, don't let me spoil your battle for you.' Major Griffin's 'A' Coy repelled and broke up a determined counter attack: 'The enemy gave us no respite. Their final assault met the fire of enemy Sten, Bren, rifle in our Coy HQ at 30 yards range.'

Two hundred and fifty prisoners were taken in the two actions but both sides suffered many casualties. The East Lancs had eighty-five battle casualties in the two weeks 9–23 August. The pursuit continued with 1 Ox and Bucks ordered to seize the important crossroads on the main Thury-Harcourt to Falaise road, some two miles south-west of 'Boiled Halibut'. 'B' Coy under Major Taylor were to follow behind 'C' Coy under Major Jim Callingham. In thick early morning mist on the 13th they reached the crossroads which turned out to be well defended by the enemy in and around the half dozen houses, with a Tiger tank in support. Sgt Jim Kirk in a flank attack was involved in a four hour battle. Lt Norman Davis reached the crossroads and silenced the Tiger tanks and both company commanders (with Davis) were awarded the MC. But at 10.00 hrs Lt Col Hare withdrew both companies to allow for gunner support and by mid afternoon 'A' and 'D' Coys were entirely successful. After spending the night at Acqueville, 'A' and 'D' Coys were loaned to 4 RWF to advance due south between the Bois de St Clair and Bois Saurier. On the way Major Rupert Livingstone, 'A' Coy was killed by a Spandau burst.

Bud Abbot was with 5 Troop, 'C' Sqn of the Recce Regt. Les Logis farm near Martainville was held by SS troops. He recalls: 'The advancing section on clearing the wheat field became the target for some well hidden 88s covered by the buildings. Two carriers were hit immediately, the occupants were killed or wounded. My gunner and I were firing away at the enemy entrenched in the hedgerow by the farm.' The troop officer, Lt 'Timber' Woods, was killed by a Spandau burst as were three other ranks. Lt Peter Utley was ordered to send his troop towards Bonnoeuil. His leading HAC had been hit and was burning, 'I crawled forward to it and recognised Tpr Stevens the driver. He was blackened, in a bad way, told me the Sgt and Corporal were both dead.'

4 RWF had helped clear Acqueville of snipers and they were ordered to advance nearly two miles due south at night. Major Roberts 'B' Coy found his road barred at Les Logis where the Recce carriers had been shot up. But by the morning the battalion was half a mile from Les Logis astride the enemy's line of retreat. The opposition who had been by-passed in the dark consisted of a strong Adolf Hitler SS battalion supported by tanks. 'D' Coy of the Ox and Bucks now joined 4 RWF at 07.00 hrs. Some mortaring and Spandau fire was a prelude to Battalion HQ being shelled by a Panther tank. Shortly afterwards

a heavier attack came in with 70 infantry in half tracks supported by six tanks who fell on 'B' Coy Ox and Bucks. Sgt Gordon Hay was the hero of the hour:

> Lt Donald Harvey of 244 Field Coy RE on attachment to recce a nearby bridge shouted Piat! Piat! Piat! over the noise of the shouting by the German PZ Grenadiers. We found shelter behind a knocked out Brengun carrier, and fired the PIAT from a kneeling position at about 50 yds. At first I missed and was knocked over by the recoil. I moved closer and got a direct hit. The impact crippled the armoured personnel carrier killing its occupants. Boxes of ammo aboard exploded causing confusion amongst the Germans. We then reached the gap in the hedge. Lt Harvey, an inspiration, was shouting 'Come on, Come on, let's get them.' I fired a shot at the nearest tank but missed. [The Piat bomb weights 2½lbs, has a range of 115 yards and in short range tests only had a 57% hit rate.] I had another go and hit it in the hull, then hit it in the tracks. It came to a halt with smoke billowing from its turret. It was a massive Tiger.

Sgt Hay, inspired by Lt Harvey and provided with more bombs by Pte Hannessley, then destroyed two more Panthers. Lt Harvey was killed, was recommended for a VC but received a posthumous mention in despatches. Sgt Hay was recommended for the DCM and was awarded the MM.

At 16.00 hrs the battalion area was heavily shelled by *British* medium guns and caused 'D' Coy twenty casualties. A stream of British armour now came up and the battle was over. The Adolf Hitler SS lost 30 killed and 150 taken

Wehrmacht PoWs in Normandy

prisoner and had 5 tanks and 2 half-tracks knocked out. No wonder General 'Bobby' Ross sent both units his congratulations.

Irfon Roberts, Signals Officer 4 RWF saw 'one batch of prisoners who could hardly conceal their relief that it was all over for them. By contrast an SS man, physically almost a sheer caricature of the 'Teutonic brute', heavily built, bull-necked and glowering, radiated an almost palpable sense of hatred and fury at having been captured.'

The 2 Mons had a major role in the capture of Les Logis village. The attack in thick morning mist on the 14th was costly (fifty casualties including seventeen killed) but the enemy had retreated by 17.30. Later 4 RWF destroyed the three Panthers which had caused much of the damage and the advance to Hill 201 and the village of Leffard, three miles ahead, continued. The Mons were loaned to 158 Brigade for the massive set piece attack on Leffard on the 15th. Lt Purvis, 'C' Coy ran out of Bren ammo, captured several Spandaus and used them to stem a counter-attack. By nightfall the Mons were in a sadly battered state having lost another fifty casualties including ten killed, but the way was clear for 158 Brigade and supporting armour to go through. After dark Major Tyler, the temporary CO [Lt Col Kempster had been promoted to GSO1 3rd British Division], visiting 'C' Coy, collected six men and 'arrested' seventy-five Germans hiding in a building. By 21.30 hrs Leffard was firmly held with forty dead Germans and over 100 prisoners taken. In two days the Mons had suffered 144 casualties. Lt Col F. H. Brooke arrived as their new CO. A brand new 'B' Coy arrived from 5 East Lancs of the dismembered 59 Pithead Division and the depleted 'A' and 'B' had merged to form one company. On the 19th a night attack on Necy was followed two days later by a successful action when 'B' Coy destroyed and captured two out of three Tiger tanks, capturing 100 prisoners. Major Hughes' pistol and Capt Thomson's Hotchkiss [497 Bty Co and OP team] were curiously ineffective against one of the Tigers whose 88 mm gun hit a steel telegraph post which collapsed on the OP carrier.

1/5 Welch had three days out of the line after their part in taking of Fresney. The Divisional Concert Party, mobile baths and canteens helped restore morale for on the 15th they were on the move south to cut the main road into Falaise from the west. On the 16th, a mile beyond Leffard, they encountered heavy shelling, and moved through the woods of Bois du Roi to the village of Martigny sur L'Ante to meet their supporting tanks at the crossroads. They turned left to search the highground with their objective the Falaise road and road crossing. The 'B' Coy were on the left, 'C' on the right but by 19.30 hrs the situation was desperate. There was a complete breakdown of radio communication between Battalion HQ and the two attacking companies. A message from Brigade came down 'standfast, do NOT cross main Falaise road'. Unfortunately 'B' Coy crossed it at 20.00 hrs. Eventually five hours later Lt Tasker Watkins with just twenty-seven members of his company returned. They had reached their objective across booby trapped fields, repelled a counter-attack and killed fifty-five Germans of the Bakery and Slaughter House Coys of *271 Infantry Division* who had had no food and little water for the last five days. Lt Watkins had charged two enemy posts and led a bayonet charge. At dusk they were alone and surrounded and Watkins decided to rejoin the battalion with the survivors, having had thirty-three casualties. He was later awarded the Victoria Cross for his gallant conduct. The battalion consolidated around Hill 223.

'We met the Maquis for the first time', Capt H. Roberts, Adjutant 6 RWF, explains: 'civilians with an arm band only too eager to repay the Germans for the damage they were doing as they fell back looting, stealing stock and burning. A one-armed man who had jumped on the back of a German sniper and strangled him. A farmer with a pistol who demanded German PW to bury his cow which they had just killed for no reason, and two 'toughs' who acted as excellent scouts for our leading sections.'

The East Lancs supported by 147 RAC Sherman tanks took Noron L'abbaye and Mietre in set-piece attacks. Then Allied Lightnings dropped bombs on the battalion. 'B' Coy repriming .36 Mills grenades caused a terrific explosion, and demolished a house, causing nine casualties. They moved to St Martin de Mieux and Necy. During two days of torrential rain the mobile bath unit arrived! Reinforcements poured in, 50 from 1/5 Welch, 35 from 5th East Lancs, 143 from Lancashire Fusiliers. Someone had got their sums wrong. The battalion soon had an *extra* company who were then sent off to 7 RWF who were very short of men.

It was clear to everyone that by mid-August the attritional brutal battles of the bridgehead were now over and a new pattern was emerging of small well-defended German *retreats*.

Captain Bolland's diary entries:

Monday 14th. Regiments pushing forward. The Div has now been given the task of blocking roads leading into Falaise from S and SW. Very hot indeed and many men are suffering from 'Normandy stomach' brought about by thousands of flies [feeding on dead animals and corpses]. Prisoners are rolling in — some 250 marched down the road this afternoon. Dust is again terrible. Went through Bois Halbout this morning still burning from the recent heavy fighting. Thursday, 17th. Went back with Padre to Rear Corps HQ at St Laurel de Condel. 1st HLI were burying their dead there. Their buglers sounded the Last Post and Reveille. An impressive little ceremony. Friday, 18th. A day of considerable shooting. Our own troops are now on the high ground overlooking the German retreat routes. A very large number of prisoners were taken. What a miserable crowd they look — all nationalities except German. Went through Falaise on the way to the Regts, like CAEN this city has been completely destroyed by its 'liberators'. A pathetic sight and still burning.

John Ottewell 7 RWF suffered from a 'dose of dysentery':

> You'd be eating your rations and it would be covered in flies. You'd crush them off and carry on eating. Of course these flies had been everywhere but mostly on 'putrefying flesh.' First a high temperature sudden bouts of vomiting and stomach pains, soon to be followed later at the Field Hospital by sudden uncontrollable attempts to evacuate 'empty bowels'. The stench in those Hospital tents was overpowering. It was bloody hilarious in a cruel sort of way.

6

Morale

In four weeks of attritional fighting in the Bridgehead the Division had taken heavy casualties; 32 officers and 269 other ranks had been killed, 75 officers and 1326 wounded and a further 17 officers and 218 other ranks were missing, certainly captured, possibly killed or wounded. Of those keen, well-trained but 'green' young soldiers who had spent four years preparing for Overlord, already 1937 were *hors de combat*.

General 'Bobby' Ross decided for a variety of reasons to realign the three Royal Welch Fusilier Battalions (they all had new COs and a flood of intake reinforcements). So 4 RWF joined 71st Brigade replacing 1st East Lancs and 6 RWF went to 160 Brigade replacing 1/5th Welch Regiment. There was some resentment at first and morale was certainly not at its peak.

Major Nick Cutcliffe, 4 RWF, after several abortive raids and patrols:

> I wasn't at all happy about the tactics we had employed. In every operation so far we had been put in with, to my mind, *grossly* inadequate preparation, and what was still worse, in 'penny packets'. To round off these two tactical crimes, we had reinforced failure rather than success. I felt that our withdrawal from the outskirts of Evrecy should never have taken place. Morale was as bad as it could be. We were all very weary. I spoke to Silas Jones, our Brigadier [who was replaced in August] about the shell shock cases who were rapidly draining our strength [380 in the Division who were evacuated to the UK]. It was infectious and if one man in a slit-trench started to go under, it was probable that his companion would follow suit. H..., I knew, was on the verge and during heavy shelling I would sit and hold his hand tightly. But it was no good. After struggling with himself for a day or so he broke down and cried and had to be sent away. In the circumstances I was not sorry to lose these men.

Corporal Sidney Griffiths, 'A' Coy 4 RWF describes another similar incident: 'The shelling continued for quite a while and was heavy. The blast of near misses seemingly bouncing our brains about like ping pong balls within our heads. Fusilier George Reynolds began to cringe and break up (i.e. becoming shell shocked).' Later: 'I spotted the body of young Roberts lying on the ground, half his face was shot away, and left forearm dangling. The upper arm had been shot away. I looked down at him (he was only 18½ years). I thought what would your Mother say if she saw you now.' And: 'When I got to my trench George R[eynolds] was by now in a state of great shock and had his hands round Fusilier Joe Collard's throat. I shouted at him to let go, he didn't. I hit him with my fist. He still didn't let go. I couldn't prise his hands away, so I hit him on his steel helmet with the butt of my Stengun. Lt Ireland arrived. I had already reported Fusilier Reynolds suffering from battle exhaustion. Stretcher bearers took George away. This was the last I saw of him.'

Nick Cutcliffe again, 'Another worry was that shell shock was about the easiest thing to malinger. It was largely a question of willpower, but not entirely. Some men, I knew, tried very hard to keep their heads above water and with those one had to speak in a kindly and sympathetic way. Others needed a sharp word — a *mental* shaking by the shoulders or slap in the face. But although this treatment might delay the breakdown, I don't think it prevented it.' When 6 RWF relieved 4 RWF, Nick's company moved off back to the 'rest' area south of Tourville. 'They looked an undisciplined rabble and I was speechless with fury.' And on arrival, 'gathered them together to tell them exactly what I thought of them. I told them they were soldiers and must expect shelling and casualties. However unpleasant the last few days [attacks on Evrecy] that was no excuse for this unsoldierly mob. They looked rather sheepish.'

Nevertheless, it was a hellish life for the very few soldiers up at the sharp end, and as these two accounts — one by a company commander, one by a corporal — demonstrate.

Mostyn Thomas 1/5 Welch described life on the receiving end:

> Our reception was concentrated artillery heavyweight shells. Mortars and small arms fire. Sleep was almost impossible. Hunched in the bottom of your hole, legs crossed up to your chest with the small pack across the knees to keep the rain off. Your mate standing guard in his half. What rest you could get constantly being interrupted by alarms or duties. When on the receiving end of fire, both crouched in the pit, assessing what was happening above, watching the face of the other, gasping for air when a new explosion saturated the space with a blue vapour and the stink of explosives. When you could judge the best time to look over the edge, the cries of stretcher bearers bring you to your feet to find out what was happening…

Major R. N. Deane, 'A' Coy 2 Mons wrote of their slit trench life at Mondrainville:

It became our home and had a fair chance of becoming one's last habitation on the face of the abused earth. Almost every day some domestic improvement was carried out; a little scraped out here to fit a 'knees-up' sleep position, a piece of head-cover against flying metal, a recess pried out for a cigarette tin or Sten gun magazine. I would lean on the edge of it at stand-to, looking out towards the sunset horizon and the coming stars, like any suburbanite leaning on his gateway after an evening of improving his garden. But reveries were subject to cruel and explosive interruptions. One night my next-door neighbours had a shell come at a slant slap into their home in the ground. On such tragedies one felt nothing but blazing anger. A senior officer stood up against the starry sky and, over the moans of the wounded, shook his fist and threatened the enemy with all they eventually got. The next 'crump' made one hug the lowest extremity of the trench with a naked feeling at the base of the spine. Then there were the 'duds', which hit the ground with sickening thuds, and left an expectation where there should have been an explosion.

Major General Ross was a highly experienced commander and knew how vital the battle was to maintain morale, as Capt David Bolland's diary entry for Tuesday, 25 July indicates:

53 Div relieved 43 Div — the front line now runs all the way from Bougy to the river Orne. Jim Cooper, the Divisional entertainment's officer now has an excellent little theatre, complete with seats at Marcelet. He runs five shows in a day there — two Div concerts, two films and one ENSA. All are packed and regiments do their own bookings direct at the box office, so that everyone gets what they want.

One of the other key features for morale was the certain knowledge that a battle casualty would be treated swiftly and efficiently. David Bolland wrote to his mother on 15 July:

Most of the planes you see are troop carrying ambulance planes. There is a fantastic amount of air evacuation. When possible every case is flown back. Others wait at the base hospital until they are fit to travel by air. The whole medical arrangements are first class. I often look in to the Field Ambulances and have seen the excellent work being done there. They get right up into the front line and work ceaselessly through all the bombing, shelling and mortaring that goes on around them. *At least one in every four vehicles on the road is an ambulance*, to get their casualties back to the Field Dressing Station and Hospitals further back. The MO's say the equipment provided in the hospital is far better than anything they have come across before.

The French memorial stone to the British soldiers who died at Baron and Hill 112

NOTRE DAME DE BARON

VEILLE SUR TES ENFANTS

MORTS AU CHAMP D'HONNEUR

VICTIMES CIVILES DES COMBATS

ET

SUR LES SOLDATS BRITANNIQUES

TOMBÉS SUR TON SOL

PASSANT SOUVIENS TOI

QU'ILS ONT VERSÉ LEUR SANG

POUR TA LIBERTÉ

Below: Major R.N. Dean, 'A' Company 2nd Monmouthshires' impression of Hill 112

" The slit-trench was a hole in the ground peculiar to this war. It was the invention of cold logic and it combined a maximum of protection with a minimum of comfort.

And in those lengthy summer periods of sitting tight in Normandy and being shelled day in, day out, and nights too, this inadequate hole in the ground became " home " for many, and had a fair chance of being one's last habitation on the face of the abused earth. Almost every day, some domestic improvement was carried out on this limited bit of inverted architecture ; a little scraped out here to fit a knees-up sleep position—a piece of head-cover provided against flying metal—a recess pried out for a cigarette tin or sten gun magazine. And after a time on Hill 112 I found I had become attached to my " home," and would lean on the edge of it at an evening " stand-to," looking out towards the sunset horizon and the coming stars, like any suburbanite leaning on his gateway after an evening of improving his garden. But reveries were subject here to the most cruel and explosive inter-ruptions.

"Nothing grew on Hill 112 except bleached grass. The few scruffy hedgerow trees were in the process of dusty dying after weeks and months of shelling. I don't think I ever heard a bird in Normandy, though I did see a dead one blasted in a hedge. Dust was part of the atmosphere—powdery white dust. Smell too was an element of the atmosphere—a difficult smell to imagine, and a nasty one to analyse, though it was the German side of 112 which was worst in that respect.

"Approaching 112 from the rear, by the much shelled Baron road, one could work forward by dusty hedgerows honeycombed with funk-holes, to a point where the hedgerows stopped and one was confronted with the open hill itself. This was a parched bald slope rising to a skyline over which an Air O.P. usually hummed, dipping and dodging in the sky. Towards this bare skyline went all manner of whispering shells, warbling mortar-bombs and screaming missiles from our gun-lines in rear. Back across the summer skyline came the howling, rushing 'swoosh' of German shells and the occasional 'moaning minny.'

7
The Killing Ground: closing the Falaise-Argentan gap

By 18 August the Division was close to Falaise, a mile or so west of Noron L'Abbaye. On the next day the Polish Armoured Division linked up with American troops, advancing from the south, at Chambois — and closed the famous gap. The Canadians had finally captured Falaise. The Allied airforces had created appalling damage. Mile upon mile, not a yard that was not littered with wreckage of tanks, AFVs, guns and thousands of mutilated stinking corpses decaying in the hot sun. Captain Roberts, 6 RWF wrote:

> We were on high ground at Martigney from which we could see across the Falaise Gap, an extraordinary panorama, with the dust clouds of fleeing German transport columns, the smoke of the transport burning and the bursting shells of our own barrage with the Typhoons swooping down to support 71 Brigade at that time leading the advance. The next day we moved by transport through Falaise. It was devastated and the ruins were still smoking. We relieved 4 RWF on the high ground to the south of the town. The front was very confused, shells coming from all directions. It was hard to know which were ours and which were the enemy's. The Germans were completely disorganised.

A lesser foe would have given up completely. Individual fanatics, usually very young, would snipe first and then try to surrender. 6 RWF had a bloody nose at Ronai, eight miles south of Falaise, one of the last escape routes, and Major Grindley's 'C' Coy took several casualties including a Canloan officer, Lt Main, and the Dutch Lt E. Kahn, both killed. Four thousand prisoners were now in the bag — SS, Wehrmacht, Poles, Russians, Mongols even Chinese and Hindu.

Captain Bolland's diary: 'Saturday 19th. These days are certainly the gunners paradise — targets all round him. The OPs could almost shoot blind and be certain of killing Huns. The 'German Killing Ground' has now been defined. Sunday 20th. Throughout the day PW rolled in hundreds at a time. The PW cage is near Div HQ. It always is, to assist interrogation by the 'I' boys.'

Welshmen meet the Yanks in Trun

The Recce Regiment's HQ was in the village of Merri (south-east of Falaise). They had first met up with the Canadians on the 16th, and on the 21st met the Americans at Trun, the first British troops to do so. Major A. S. D. Graessers 'A' Sqn had worked the twelve mile road east from Falaise to Trun and helped capture between two and three thousand prisoners in the area Villedieu-les-Bailleul and St Lambert-sur-Dives. They also over-ran a German field hospital and retrieved some 53rd Division wounded. At one stage they had gathered in about 5000 prisoners, 'but many of them we gave away to the Canadians and other units'. The Provost Sergeant, Roberts, had problems with the huge pile of collected Luger pistols and other small arms and Philip Cowburn, the Recce historian recorded:

> Around Chambois [north-east of Argentan] we passed five miles of continuous destruction — destroyed armour, transport, horses, men, carts, staff cars, trucks of all types. The devastation of men and material was past belief. Huge tanks just knocked off the side of the road and black from burning, dozens of them with the crews hanging half-in, half-out of turrets and escape hatches. Men lying dead everywhere. Horses dead, swollen and smelling hideously.

But amongst the wreckage the will to fight back was still there. 'Bud' Abbott and 'C' Sqn Recce were clearing the Bois St André, south-east of Falaise. An 88 mm gun hit the carrier he was driving. The first shell killed Tommy Palmer and the second shell Trooper Mason. Bud was thrown out, got a lift on Sgt Cox's carrier and a third shell hit 'Dai' in the chest killing him instantly.

The Ox and Bucks had captured Pierrefitte in a night action on 19th and stayed there for a week. Their CO, Lt Col James Hare wrote:

The wrecked machinery of war

21st August. With the hunt up as it has been, I've had no time at all. We've marched miles through the night with no idea when and where we shall come across the Bosch, and then attacked the next day. It's a very wearing war, with plan and counter-plan hustled into battle and hustled on again from our objectives. Only eight of my original officers remain, but thank heaven, all but one of my sergeant-majors. Morale could not be better and the troops are always smiling. Willing and cheerful. I could wish for nothing more. We have been lucky, too, in avoiding tight places.

Reinforcements arrived from 8th Bn the Kings Regiment, and from the Royal Norfolk Regiment. Alan Moorhead, the *Daily Telegraph* correspondent, visited the Ox and Bucks and the regimental band and bugles appeared. Their shining instruments and the smart parade and procession looked out of place amongst the destruction all round. The battalion went on a route march of twelve miles into the Falaise Pocket — a grotesque bizarre march past the wrecked machinery of war and the burnt, mutilated fly-infested corpses.

1 HLI took Montabard on the 20th:

My 16 Platoon, 'D' Coy 1 HLI was in the thick of it. We were pressing forward through this frightful mess of burnt lorries, tanks, dead Germans and horses due to the RAF Typhoons and came upon a German Paymaster's truck. The crew were dead and the contents were strewn across the road in thousands of notes. Though I had never been abroad before, I recognised German, Dutch, Belgian and French notes of all denominations. Tired as we were we picked up as many as we could and stuffed them into the pannier amongst the oily tools on the Brengun carrier. When we reached Antwerp the dirty notes gave each person in 16 platoon about fifty pounds, a lot of money in 1944. [Lt G C R L Pender]

Fusilier John Ottewell, 7 RWF:

Flies were everywhere, millions of them droning about the ears as we passed burnt out tanks with blackened swollen, grinning corpses hanging out of turrets, spread out in great heaps along the roadside. There were SS Staff Officers Cars piled full of 'loot'. Some were dead in their vehicles. Funeral pyres blackened the sky on to the horizon's rim. RAF Typhoons were having a field day passing through Falaise. French civilians were piling great heaps of German jackboots outside the village school. Children would run alongside us shouting 'Bon Chance, Tommy, Vivent Les Anglais, cigarettes pour Papa, chocolat pour Mama.' One running in front was wearing a bloodstained jackboot shouting, 'Les sales Boches sont partis.' Something out of Dantes' Inferno. Long blue grey lines, four abreast, a far as the eye could see, dischevelled, capless, bombardment shocked German troops, with eyes averted from our stares. They came by in their thousands. Hitler's pride of bygone battles, broken men, no longer singing the Horst Wessel and Lili Marlene.

Ron Ludgater and his pals of 1st Manchesters, 'rounded up 20 big farm horses made rope bridles, got on their backs from the top of a farm wall and set off as a [sheriffs] posse to bring in hundreds of German PoWs and herd them back to the cages being assembled at the rear.' And Major Nick Cutcliffe, 4 RWF: 'At last we thought we could rest, get a proper meal and some sleep. We had done an attack the previous day, consolidated and dug in, carried out a relief and a long all-night march through enemy country; had a dust up on the objective, again dug in and fought an all day battle. But it was not to be.' 4 RWF moved to Ronai six miles south-east of Falaise. Nick's company dug in next to Battalion HQ:

I had settled down, well in my trench when 3 mortar bombs fell in my Coy HQ, 3 fellows were hurt. I went down to the RAP with them, returned to my slit and sat on the edge. There was another deafening explosion behind me. I felt a kick like a mule in my arm. It was dangling in an absurd fashion. I remember thinking as I walked 70 yards to the RAP how well I had chosen the time and place to be wounded. My great dread had been of being hurt during a night attack through standing corn and of lying helpless, unseen. 1700hrs 19th August. From the RAP, ambulance to FDS, ambulance to CCS, theatre operation before dawn on 20th and ambulance to 101 General Hospital at Bayeux.

Nick's watch, silver cigarette case, wallet etc were stolen 'presumably by the RAMC orderlies in the Base Hospital'. On 26 August he was taken by ambulance to the airfield, Dakota to Oxford, ambulance train to Swansea. 'I was home.'

In 13 FDS Corporal Isherwood noted in his diary:

19th August. On the operating table was a little French girl pale, emaciated with shrapnel wounds. Her wounds were being dressed by the Captain with Morris assisting. Harry and 'sticky' carried the tot, labelled with name and address, though her house was probably a heap of rubble, on a stretcher to an ambulance to evacuate her with two East Lancashire lads with severe mine wounds. We kept a mixed bag of sick and wounded: our own troops, German soldiers, civilians — men, women and children.

Captain Roberts, 6 RWF continued:

Owing to the number of casualties in 6 RWF and the lack of reinforcements 'D' Coy were disbanded, a platoon joining each of the other three. Our own 'R' [Reserve] Coy containing many picked men who we had reserved on purpose were drafted *before* our arrival in Normandy to reinforce the assault division. Throughout Normandy, rifle companies seldom went into battle 50 strong. *Depending on the leaders available,* Coy COs had to decide between two full platoons or three weak platoons of only two sections. It was unusual to have more than two officers per company. Reinforcements came through slowly and seldom from Welsh regiments. When the battle of Normandy was over 6 RWF had only 14 of their original officers left. Seven had been killed and 56 ORs KIA. It had been an infantry man's battle, each small field and hedge had to be dearly bought and held by sheer guts under ceaseless fire. It was over but we had left many friends buried in Normandy.

Up to 31 August the Division had lost in the killing grounds of Normandy:

Killed	52 Officers	533 ORs
Wounded	145 Officers	2711 ORs
Missing	18 Officers	360 ORs

La place Belle-Croix, Falaise, after the bombardment of 18 August 1944

Another view of La place Belle-Croix, Falaise

8

Hot pursuit:
'cognac and kisses'

There was little doubt that the Allied Armies had — eventually — won a smashing victory in Normandy. Montgomery's tactics had worked perfectly — painfully, yes — but perfectly. At great cost and with brave tenacity the infantry and armour of 21st Army Group had borne the brunt for ten weeks whilst Patton's magnificent 'cavalry' charged on the right wing to Brittany, the Seine, and the liberation of Paris. Seasoned warriors were taking bets on the end of the war by Christmas, perhaps even earlier. It was a time of great optimism. The 20 August found 71st and 158 Brigades resting in the Ronai-Montabard-St André Forest area and 160 Brigade continued to mop up stragglers.

The German losses had been staggering. At least 10,000 had been killed and 40,000 captured during the closing of the 'Pocket'. Nearly 350 tanks and SPs had been destroyed, as had 250 guns and about 2500 lorries. Five SS Panzer divisions (*1,2,9,10 and 12*) had been devastated. Also *2, 21 and 116 Panzer Divisions* had only six weakened battalions and twenty tanks left between them. Nevertheless about 20,000 German troops, twenty-four tanks and sixty guns were eventually ferried east of the Seine — the bridges all being blown.

Mopping up, collecting stragglers, integration of new reinforcement took place. But on the 25th the Welsh Division was on the move northwards towards the Acquigny-Ecardinville-Evreux area south of the Seine. In Operation Neptune, 43rd Wessex Wyvern Division were fighting a five day battle to force a bridgehead at Vernon. When that was accomplished Monty unleashed his greyhounds. 11th Armoured headed for Antwerp via Amiens, 7th Armoured for Ghent and the lucky Guards Armoured for Brussels.

✻   ✻   ✻

On the way a few moments of peace; on 26 August 83 Field Regt RA had reached Sebecourt as Rev H. E. W. Slade, CF, their chaplain recounts:

War is mostly an unexplained mystery illuminated by moments of understanding. At least that is how it appears from the Chaplain's end. After a day of constant movement and uncertainty along dusty roads littered with the wreckage of German transport and occasionally made alive by groups of cheering and bewildered French civilians, we came to Sebecourt in the evening. It was a small village with a green and a church, bomb damaged, but still inviting us to use it on this Sunday evening. There seemed little chance of that. The hot meal had still to be cooked. There was the usual scramble for somewhere to sleep. But the church continued its silent invitation, and at 7.30pm with the evening meal disposed of and the billets arranged, I let it be known that Evensong would take place in that church at 8pm.

Long experience had schooled me to expect little. Perhaps one or two gunners and the rest — angels, archangels and the whole company of heaven. But this was a moment of illumination, not only for myself but for the whole regiment. The gunners came into that church as to their home, so did the other bewildered French villagers, and, as in all moments of illumination, the service conducted itself and the light in our darkness and the peace which passeth understanding were given. For some of us that evening moment seemed the end, the glory of all that was now behind in Normandy. Later experience was to reveal that it was not the end. It was but a breathing-space in a campaign but half-completed, yet it remains a Mount of Transfiguration, and though we have now come down, we look back to that moment and in its light know that all will one day be well.

The Recce Regiment had a certain amount of fighting to clear north of Les Andelys but on 1 September achieved a fifty-five mile 'dash' through Forges Les Eaux, Beaufresne and Beauchamps where their cars were pelted with flowers and fruit, occasionally bottles of cognac and kisses. Just after the river Somme was crossed on the 2nd at Picquiny, resistance increased. To make matters worse four casualties were caused by one troop firing on another. Flixecourt had enough enemy and 88mms to hold up 'B' Sqn until the Manchesters' Vickers MMGs helped resolve the problem. 'A' Sqn cleared Domart and 'C' Sqn reached St Riquier. David Henderson, a carrier driver with 'C' wrote: 'Dark and raining when we arrived. We noticed a lot of chaps with horses and carts. We thought they were civilians. Our No. 5 troop, seven carriers to begin with, belted along suspecting nothing. The leading carrier turned a sharp bend and bumped into a heavy truck pulling a gun. We emptied a magazine into the front cab which blew up and chased two escaping Jerries with tracer bullets.' Henderson's carrier now led: 'A blinding flash — it stopped dead. "Ambush — Bale Out." We found a side lane and scrambled on to the three remaining carriers. Then we bumped into some horsedrawn vehicles with 88 mm guns behind.' Eventually only one carrier was left intact, 'we piled on all 20 of us and slipped off into a field.' The next few days rearguard pockets had to be dealt with round St. Pol, across the rivers Ternoise and Hesdin. And so to Lille by devious routes through Aubigny, Noeux-Les-Mines, Carvin and Seclin. On the 7th Belgium was entered. A bizarre episode ensued when a wireless report

53rd Recce, Lambersant/Lille 6th Sept 1944

indicated that a German general and 500 men at Ypres would surrender if asked nicely. Lt A. A. Pounder, 'C' Sqn with three cars went off to collect them and vanished. The complete party had been captured by a clever bluff but all survived. On the same day the whole regiment had a furious battle in the streets of Moorsele, helped by the SP guns of 340 Bty against seventeen year old Hitler Jugend lads who left a hundred dead and wounded behind.

71 Brigade was on the move again on 26 August. For the first few miles around Trun and the river Dives movement was difficult and slow because of destroyed German equipment and bombed roads. Their route lay through Orville, Mesnil Rousset, the Forêt de Conches, past Evreux and across the Seine. Most of the troops travelled by troop carrying vehicles, the weather was good and the joys of 'liberation' were immense:

> Names, dates I cannot remember — it was an endless nightmare of marching, sometimes lifted by Infantry personnel 3 ton trucks with Jocks exhausted in the back and out for the count. Myself in the front with an RASC driver either trying to follow the truck in front in daylight, or in darkness, the little white night light on the back axle of the TCV in front. It was only by luck that the RASC driver did not go to sleep and crash. 16 Platoon always seemed to be in the vanguard of 'D' Coy 1HLI. My Jocks took a pride in it and christened ourselves 'The Bumpers'. We crossed the Seine on 30th August, the Somme [Picquigny] on 2nd September, through Givenchy and Menin where we stayed the night and watched the Last Post being sounded at the Menin Gate in memory of the Allied Armies

Liberation of Lille

dead of 1914-18, played by the towns fire brigade. All the way to Antwerp was one endless nightmare. There were some compensations, flowers, wine, fruit and pretty girls who all cheered their liberators to the highest. The Jocks showered the children and girls with chocolate and food. [Lt Pender, 1HLI]

2 Mons led 4 Welch via Trun and Chambois where their bivouac area was contaminated with German dead, through the green valley of the river Risle. After the Seine crossing through the Forêt de Lyons, Argueil, Aumale, over the Somme at Abbeville to Hesdin. Flying bomb sites were spotted. The East Lancs started from Bailleul to Mardilly with the Bicycle company using their machines. Many men bathed in the river Touques, and many captured small German trailers appeared, to carry anti-tank and anti-personnel mines, extra wireless batteries (and probably other recent acquisitions) towed behind 15cwt and 3 tonners. Across the Seine to Le Mesnil Virreleve, Bosquentin to Domart. The hard work had already been done by the three armoured divisions. Brussels, Antwerp and Ghent — prime targets — had all been taken. So 53rd Welch had few actions of note. Wood clearing, mopping up. The gunner regiments crossed the Seine on 29th. At Grossat a target was engaged at Valhoun. Only small-scale maps were available. Sometimes batteries carried their own infantry in their vehicles. As each town or village was entered the follow-up 'liberation' troops received a marvellous welcome, particularly at Cauchy. Once a captured V bomb site was used as a gun position. There were several cases of small ambushes being laid by the Germans. Once a party of five 2 Mons officers were ambushed in the dark, two wounded, one made a prisoner. The FFI/Maquis were always helpful. The Ox and Bucks met a well-mannered Old Harrovian who gave accurate military information at Bois Branger, but unpleasant bits of mob law against recent collaborators were noted. 4 Welch had some fierce street fighting at St Pol on 3 September, 220 prisoners being taken, and the population went wild with excitement.

Corporal Bert Isherwood, 13 FDS encountered in Marzingarbec on 6 September a particularly savage execution by the Maquis of four men and a woman in front of Major McClaren and Ted Dwyer's ambulance team, 'with machine pistols they opened fire, each FFI man shooting off an entire magazine of bullets into the target bodies. Their chopped up bodies finally lay in small dehumanised heaps. A cold calculated organised, *maybe* justified killing. At the same time the throng lining our route cheered us as their liberators.'

The 1/5 Welch route to Antwerp was via Muids (Seine crossing), La Mesnil Virreleve, Gourney-en-Bray where the FFI shot a priest, Le Heronde to Surcamp, a night journey of eighty miles. Then Lillers via St Pol. Sgt Machin recorded:

Here the civilians gave us a rousing welcome. The usual wine and beer drinking, handshaking, laughing and talking, took place. I suppose that the language was a difficulty on such occasions, but it did not seriously interfere. After all, one did not have to *ask* for a glass of beer, it was brought to you. If a pretty girl felt like kissing you, well, who wanted to stop her! At Lillers the FFI helped us locate a Coy of enemy infantry making a hasty exit. Our 3 " mortars and the Manchesters Vickers MGs assisted them!

Then to Sailly, Wervicq via Armentieres, 'where the town square was carpeted with locks of shorn mademoiselles who had associated too closely with the Germans', then to Menin, Oudenarde, Alost and Boom to Antwerp.

Ron Ludgater, a despatch rider with 1st Manchesters, spent several days in Antwerp: 'I went scrounging food of sorts and vegetables, went swimming, rode on a tram and slept on a billiard table in a big mansion in Hoboken.' Ron had suffered minor wounds at Esquay, another on the way north of Bethune (where he saw the gallant Resistance movement busy shaving heads and abusing French girls said to be collaborators). He also saw there, 'A German officer hanging from his ankles from the top of a flagpole, obviously beaten to death and then strung up.'

Captain Tim Dumas of 4 RWF, having recovered from his wound in Normandy rejoined the battalion a month later:

Our new CO. Lt Col Tedder appointed me OC 'C' Coy as Nick Cutcliffe had been badly wounded. Very few of the Majors and Captains who had come out with us from England had survived. Tom Cumberland the 2 i/c, and RH Roberts OC 'B' Coy were the only majors, the commanders of 'A', 'C', 'D' and HQ Coy all having been killed in July. 43 Div transport was used to move the Division across N France to Holland and Belgium. In Antwerp we guarded a lock gate which if destroyed would have emptied the harbour. Looking down the Scheldt we could see Germans crossing by boat some ¾ mile away so we aimed Brens and rifles at a high angle to discourage them.

        *   *   *

'Travelling at night through the Flanders plain was an eerie and poignant experience. In the fading light the trench lines of WWI were vaguely discernible. With closed eyes one [Fusilier John Ottewell 7 RWF] could almost visualise their "No Man's Land" screaming and cheering as they waded through the slopping mud to oblivion. Somebody struck up "Roses Are Blooming In Picardy". Within minutes the entire convoy, the Welsh "Treorchy Male Voice" in muted harmony, tenors and baritones were rendering that "tearful" love song… '

At Fleurbaix in Belgium, the GOC established Division HQ — fleetingly — where he had spent the winter of 1914-15 in trench warfare.

So eventually 53rd Welsh arrived on 8 September in Antwerp to a tremendous welcome to tidy up after 11th Armoured Division's five-day town battles. Apart from some enemy in Merxem, the northeast suburb, the Division acted for a week as a garrison. Sapper Ned Petty:

> The Div took over a nice place in Antwerp known as 53rd Divisional club, good for 48hrs leave. A real eye-opener. I went there straight from life in the fields. It wasn't very smart. However, showers were provided, clean sheets and beds were a real luxury. All the meals were very good. Each table had cigarettes, bars of chocolate. Boots left outside the bedroom door at night were cleaned by morning. I saw the 'Merry Widow' show, playing from London. I enjoyed it.

Bert Isherwood, 13 FDS met the Steenackers-Sunen family; Edward an insurance clerk, Alice a nurse. They told him that a German practice invasion force in invasion barges, with E boats escorting, had sailed halfway across the Channel, and were spotted by the RAF and bombed with incendiaries. 'The whole force was enveloped in flames. Few returned, all were badly burned.'

The 1HLI entered Antwerp on the 9th again to scenes of wildest joy:

> We found ourselves in the trenches dug by British Marines in their ill fated attempt to defend the City in 1914. Next to us were the HLI of Canada on our left with 16 platoon next to them. We had several Canloan officers in the Bn. We soon had a good liaison with them. A charming young gunner FOO officer decided to make an OP in a tree above my platoon HQ. Shortly afterwards he lay at my feet with bullets in his head. I had warned him not to climb the tree. [Lt Pender]

The RQMS of 1 East Lancs had been ordered to leave 147 bicycles behind under lock and key in Fleurbaix. Three days later he returned to find *all* the population riding them. The Marine and Gendarmerie were persuaded to round them up! 81st Field Regt had gun positions in the southern suburbs. Wally Brereton 'found a nice little bar which became our regular haunt. It had a huge fairground-type organ with deafening noise. Many a happy evening was spent dancing with the local girls. The "phoney peace" ended when the Captain said we were going to set up an OP in the dock area!' All three gunner regiments pounded away at the German defenders in Merxem. RWF patrols sneaked over the Turnhout canal and set ambushes. 4 RWF 'Lockforce' was particularly active.

On 13 September, Field Marshal Montgomery visited the Division and talked to many officers and men, and two days later the real war started up again.

Monty

9
The Lommel Bridgehead

As part of 12 Corps, the Division's next task was to help develop and protect the left base and then the left flanks of Monty's ambitious operation 'Market Garden'. 8 Corps with the author's 11th Armoured Division had the unenviable task of guarding the right flank with the Siegfried line troops to their east. 30 Corps had the most difficult task of all of reaching and protecting the three airborne drops on the route north from Eindhoven, Nijmegen to Arnhem. The next move then was some thirty-six miles due east (leaving 7th Armoured Division to hold Antwerp) to force the key Canal de Jonction north of Lommel. The Recce Regiment and 158 Brigade — who were to make the actual assault crossing — led on the afternoon of 15 September for Steelen. The following day the Recce cars were making the long easterly trek to Vorst with a view to crossing the Albert canal at Beeringen, then turning north to Bourg Leopold into Holland and forcing the Lommel bridgehead. On Sunday 17th the skies were filled with the huge airborne armada on its way to

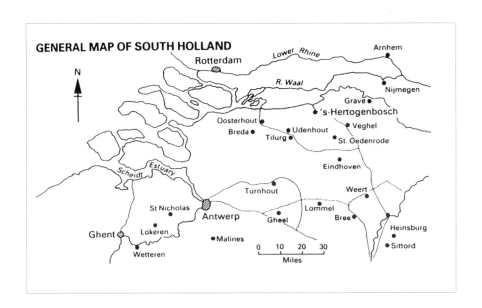

GENERAL MAP OF SOUTH HOLLAND

Nijmegen with hundreds of gliders and troop carriers. David Henderson 'C' Sqn:

> We moved very slowly up to the bridgehead area [Beeringen]. Everybody wanted and expected priority and things became chaotic after nightfall. It was pitch dark and raining cats and dogs. We were soaked through. The kit was wet and the food sopping. I for one was dead-beat.

THE BRIDGEHEAD

The assault on a two battalion front on both sides of a demolished bridge was by 1 East Lancs on the left, 7 RWF on the right. About six miles to the west 15th Scottish Division was also carrying out an assault crossing at Gheel. The Canal de Jonction (de la Meuse) was two and-a-half miles running east-west. A steep 'bund' runs along its length crowned by a dense strip of young fir trees. The crossing points for the East Lancs were about 200 yards apart. The 50 yards width of the canal would be crossed by 16 class V rafts built by the Pioneers and REs, holding eighteen men each. A 'flight' of two boats would thus take a platoon. The 2 Mons carried out duties of 'obstacle company' with carrying parties, ferrymen, generally assisting the assaulting companies of 'D' Coy on the right, 'C' Coy on the left. A substantial fire plan from seven Field Regts, two Medium Regts plus the Manchesters 4.2-inch mortar and MMG would provide supporting barrages. Opposition was to be from dedicated German paratroopers who fought with courage and great skill.

At 23.30 hrs on 16 September the East Lancs boats went down the steep stone-faced bank into the water. It was a dark night, belting with rain and visibility only 10-15 yards. Although on the right flank two boats sank with two men drowned, both companies got across relatively unscathed. The move through narrow rides in thick forest at angles to advance meant that all companies became isolated, lost in the dark. Predictably wireless communications broke down. Lt Col Burden tracked down his leading companies, ordered them to halt and advance again at first light. At dawn three out of four companies had 'changed' places, only 'C' was in the right place. Moreover most enemy forces had been bypassed in the dark, who then opened fire briskly on the rafting operations on the canal. Confused fighting went on all day on the 17th. Major Griffin led 'A' Coy in four separate attacks on isolated fortified huts in the woods. By the time 1/5 Welch came through in the evening the East Lancs had thirty casualties including Major Genese, Major Nicoll, Captains Carter and Till and Lt Sharlot.

7 RWF made their first ever assault water crossing according to plan, although 'A' Coy on the right met heavy Spandau fire. 'B' and 'C' were quickly

across the canal and cleared the far bank towards 'A'. 'D' Coy of 1/5 Welch was borrowed and by 05.00 on 18th all five companies were dug in on their objective. Lt Col Dickson then pushed 'C' and 'D' at 11.00 towards the Heider Heide, again with success. The 7 RWF suffered thirty-four casualties, captured twenty-eight prisoners and did a lot of damage to the enemy paratroopers.

Pte Laurie Woolard, 2 Mons:

> We put up the 3" mortars behind a farmhouse on the Albert Canal. No sooner did the Bn move to cross the canal, when suddenly out of the woodland on the other side appeared some 88s. Back came the infantry and we were asked for back up fire. A 3" mortar lowest range is 500 yds. No.1 mortar fired the first bomb which went well behind the 88s. We tried to place some stones under the mortar legs to get the range down. But the 88s [crews] had seen the explosive material rise over the barn top and we had had it. They just pointed their guns at it. All I remember was a big bang and somebody dragged me to a farmhouse where I was given morphine, put on a Red Cross carrier.

Laurie went to Brussels and eventually back to Newtown in Wales, with a badly injured right arm.

On 13 September Lt Col Harington, CO of the Manchesters had been promoted to be Division GSO1, and was replaced a week later by Lt Col Earle. The CO of 71 Anti-Tank Regt was captured on the same day that Brigadier Bloomfield and two of his staff were wounded. 116 LAA Regt had been 'reorganised' into RASC platoons as the Luftwaffe threat had diminished. From late September the Recce Regt acted mainly as infantry in defensive positions.

Escaut Canal

1/5 Welsh had left Hove, for Osterloo, to the Brigade bridging area at Kattenboche, and to Heide. 'The enemy was strongly opposing the 7 RWF and East Lancs crossing. The Luftwaffe was in rare evidence and slit trenches were useful. We crossed [Sgt Machin] the canal at 12.40 hrs on 18th and proceeded to Luyksgester without seeing a single German. Bn HQ managed by mistake to enter L[uyksgester] first. The next day we were ordered back to the canal crossing area to help clear the northern banks, and move west to help 15th Scottish.'

The following morning Lt Col Gibson was shot by a sniper and died of his wounds. Bill Tudor Owen wrote: 'I was at his side when he was shot on the towpath of the Escaut Canal near Lommel. He displayed no fear or anxiety and strolled down the path passing on his right a thick plantation of conifers with a series of rides. I was horrified and started to think of myself as a Jinx [Bill was by the side of three successive COs as they were wounded or killed]. In a static position Colonel Gibson would search me out saying, "Get binoculars and a Bren, we're going to harass the Hun", and harass them we did.' From Steemsel 1/5 Welch captured Hoogeloon on 21st with a bag of sixty-one prisoners. However, Major Goldsmid led his two troops of Recce cars and carriers into the village and was mainly responsible for the enemy's 200 casualties. On the 18th 6 RWF led 160 Brigade across the canal and next day 71 Brigade followed.

For the next two weeks the Division was involved in half a dozen nasty unit battles which are described chronologically. The Recce Regt, now across the canal, 'fought our way into this country of moorland, wood and marsh, occupied by a resolute battle group of 6th German Parachute Regiment. All squadrons fought with distinction round the villages of Reusel, Bladel, Eersel, Hoogeloon, Casteren, Netersel, Middelbeers and Hilvarenbeek in that corner of north-west Brabant', wrote Philip Cowburn, the Recce historian.

On the 19th, 4 Welch advanced at 07.00 towards Wilreit, but were held up at Postel by a force of 600 parachutists behind minefields. 'A' Coy was blocked by 88 mm mortar and MG fire and 'D' Coy was badly ambushed in thick woods, losing two officers and many men. They got out as best they could, some lay motionless for six hours until darkness. Another attack was made round the right flank to the north-west, but part of 'B' Coy was surrounded. Wireless in the woods made communications impossible. Eventually, 4 Welch got back with many prisoners taken and concentrated west of Wilreit.

The next day 4 RWF attacked and captured Wintelre having passed through 158 Brigade's bridgehead on the 19th. The village, ten miles inland was strongly held and it took a two-day battle to clear it. 'A' Coy was counter-attacked near Bysterveld and suffered badly and 'D' Coy was under heavy fire from Hoogeind. The village church spire was an enemy OP. Eventually at 14.30 on the 21st after a heavy concentration of divisional artillery fire, the enemy started to give up and by the evening the village was taken. The enemy lost sixty killed, many more wounded and 4 RWF took 168 prisoners, plus eleven enemy guns of various calibres. But the Fusiliers had eighty casualties, 'B' Coy alone losing thirty-three. Unfortunately Brigadier Bloomfield, following 4 RWF into the village was badly wounded. The Brigade without firm management played 'Musical Chairs' for the next few days. 4 RWF were told to stay in Wintelre for a few days and dug in. They were promptly moved on the 22nd to relieve 7 RWF at Westel-Biers. 7 RWF moved to Hoogeloon, then by vehicle to Duizel. 4 RWF settled in again. 7 RWF were ordered back to their recent positions. And 4 RWF? They returned to Wintelre! Not very good staff work for hundreds of exhausted Fusiliers. The moves were *not* explained to the COs, certainly not to the rank and file. Brigadier M. Elrington arrived to command 71st Brigade on 28 September. The rest of 71 Brigade were more fortunate. 1HLI captured Oostelbeers and Middelbeers, two villages three miles north-west of Wintelre — but only after a three-day battle.

Lt G. C. R. L. Pender with 16 Platoon, 'D' Coy 1HLI, took part in the capture of the two large villages:

> 'D' Coy was commanded by Major W Bowie, Capt McEwan was 2 i/c and 17 and 18 platoons were led by Sgts. We started in wooded country at mid-day on 21st just south of Middelbeers 'C' Coy was directed on to Oostelbeers and the rest of the Bn on to Middelbeers. But by 04.30 in the morning we had come up against stiff opposition. Nevertheless 'C' took their village and we attacked ours against well dug in enemy, who had placed a road block on the road running SE-NW leading to the church. About 06.00 one of our tanks charged in front of my position with the Assault Pioneers Platoon CO huddled behind the turret, wearing a bonnet, clutching a bag of demolition charges. The tank smashed the roadblock but then was 'brewed up'. The command radio failed to work so Major Kindersley 'A' Coy CO took over command and passed through 'D' into the centre of town. They were forced off their objective leaving Sgt MacDonald's platoon behind. They were surrounded, fought to the last and 15 wounded survivors were made prisoners. Then Capt. McEwan took a fighting patrol of selected Jocks from 17 and 18 Platoons into the south of the town, captured the houses and church to the west. Our losses were 59 KIA, wounded and PW. We captured 68 and 27 dead were counted on the field. We also acquired 33 MGs, 5 bazookas, 7 field guns. We stayed in the two villages until 3rd October.

Major Kindersley was awarded the DSO for this action. Major John Lloyd, 2 i/c 81st Field Regt wrote:

> 4 RWF were advancing up the road towards the small town of Middelbeers. We set off to catch them up and look for the next gun area. The Bn seemed to have

made a fairly rapid advance as we drove along quite a long way without finding
them. [Eventually], we found a suitable location, parked my staff car, went in a
jeep with the survey officer to inspect the area.

Major Lloyd sent a wireless message back to the battery commanders
indicating the RV of the new area: 'The BC with 4 RWF called me up and
said, 'You may be quite happy where you are but you are 3 miles *ahead* of our
leading company!'' [4 RWF had pulled off the road for *tea*, so Major Lloyd
had missed them on the way].

Gunner Wally Brereton, 81st Field Regiment:

The HLI along with Roger Fox [OP carrier] started off on one of the longest
marches of the campaign to Middelbeers. There were two church steeples in the
village, one with a slender spire, the other a square solid tower with a short
blunt point. The latter would make the best OP. The enemy had constructed a
barricade of furniture at the end of the village street, defended by unseen snipers.
The first AFV was knocked out by an A/Tk gun, the second was more successful.
We could see the HLI infantry now in force making their way up dodging from
tree to tree, wall to wall. Already there were casualties. The MO had a RAP in a
large barn near the original barricade.

As Wally was drinking half a bottle of wine acquired in Antwerp, mortar
bombs exploded all round the barn which was their OP. When they moved
the OP to the church spire a 88 mm shell hit it wounding Capt Peter Green
the FOO and Wally too. The HLI reached the next village of Oostelbeers:
'We then heard that the battle for Arnhem had failed. When the survivors of
the Airborne Division were retreating back across the river, I was sitting in a
Dutch barn with my head bandaged.'

The Ox and Bucks were ordered to infiltrate the enemy lines towards the
Wilhelmina Canal, twenty miles north and parallel to the Junction Canal. So
on 19 September they crossed the Escaut Canal by pontoon bridge, ten miles
south-west of Valkensward and then via Meerveldhoven, near Eindhoven
passed Oerle, Hoogeind and Scherpendhering to the village of De Kruisberg.
On the way at Eijkereind an entire school of novice priests turned out on the
road to sing 'God Save the King'. After many adventures the battalion arrived
at the blown bridge at Oirscot on the Wilhelmina Canal, west of Best. 'D' Coy
moved along to clear the south bank of panzer grenadiers of *Kampfgruppe
Zedlitz* but they were counter-attacked, heavily shelled and lost six men killed
and nine wounded. Lt Col Hare took over command of 71 Brigade for a week
when Brigadier Blomfield was wounded.

After 158 Brigade had made the initial bridgehead north of Lommel they
moved north on 21st to Eerzel, Duizel and Hapert which had been previously

occupied by 71 Brigade. The next day the East Lancashires attacked the village of Bladel halfway between Reusel and Hapert. On the way their Bren gun carrier platoon under Capt Dawson and Sgt Fish, had cut loose in the fields of standing corn crops and in their five ton tracked carriers had hunted the fields like greyhounds, herding back forty prisoners. The advance of one and-a-half miles from Hapert west towards Bladel was over exposed country, an unsecured start line, a broken road bridge and a stream full of water.

Major J. F. Lake:

> My 'D' Coy played a leading part in the capture of Bladel. It was a very costly attack. We came under small arms fire as we entered the FUP NW of Halpert, the enemy having infiltrated during the night. I ordered 16 PL to smoke off our right flank with their 2" mortar and the CO [Lt Col Burden] ordered 'C' Coy to form a defensive right flank. We fought our way across the green swampy fields, the only cover being shallow wet ditches. Sgt Whitehouse commanding 16 PL was killed outright, but 17 Pl under Lt Fitchett advancing along the axis of the main road cleared the enemy in front, but were checked by MG fire from a farmhouse. L/Corp Boardman, the Company runner moved tirelessly from PL to PL. Once in the town enemy resistance seemed to collapse.

Unfortunately 18 Platoon under Lt Crewe disappeared up the Hulsel road and were killed, wounded or captured. The next day a German counter-attack was repulsed but cost the East Lancs twenty-one casualties, and 'D' Coy was reduced to half strength after its gallant efforts. The East Lancs stayed in Bladel until the 28th: 'Curfew was imposed at nightfall and Nazi Party members were rounded up. The local Padre who spoke English fluently and 'Half track Henry' with his vintage armoured car and Resistance crew were of assistance.'(Major Lake)

On the 23rd 6 RWF moved to Postel, south-west of Wilreit. Their late night arrival "… was greeted by monks from the local monastery who turned out in their long white robes and greeted us [Capt. Roberts] with a local barrel organ with such tunes as 'It's a long way to Tipperary' and 'Pack up your Troubles'. We thanked them for their (noisy) welcome, begged them to be quieter as the enemy was still quite close and might shell the village. Unwillingly they condescended to silence the barrel organ."

Netersel, a village north of Bladel was jointly cleared by the Recce Regiment and 1/5 Welch. Lt Boraston, 'B' Sqn Recce: 'Our task was to hold on to the village of Netersel, prevent the enemy getting back into it. An enemy 88 mm just missed Sgt Mote's car and the next car, but we were more or less pinned down.' 'Bud' Abbot recalls: 'Here we lost "Dusty" Miller and others due to wounds from shell and mortar fire. We manned a slit trench with the Germans dug in just a field away.'

From Casteren onwards the Bosch really started to be nasty. As we [Sgt Machin] reached the bridge the enemy opened up with Spandaus. The Bn took up defensive positions. Major Campbell our FOO put down a concentration of fire on Netersel, after which a section of carriers followed by 'D' and 'C' Coys entered the village and consolidated by late afternoon. The Bosch made several energetic attempts to regain Netersel. One fighting patrol got into the centre of our area and gave us a lively time with egg and stick grenades. Sgt Townsend took out a Recce patrol and never came back. The Adjutant Capt Johnson was wounded and evacuated. An enemy 88mm worried us all day and after 20 hours of repeated attempts finally hit the Netersel church tower. [Sgt Machin]

Capt Squire, 329 Battery, and his R/T operator Bdr May, were the indomitable OP team and for several days were 'cannonaded' as they helped 1/5 Welch fend off counter-attacks. Squire received the MC and May the MM. On the 26th the Recce Regiment took over the defence of Netersel and 1/5 Welch moved to Casteren.

The 7 RWF reverted to 158 Brigade on the 21st and set off early through Veld-Hoven and Knegsel towards Vessem and spent the day clearing the village of the *937th Infantry Regiment*. 'B' and 'D' Coys took thirty-two prisoners to the delight of the inhabitants. The following day they pushed into Donk to add another twenty-two prisoners and tried to take Westelbeers. A determined enemy using flame throwers caused casualties to Major Tomlinson's 'D' Coy but a battalion attack was cancelled as 4 RWF came up to relieve 7 RWF who moved to St Oedenroede area and at once sent out patrols, as Sgt Mike Hannon 'D' Coy relates:

On 3rd October took a four man patrol into enemy lines, and got behind their forward position. Am about to stand up when two German officers walk past. I remained still and they did not see me. I returned to my men who were waiting in a ditch. As we were making our way back, we came across a group of Jerries sitting in a dug out, eating and jabbering away. We surrounded them, made them put their hands on their heads. We were marching them back to our lines when we were ambushed. The prisoners made a dash for it. We opened fire on them. A German grenade exploded as we took cover in a ditch. One of my men, Fusilier Gatenby was shot in the head. He died instantly. I tossed two hand grenades into the Jerries, and one came out with his hands on his head. We took him back for interrogation.

At Luikestel, Ron Ludgater, a despatch rider with 1 Manchesters lost his left leg and was evacuated to hospital. 'Just a colossal bang, probably a mine. The surgeon, Major Darke RAMC came to apologise for having to amputate my left leg above the knee.'

As the airborne reinforcements passed overhead on Sunday 24th, 133 Field Regiment supported 2 Mons in their attack on Voorheide. They had advanced from the De Maat and Postel area from the bridgehead and went into action at 18.00 hrs. There were minefields difficult to clear in the dark and Lt D. Evans and Corp Wheater were killed, Capt R. E. Foster and Lt M. Evans wounded. The gallant Pioneers located the mines under fire *in the darkness*, and pulled them out by hand with a cable. At 03.00 hrs 2 Mons were counter-attacked by four companies of paratroopers. Savage confused fighting took place, bazookas, grenades and Spandaus were deployed against buildings occupied by three Mons companies. All company areas were penetrated at times, complete platoons and sections surrounded. Heavy defensive fire by divisional artillery and the Manchesters 42-inch mortars saved the situation.

Major R. N. Dean, OC 'A' Coy:

> The enemy had counter-attacked out of the dark, four companies of paratroops to our three and for a time the village was in complete pandemonium where the only recipes for continued firing were to stay in a slit and shoot Germans off the windy skyline or stay in a room and shoot them off the dim windowsill. In the latter case the cost of bad shooting was a hand grenade thrown into the room, a deafening disruption of domestic rubble and someone badly hurt. The cost of speaking on a wireless set at all was the hand grenade or 'bazooka' from the Germans outside. At one time Voorheide was held by both German and British, one on the outside of the houses and the other inside. Invitations to 'surrender! You are surrounded!' were met by streams of good British verbal obscenities and a burst of automatic Sten fire from skylight or cellar peephole.

Major Hughes of 133 Field Regiment won the MC here. He ordered fire on his own position *between* the forward companies and Battalion HQ. 'C' Coy called for defensive fire when the enemy counter-attack was 50 yards away. The *6th German Regiment* parachutists left over sixty casualties on the ground. The Mons lost eighteen killed, twenty-two wounded and seven prisoners. Majors Chaston and Morgan received MCs, and Corporal Platt the MM. General Ross sent a message, 'Well done, 2nd Mons.'

Of the dozen or so battalion battles involved in the operations north of Lommel perhaps the most savage was that of the assault on Reusel on the west of the 53rd Division salient. The town was one of the road junctions, most important to the German defence and was defended by 600 paratroops of whom only 100 were destined to survive. Every house had been fortified and the divisional artillery of 25-pdrs would do little damage to the German strong points. On the 24th the carrier platoon of 6 RWF came under fire. 'A' Coy under Major O. E. H. Hughes advanced under heavy Spandau, anti-tank and artillery fire. They secured the outskirts of the village but could move no further. 'C' under Major Grindley and 'B' under Major Lord Davies were sent right flanking but they were observed and pinned down. In close fighting 'B' lost Lt Haines, Corp Bramwell, Fusiliers Smith and Mitchell all killed. The Canloan Lt P. West of 'C' Coy was hit and died of his wounds. By late afternoon after many hours of heavy fighting the three rifle companies were still hundreds of yards short of the town. Lt Col Snead-Cox decided to withdraw at nightfall. At dawn Capt Barnett led a patrol into Reusel unopposed. It was a trap as 'B', 'C' and 'D' Coys were shelled as they were forming up for a dawn attack. 'C' Coy despite heavy casualties captured some buildings on the south side but 'B' Coy were also in serious difficulties from MG fire from a church converted into a strong point. Major Lord Davies and Lt Ashmole were killed and CSM Blakely took over command. His grave was found later in Hooge Mierde, used by Germans as a first aid post during the battle. SS troops including Dutch SS mounted a bold counter-attack which forced 'C' and most of 'D' to withdraw. CSM Lloyd was killed by a shell on 'C' Coy HQ. CSM Wyle was badly wounded, taken prisoner and died of his wounds.

For a day and a half 6 RWF had tried their best and failed. Now 4 Welch attacked the following night, approaching Reusel across the front of 6 RWF, but were held up by the church strongpoint.

For three days 4 Welch grimly cleared house-to-house, street-to-street. There were many casualties in that time. The paratroopers succeeded not only in holding the attack but in infiltrating their Spandau groups, some twenty strong between platoons and companies. The fighting became very confused. The least movement drew enemy fire and mortar bombs seemed to be bursting everywhere. Sections were burnt out of houses by panzerfaust and phosphorus grenades. Stores were burnt and reserve ammo exploded. Battalion HQ had great difficulty controlling so confused a battle. Major A. J. Lewis OC 'D' Coy:

> The enemy were now all round us and a runner dashed into say he had seen them entering the basement of our Coy HQ. We dislodge them. We make a dash to the next house where we receive similar treatment. Three times we are burnt out during the afternoon before finally re-organising the Coy around a nunnery and school close to the crossroads. At one period 'D' Coy held one end of the village church and the Germans the other.

Close quarters fighting continued for three days when 4 Welch was ordered to withdraw a half section which was cut off in and around the church. They had no wireless. The German/Dutch SS opposition probably spoke English, so Sgt J. H. W. Williams came up and directed the withdrawal in the *Welsh* language. The section and the remainder of the battalion were during the day successfully withdrawn under cover of our artillery. A flight of Typhoons dived at the church firing their rockets. Anti-tank guns and 17-pdrs of the Anti-Tank Regt fired at the church and brought the steeple down but the paratroops fought on. Capt Frank Smith, 331 Battery RA and Lt Bibby both won MCs as FOOs in the Reusel battle. Major A. J. Lewis: 'Many people believed in the protection of God during that withdrawal. We certainly seemed to be protected by some Divine Power.' 4 Welch withdrew on 28 September and 6 RWF found Reusel empty on 3 October.

RQMS Pat Cullen 4 Welch was bringing up a convoy of his trucks and a jeep full of reinforcements, mostly returning to their unit having recovered from wounds received in Normandy. Rounding a bend in the road, they were stopped by a Sister of Mercy in a black habit. She showed them a terrified sixteen-year-old girl who had had her left hand hacked off at the wrist. She had been caught by the Germans taking water to an Allied flyer hiding in a ditch. 'After this, I told the men what had happened and said 'Know your enemy!'

Captain David Bolland's diary:

Wednesday, 27th September. 83 Field Regt went off with 158 Bde towards Schinder where Jerry is being troublesome trying to cut our lines of communication — again — north of Eindhoven. The BBC announced that the Airborne troops have been withdrawn from Arnhem. This came as a bitter pill to most of us who knew just how much effort had been put into the whole thing. Many lives must have been lost. Friday, 29th. To HQRA, a visit by the Inspector RA and BRA Second Army. How typical the RA was of the Regular Army, slightly patronising towards the wartime soldiers and full of his stories about all his pals. Tuesday, 3rd October. Visited 31 RHU, 30 miles SW of Brussels. Very cold, very wet and very cross. Still crosser when I discovered we were only to get 56 out of our 190 bodies. [reinforcements for the Divisional Artillery Regiments]. On 6th October 160 Bde and 71 Bde moved NE to a defensive position about Elst, a few miles south of Arnhem into a defensive position. 158 Bde had already moved through Eindhoven to St Oedenrode.

Capt Tim Dumas of 4 RWF wrote about morale:

As a Coy CO I must say that one had complete confidence that any battle or engagement would in the end be successful. We had complete air superiority and good weapons. But the German 88 gun was worrying for an infantryman; an incoming shell could normally be heard and allow one to get down, whilst the 88 exploded before you could hear it coming. A quite senior Fusilier Barden, a Cockney from Kent said to me, during another bombardment in Bemmell. 'Them little things can't 'urt yer'. The next moment he was dead. A mortar bomb had landed right by him.

Infantry in Kangaroo on the way to 's Hertogensbosch

10

Garrisoning the 'Island': 'Weather wet and stormy'

The two weeks expanding the Lommel bridgehead and evicting German paratroopers out of a dozen well defended villages had taken their toll of 53rd Division. In theory the next task — that of defending half of the so-called 'Island' should have been initially more pleasant. The Germans had flooded much of the area south of Arnhem and mounted a series of small but determined counter-attacks with a view to 'retrieving' the vital road and road bridges at Nijmegen.

When the East Lancs moved into the 'Island' the area between the rivers around Arnhem-Nijmegen, they occupied defensive positions from 28 September-19 October. There were artillery duels, a programme of patrol and raids in an area littered with destroyed Shermans, Cromwells and Stewart tanks mainly from the Guards Armoured Division. It was a flat dismal area of deep wide ditches, thick rectangular tree plantations and occasional fruit tree orchards. Two church spires at Schindle and Weiboche provided OP points. On 29 September they were rudely disturbed by six Typhoons who attacked 'A' Coy with rockets and MG fire, despite red smoke signals! The 7 RWF were dug in on the right flank, and 1/5 Welch on the left flank in and around a monastery. Private Bannister, 'D' Coy 1/5 Welch was there on sentry duty. On a dark, cold night he was wearing, perhaps rashly, a German sniper's hood and coat. Capt Smedley on his way from his Mortars to Battalion HQ was challenged in a Cockney accent 'Halt, goes there?'. The 'German' was rudely assaulted and was tumbled down the monastery steps. He recovered and fired a shot at his quarry who had gone. An officer of 'D' Coy complained to Battalion HQ how an enemy *patrol* had beaten up his sentry! Lt Col Nelson Smith had arrived at St Odenrode to take command of the 1/5 Welch.

7 RWF fired about 200 bombs a day on targets selected by patrols. Sgt Dunbell and L/Corp Benson led successful patrols, but on 14 October 'B' Coy suffered two determined attacks. Major Barber called for SOS fire and they were repulsed. L/Corp Morgan alone fired forty-two magazines from his Bren gun. Lt Col Dickson, then in Nijmegen, hurried back, but arrived too late for the fun. Capt D. M. Evans wrote: 'To those compelled to live in

a hole in the ground, Holland extends scant welcome. Water lies near the surface and trenches collapse without warning. Matters were not helped by the drab monotony of the countryside and the confusion caused by the unpronounceable names full of Beer and the pubs emptied of it, by an enemy always on the move.'

6 RWF now commanded by Lt Col K. G. Exham (from the 49 Polar Bear Division) since Lt Col Stead-Cox had been invalided out, were ensconced around Elst. Battalion HQ in a large farm was known as 'stonk Hall'. Coy HQs were mostly in cellars of gutted farm buildings. The main enemy positions were along the Rijn Wetering canal, behind which were the high grounds overlooking all the British positions.

Capt Hugh Roberts, Adjutant 6 RWF:

We were in brigade reserve. The weather was wet and stormy, the flat rain-soaked Dutch landscape was dreary and depressing. Men had covered shelters among the apple trees, lined with straw, reasonably dry and warm. When we went into the line to relieve 4 Welch, the landmarks were a destroyed ambulance, a burnt out half-track, a knocked out Tiger tank. Gutted farmhouses provided cellar accommodation known as JOE's DIVE or ANDY's HEDGE. The enemy were 150 yards away guarding 'JERRY's BRIDGE'. Our Bn position was astride an unfinished autobahn. We sent fighting patrols out to dominate No Mans Land. 17 pdrs from the A/Tk regiment supported us, and a Bn of 82 US Airborne were on our right.

After the severe casualties at Reusel, 4 Welch reorganised at Bladel and moved on to the Island on 7 October, also astride the unfinished autobahn. Movement was very restricted, really a battle of wits, in choice of observation posts and patrolling ground. They laid minefields, and found half a dozen young pigs running loose, so roast pork was a welcome change of menu.

For ten days Ressem was the wet and miserable home for the Ox and Bucks. Lt Geoffrey Fuller took a patrol out on 11 October to a brickworks near the river Waal and found it crammed full with displaced persons (DPs) and German slave labour from Poland and Russia. Food and medical supplies were quickly brought in. Several torpedo-like 'weapons' used by German frogmen were discovered and guarded as constant attempts were being made to destroy the vital Nijmegen bridges. Two privates of 'D' Coy guarding them were hit by mortar fragments and died of their wounds. Eventually on the 18th the battalion moved back to Harpen.

4 RWF moved several times in this three week period. They were not on the Island but back initially at Westelbeers, where they were badly shelled on 28th during a pay parade, causing ten casualties. On 1 October 'A' Coy had two early morning attacks on them but accepted five prisoners. The next day the

battalion moved to Netersel and Kastern, on the 4th to Diessen and Hilvaren Beek, and on the 6th to Wintelre. Eventually they arrived on the Island at Bemmel and Baal, three miles north of Nijmegen where they were constantly shelled.

The Recce Regt moved onto the Island to relieve 61st Recce of Tyne Tees Division and spent a week in the orchards at Lent, Oosterhout and Ressem out of contact with the enemy and then eastwards to Zetten and Andelst under command of 101 US Airborne. On 18 October they moved back over the river Waal to Reek, near the Grave bridge.

The Divisional artillery was in action most of the time during the 53rd's occupation of the Island. The popular CO of 81st (Welch) Field Regiment was wounded. His adjutant, Michael Dowding, explains:

> Puffin Tyler our CO was always right up at the sharp end — wriggling into inaccessible and dangerous OPs — ensuring they were well manned. He was a great ally of every Brigadier whose Brigade we were supporting. As Adjutant I was mainly back in the gun area alternating in charge there with John Lloyd, our 2 i/c. Once the forward moves started in Normandy 'Puffin' was irrepressible in getting the guns forward with great zest to ensure we could react to seemingly impossible targets next morning. The only criticism I ever had of him was the extent he exposed us to shoot, shell and mortaring at the sharp end! One of the first jet fighters — an ME 323 — dropped a bomb near Nijmegen and a splinter hit Puffin in the arm. He was evacuated in great pain on 7th October.

On 13 October the German attacks in company strength on 7 RWF and East Lancashires needed Capt K. A. Holme, 460 Bty to fire not only many DF targets to protect the infantry, but Corps Artillery was also put at his disposal! Eventually four German ambulances appeared in full view of the 158 Brigade front line and spent two hours collecting their wounded. 83 Field Regiment on the same day received a direct hit on 330 Bty CP causing twelve casualties. Both CP officers were killed and the battery captain wounded. On the night of 15th/16th Operation 'Winkle' was fired to attract deserters from the Weibosch area. A heavy fire programme up to 16.00 hrs, then an amplifier repeated twice a moving appeal to desert under cover of a smokescreen. There was no response! Captain David Bolland, Staff Captain RA diary:

> Monday, 16th. Held our A/Q conference at the German IA restaurant, Nijmegen. Lt Col Neilson [A/Q], Lt Col Kerr [ADOS] and Macewan [DADOS] and Bill Woodward, Senior supply officer. The CRA came for a short time, with Lt Col Townsend from Military Operations Branch who gave an excellent talk on the war situation. All QMs, battery captains and BSMs also present. It rained all day. The roads on the Island are getting appalling.

Nijmegen Bridge

13 FDS moved from Steensel and Corp Bert Isherwood noted:

> Div is in action [26 Sept] in the Reusel, Bladel, Hapert area. George Stout and Hudson were stopped by a German patrol whilst driving their ambulance full of wounded through enemy lines. The patrol checked the load and let them go through safely. The evacuation of casualties continues during the night and early hours.
>
> On 8th October to Grave and 9th October to Nijmegen. The unit sets up to receive casualties. Within half an hour the ambulances are rolling down the street bringing wounded in from the city itself, but mostly from the Arnhem side of the Waalbrug (i.e. the Island). 10th October 13 FDS crosses the Waal this morning to a large farmhouse near Elst, under constant German gunfire. We have to run the gauntlet going across the bridge. A stonk of 88m came down on the approach, we and the MPs dived into slit trenches. The first 30 feet of the bridge has been damaged by the enemy demolition charge.

On 19 October, both 158 and 161 Brigade were withdrawn from the defence of the Island and spent a few days of rest at Zandstraat and Ravenstein.

11

The taking of 's-Hertogenbosch: Operations Pheasant and Alan

On 16 October Field Marshal Montgomery issued orders making the clearance of the rivers around Antwerp the sole priority for 21 Army Group. This meant switching 2nd Army westwards. Although 11th Armoured Division had taken the city early in September, this vital port was not cleared for incoming shipping. Supplies were still being sourced from the far-off Normandy beachhead. Operation Pheasant was the name given to this huge task with the Canadian 1st Army attacking northwards from the Antwerp area, and Second Army's 12 Corps thrusting westwards from the Nijmegen salient. The three British Armies involved were 15th Scottish directed on Tilburg, 51st Highland on Boxtel and 53rd Welsh on 's-Hertogenbosch (Den Bosch). 7th Armoured Division — the Desert Rats — would then drive westwards passing through 51st Highland Division. Operation Alan was the codename for the taking of 's-Hertogenbosch, a town of about 50,000 population, intersected by waterways, the river Dommel, river Dieze and the Zuid Willems Vaart Canal. The town was a typical late medieval fortress with ramparts, moats and a citadel. The only approach was from the east and north- east, a wedge shaped area dotted with fortified villages. The nearest secure startline was around the village of Geffen, eight miles to the north-east.

Most of Generaloberst von Zangen's fifteenth Armee supply lines ran through the town and its defences were entrusted to General Lieutenant Friedrich Neumann's *712 Infanterie Division*. The 12,000 German troops consisted of two battalions of *732 Grenadier Regt*, one of *745 Grenadier Regt*, three training battalions of paratroops, plus *Feld-Ersantz Battalion 347*. Neumann had no armour, but had thirty guns including eleven anti-tank. Two parallel defence lines were constructed from north to south, *745 Regt* from the Maas-Nuland: *732 Regt* astride main road east to Nijmegen; and *Kampf Gruppe* of two parachute battalions from Doornhoek to the canal.

For Operation Alan, Major General Ross had the Cromwells of 5th Inniskilling Dragoon Guards (the Skins), flame throwers of 141 RAC (the Buffs), Flails, AVREs and Kangaroo personnel carriers under command. The plan of attack would start with 160 Brigade to the north astride the

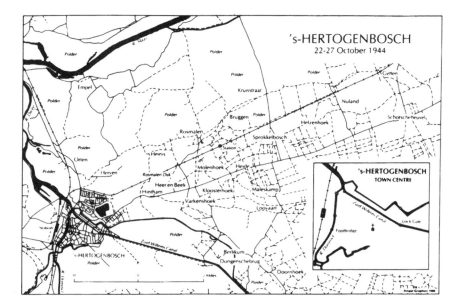

Operation Alan – the capture of Den Bosch

Nijmegen-Den Bosch railway line and 71 Brigade to the south astride the main Nijmegen-Den Bosch road. 158 Brigade was in reserve but the East Lancs were to be ready in Kangaroos to make a bold charge right through into the town. If all went well Den Bosch would be reached on the first day. In the event in a pitched battle between one attacking and one defending division it would take six days. 53rd Welsh start line was between Geffen and Bruggen.

D-DAY 22 OCTOBER: 'KEEP UNDER OUR BARRAGE'

At 04.30 hrs 12 Corps artillery, six field, two medium and a heavy regiment — over 200 guns — put down concentrations on all known defensive posts. H-hour was 06.30 hrs and Brigadier C. F. C. Coleman's 160 Brigade attacked with 2 Mons on the north side of the railway embankment, 4 Welch with Crocodiles to the south. A Sqn of the Skins supported each attack with their Cromwell tanks.

Lt Col Brooke's 2 Mons had arrived on the scene via Oosterhout-Haren to the start line of Geffen. The Pioneers cleared the minefields and with magnificent support from the Skins, who lost tanks to SP guns, in a large wood between the railway line and Kruisstraat, advanced 3000 yards. For the loss of six casualties they took 255 prisoners and left many dead of *745 Regiment* on the way. Sgts Niblett and Davis commanded platoons with dash and skill, both won MM's; as did Pte Warren, a Bren gunner who took prisoner an enemy mortar crew of four, single handed. 'D' Coy moved into Kruisstraat and at 15.00 hrs East Lancs came through in Kangaroos.

The 4 Welch under Lt Col J. M. K. Spurling were directed on Nuland, a village 1500 yards ahead, with a 15-feet anti-tank ditch defended by *712 Fusilier Bn*, starting from Oss, towards the FUP west of Geffen. Major Arthur (Zonc) Lewis OC 'A' Coy wrote:

> Down came their DF shells, but we were so quick that we were under their shell range before they could adjust. The attack was now in full swing, despite shells bursting everywhere we pressed on at top speed, trying to keep under our barrage, never allowing ourselves to be pinned down. Lt Andrew Wilson's 141 RAC 'Crocs' sped past us belching flame and we went in on top of the flame with fixed bayonets. Into the trenches went the men, grenades first, then bayonets.

By 07.45 hrs Nuland was cleared. Two enemy battalions were now on the run and the roads were being cleared of mines. '80 Germans were defending a burnt out factory on the lateral road. Some of our tanks (the Skins) had been knocked out and the Crocs had been bogged down or stripped tracks or used up all their flame. But with two tanks supporting us we stormed and took the factory. "B" Coy passed through.' (Major Lewis). By nightfall 4 Welch were 2200 yards west of Nuland and Oberst Wust, OC *745 Grenadier Regt* and Hauptmann Siebecker, OC *712 Fusilier Bn* and over fifty prisoners were taken. It had been a text book attack with all arms co-operating superbly. However, the enemy put in a textbook counter-attack in the night on 'A' and 'D' Coys position. All the Bren gun ammo was finished as panzerfaust fire came in. However, Major 'Zonc' Lewis had captured some German Spandaus during the day, with ammo, 'so we brought these into action and the enemy withdrew'. But 4 Welch had fallen well behind 2 Mons and did not reach their vital 'phase line' in time for 'saucepan' to begin.

✻   ✻   ✻

On the southern flank the attack by Brigadier 'Goldfish' Elrington's 71 Brigade also started at H-Hour, 1HLI under Lt Col Macleod were on the right and 4 RWF under Lt Col H. J. Tedder on the left. Opposing them were two battalions of *732 Regt*; with another battalion in reserve. It was heavily wooded country and the *Grenadiers* fought all the way.

Lt Pender 1HLI: 'Before the attack 16 and 18 platoons were in line, standing in a 6-foot ditch which was the start line. Ian Maclean and myself were conferring as we watched German MG bullets cut a telegraph pole above us in half. Suddenly Ian fell down and cried out that he had been hit. I thought he was larking, but he had been wounded in his bottom.' The axis for 71 Brigade lay west through Maleskamp and Vorkenshoek to Hintham. Supporting tanks were hampered by drainage ditches. 'A' Coy 4 RWF lost all their officers in the fierce — and slow — wood clearing. By the end of the day their objectives were reached. No food could be brought up as there were no tracks. At noon Brigadier Elrington slightly worried, committed his reserve battalion, the Ox and Bucks who mopped up behind 1HLI, The large woods south of Jachlust-Heide road remained a threat until Heide was taken. Early in the morning of 23rd 'C' Coy were counter-attacked by thirty-forty Germans who later surrendered including a regimental commander, a battalion commander, a company commander and an RSM.

*   *   *

Codeword 'saucepan' was a gamble. General 'Bobby' Ross intended to launch an armoured column preferably south of the railway line passing through 4 Welch into the heart of the two defences, or to the north where the route was poorer. At 15.00 hrs, about three hours late, an immense column of 111 vehicles started off through 2 Mons in Kruisstraat, led by 'A' Sqn 53 Recce, 'B' Sqn Skins, five flail tanks, 1 East Lancs plus 202 Field Ambulance, M-10 SP guns, an anti-tank batterty, AVREs and many Wasps. Philip Cowburn, Recce historian: 'A mass of echelon traffic on the roads but "A" Sqn was soon involved with enemy bypassed by our infantry. The leading Recce car was hit by a panzerfaust, a Cromwell was blown up by a mine and the long column halted. "D" Coy East Lancs debussed from their Kangaroos and drove the enemy back 1000 yds whilst Flails breached the minefield. It was dusk.' 'saucepan' had failed and the Division was still five miles from the town centre.

J. J. 'Dinty' Moore was 2 i/c 'D' Coy, Ox and Bucks:

As we dug in [on the night of 22/23rd] the German mortars opened up with a barrage right on target at their first attempt. For the next few hours we took a terrific battering. It was a bad spot to be in as it was so easy to range on [a track near Nuland]. For an hour we were continually mortared. I was in a slit trench with Major Ivor Jenkins, the OC, next to the signallers trench. Hundreds of bombs landed around us, seemingly without any damage. Finally it went dark. ['D' Coy now suffered even more under 'friendly' fire.] It had caused us no casualties but to our left 'A' Coy had suffered badly. We continued to dig. I started a slit trench of my own, got down to about 45cms and gave it up. At least it was deep enough to sleep in. Hunger was our next worry. We had had nothing to eat since 5am and no meals came up for us. The meal arrived at 0100hrs, hot stew, tea and pudding, delicious and most welcome. But one section of 18 Platoon were never relieved to collect their meals.

D+1 23 OCTOBER: 'IN LIKE DEMONS'

Before dawn 2 Mons passed through the East Lancs and pushed on towards Rosmalen. During the night General Neumann radioed *88 Korps* and was sent reinforcements of a battalion of infantry from *481 Regt*, plus five anti-tank towed guns and three howitzer batteries. General 'Bobby' Ross now saw an opportunity to outflank, perhaps surround *732* and *745 Regts* in the woods astride the main road facing 71 Brigade.

2 Mons with a troop of Skins' Cromwells and four Crocodiles flamed the enemy out of Bruggen, a hamlet on the dyke road halfway to Rosmalen. When the leading platoon commander was wounded L/Corporal GG Davies took charge, led a bayonet charge, killed fourteen enemy, and later received the MM. Major R. N. Deane, OC 'A' Coy ordered the Crocs and his reserve platoon to attack two houses where dyke and road met:

> It worked like a charm. The boys went in like demons and went straight through, shooting from the hip any Bosch who hadn't dived for cover from the flame, which was terrific. It was great fun. The boys were really wild and I saw the most harmless lads bayoneting Bosch and shooting them as they ran away. The really close infantry and tank co-operation and the whole party became a mass of fighting. Result: we killed many and captured 42, losing 15 wounded and 1 killed. Outside a big air-raid shelter, I threw a grenade [just to hear the bang!] and out came six Jerries shouting some war cry. I was pleased to see some of my boys appear out of the hedge just in time.

'C' Coy on the left working with 4 Welch cleared strips of wood south of Bruggen, and 'D' Coy passing through Bruggen cleared Rosmalen, which *Bataillon Wittstock* had abandoned without orders. But *88 Korps* now sent nine SP assault guns, Stug 111s to help the hard pressed German defenders. General Neumann launched a counter-attack at 16.00 hrs against 4 Welch at Rosmalen but five SPs were quickly knocked out, and the rest escaped back to Hintham. Everyone praised the Skins magnificent support who helped knock out twelve enemy guns, and the German counter-attack, after several hours of hard fighting, was thrown back. By 17.30 hrs 2 Mons had taken their objectives, captured 117 prisoners and killed 48 Germans for the loss of 40 casualties. Major Deane and Lt Rowland who commanded the carrier platoon and Wasps, received MCs. 6 RWF came through directed on the town centre.

As planned, 71 Brigade did not push ahead *too* strongly and 4 RWF and 1HLI kept *732 Regt* fully occupied at Maleskamp; south-east of Rosmalen. Capt Tim Dumas: 'Colonel Tedder ordered me to clear a wood with 'C' Coy across a field in front of 'D' Coy position.' Dumas encountered a German. 'We were both quite astonished but I was quicker to point my rifle at him.'

The wood in front was occupied by the enemy. 'A nasty little action followed in which Corporal Valentine was killed. We over-ran a German Coy HQ with phone intact. I turned the handle and a German voice answered, 'Ja'. I did not reply!' The Ox and Bucks protecting 160 Brigade's flanks cleared their woods and reached Heer en Beek. By then the German main forces were in full retreat.

General 'Bobby' Ross, after the failure of Saucepan, planned now an ambitious night attack. 6 RWF of 160 Bde were to cut the main road at Hintham, *behind* the German defence and 1 East Lancs and 1/5 Welch of 158 Brigade were to make a night march along the line of the railway into the town. Then 7 RWF would pass through 6 RWF and attack into the town along the main road from Hintham.

THE NIGHT ASSAULT 23/24 OCTOBER D + 2: 'SOUND OF SWEET MUSIC'

Air photographs had been issued to company commanders and under Monty's Moonlight by searchlights a substantial fire plan – named Chicago — from 200 guns would help sweep the Division onwards. At the crucial moment Brigadier G. B. Sugden of 158 Brigade fell ill and had to be evacuated.

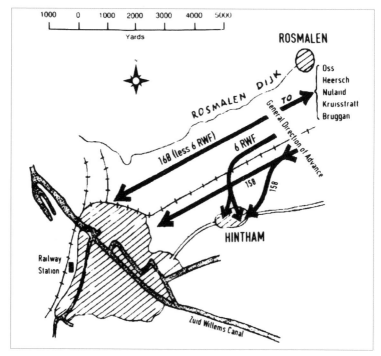

Operation Alan - final stages

At dusk Lt Col K. G. Exham's 6 RWF moved down the railway line, and 'C' Coy quickly took the hamlet of Varkenshoek east of Hintham and beat off a counter-attack. 'D' Coy had a short fight to secure Heer en Beek crossroads a few hundred yards north of 'C', but 'B' moving down the Rosmalen Dijk were halted by three solid stone strong-points, well defended and surrounded by a deep ditch full of wire. 'A' Coy led by Canloan Capt R. G. Marsh reached the village of Hintham by 22.00 hrs taking twenty surprised prisoners on the way. The CO had a difficult time; his carrier stripped a track and slipped down the embankment. Then his jeep caught fire going through Bruggen. However the East Riding Yeomanry Shermans gave good support; 'A' Coy had infiltrated into the main German defences, were surrounded and had to withstand ferocious attacks all night. Captain D. C. Barnett, 2 i/c 'A' Coy. 'All the way to Hintham the gunners kept whizzing it over our heads just in front, and *only* just in front. This close support was terrific, but very frightening. We arrived at 22.00 hrs in Hintham and Bob [Capt Marsh the OC] told me to site Coy HQ, whilst he sited the platoons. We could hear the wounded Jerries moaning in the street outside.' Two wounded German officers were brought in: 'One miserable wretch badly wounded, thought I was going to cut his throat as I bent over him to give him a cigarette.' Later, 'the Jerries brought up an SP gun and fired point-blank at our house, seriously damaging the German PoW. 7 Platoon dashed back saying their position was untenable. Coy HQ became too crowded. A small grenade landed in the trench beside me. I was wounded in right arm and left shoulder.' More grenades followed. The CSM Evans was giving orders. 'I found Bob badly wounded and Coy HQ looking like an abattoir. Two German doctors were tending our wounded. We could hear 7 RWF in the distance and the sound of their MGs was very sweet music.' Later, 'I was told Bob had just died. Of the very brave men I served with from Normandy to Hamburg, he was the bravest.' Captain Marsh was recommended for the VC but received a posthumous Mention in Despatches. 6 RWF held out and were relieved at 10.00 hrs. That night the bombardment continued and 50,000 shells fell in 's-Hertogenbosch and destroyed the houses of Hinthamerpark inflicting many civilian casualties. At 06.15 hrs General Neumann and his staff retreated on foot into the town amidst the chaos and dark confusion.

The second part of the night assault along the railway line was underway — on foot. No carriers, tanks or anti-tank guns could proceed over the railway lines. At 02.30 hrs the East Lancs in single file, scrambling through wire fences and wading through ditches made good progress and reached the first houses of Den Bosch by 04.35 hrs, and took up a box-like defence. Half an hour later 1/5 Welch arrived and passed through into the town. It was still dark and so far a total surprise. Captain David Morgan, OC 'B' Coy found the river Dieze bridge intact:

I met the CO [Lt Col Nelson-Smith] and Bill Owen. They told me to 'bash' on straight for the bridge before it got light and seize it and hold it against the usual counter-attacks. So we forked right at a Y junction, with Jack Griffin [2 i/c] going with the leading platoon, 10 Pl, followed by 11 Pl, myself and Coy HQ then 12 Pl last. We were almost doubling at times so great was our speed.

On the way they caught twenty-five prisoners all shouting 'Kamerad' at the top of their voices. Now in the fury and fog of war Sods' law usually operates. In the next twelve hours of gallant fighting practically everything went wrong.

Three times Sgt Fear's 11 Platoon either went astray or got lost. The rest of 'B' Coy then 'bumped' a huge convoy of German ambulances, and hospital trucks full of stores blocking the route. Eventually they moved back down the road towards 'D' Coy. L/Corporal Hale cut the wires to the demolition charges plastered all over the bridge. About lunchtime all three bridges were successfully blown up. 10 Platoon soon ran out of ammunition, and were forced to surrender. Then Panther tanks appeared (probably the surviving SP guns), but Sgt Brennan's 12 Platoon had abandoned the only Piat on the middle of the bridge. The absentee platoon had the second Piat, and the third was in workshops for repair! Fortunately, an East Lancs 6 pdr anti-tank gun from the north bank knocked out the Panther/SP gun and the others withdrew. The Germans had mined the warehouses, factories and houses along the bank of the river, and proceeded to blow up Morgan, Griffin and the others. Despite L/Corp Hale using his 18 set to call up artillery fire, the situation was hopeless and most of 'B' Coy fighting bravely were put in the bag. While the drama of the Dieze bridge was being enacted, the East Lancs cleared the area south to the river Aa, which was parallel to the Zuid Willems Vaart canal. By 11.30 hrs the Skins tanks had linked up by a risky advance on the railway lines.

To man the canal line General Neumann had only two battalions left, *Ewald* and *Stendhal*, but he had been reinforced with more artillery. At 15.45 hrs 7 RWF advanced down the main road from Hintham, and with 6 RWF moved towards the river Aa bridge, now blown and under heavy fire, but a steel catwalk over the lock sluices could be crossed. An hour later Major John Dugdale, 'A' Coy 7 RWF backed by Inniskilling Cromwell fire and 141 RAC Crocs flaming support, bravely made two runs across, through barbed wire under fire. Miraculously two companies got across with only one casualty and by 19.00 hrs, 282 Coy RE started to assemble a Class 40 Bailey bridge, ready by midnight.

D+4 25 OCTOBER: '19 GERMANS IN THE LAVATORY'

The first two assaults were unfortunately not successful. To the west and in the early morning mist 6 RWF's 'B' Coy under Major C. E. Hill in assault boats tried to cross the Zuid Willems Canal. 'D' Coy gave supporting fire from the commanding ramparts of the old citadel. Point-blank Spandau fire sank the first boat, killing or wounding all the Fusiliers. A smokescreen attack at 11.00 hrs was no more successful.

The East Lancs' first attempts at 08.30 hrs to pass through the 7 RWF bridgehead ran into heavy MG fire and sniping, so a new plan was made. Both East Lancs and 1/5 Welch were ordered to move along the ramparts, the former southwards, the latter towards the north-west. The East Lancs objective was the river Dommel at the south-west edge of town. And 1/5 Welch would cross the Bailey bridge with the object of reaching the river Dommel bridge near the junction with the river Dieze. Finally 7 RWF would move into the centre of the town.

The East Lancs were supported by the East Riding Yeomanry tanks, and advanced with three companies leapfrogging, as Major A. T. Bain, OC 'C' Coy relates:

> We followed 'A' Coy with no opposition except mortar fire, as platoons moved from house to house. Sgt Maddox was hit when entering the cellar of the Barracks [Palace de Justice] and Prison. A clearing operation started and our tanks pounded the cellar windows with delay action HE at 20 yds range and Besa-ed the upper floors. 14 Platoon cleared the cellars and finally 15 Platoon tracked down 19 Germans sheltering in the lavatory! The Barracks was now on fire but the fire brigade coped with it successfully.

Major Henri Salmon, 'B' Sqn, East Riding Yeomanry gave splendid support. By 16.00 hrs Major Bremner and 'B' Coy started to clear up to a garden park but later were roughly treated by enemy fire from an SP gun after dark.

Meanwhile at 13.30 hrs 1/5 Welch had come into the bridgehead and ran across the Bailey bridge under fire and 'D' Coy reached the main square, supported by 'C' Sqn of the Yeomanry. The defenders tried to blow the four bridges over the river Dommel but they did not all collapse and two could be crossed on foot. General Neumann had now been reinforced by four Jagdpanther tanks, one of which quickly knocked out a Sherman. 1/5 Welch approached the stone bridge leading to the railway station, met Spandau and SP gunfire and took shelter in houses on the river bank. At last light 7 RWF who had been relieved at the locks by 4 Welch and had cleared the city centre, reached the Dommel midway between East Lancs and 1/5 Welch. At 22.00 hrs 'A' Coy linked up with 'C' in the northern bridgehead. For most of the people

Men of 'D' Coy. 1 Ox & Bucks near 's-Hertogenbosch (John Roberts)

of Den Bosch/'s-Hertogenbosch the 15 October was the day of liberation when Cathedral Square and the Market Square were cleared of the enemy. But there was a lot more fighting still to come. To man the river line the Germans had 450 men, some Stugs and Jagdpanthers under the elderly Major Riedel. Facing them from north to south were 6 RWF, 1/5 Welch, 7 RWF and 1 East Lancs.

D+5 26 OCTOBER: 'BRISK EXCHANGE OF GRENADES'

Patrols during the night had inspected the blown bridges in front of them. Brigadier Elrington decided that the East Lancs and 1/5 Welch were to rush their bridges as soon as possible and 7 RWF would pass through the most promising bridgehead. 1/5 Welch started at 11.00 hrs with tanks blasting high explosive shells into the buildings opposite. Major Barney McCall, CO 'D' Coy: 'We formed up and rushed the bridge. Two platoons and Coy HQ dashed across and occupied the first two houses on the right, supported by 'C' Coy and two ERY Shermans. We took 21 PW and occupied a yard full of hearses and stabling for horses.' Now for Sods Law again. The hapless Pte Sidwell was ordered to throw a Mills grenade outside to deter an LMG team. Of course he didn't have one. Major McCall tossed him one and Sidwell threw it. He hit the side of a door and it fell back into the room injuring McCall, CSM Evans, the Company Clerk and the hapless Pte Sidwell.

An hour later McCall was wounded again by a phosphorous grenade. The wounded CSM thought it was very funny and put out the flames with his water bottle. Then followed a brisk exchange of grenades until 7 RWF came to the rescue. Sgt Mike Hannon, 'D' Coy 7 RWF: 'It was house to house, putting in an attack across an open square, dashing to take buildings on far side with men to follow at ten second intervals. I was hit by an A/Tk shell. I could feel the hot lead burning into me. I had been hit in the head, right arm, in the chest and stomach. I was lifted on to a board by German PW back to a FDS, stretcher on a jeep eventually to a hospital in Eindsoven run by nuns.' Brigadier Elrington now ordered the East Lancs to assault the roundabout bridge at 11.45 hrs. Unbelievably Sods Law operated again. The covering smoke screen would *not* build up. Then the prevailing breeze blew the screen *away*. At zero hour the Crocodiles were *not* ready. The artillery programme of course alerted the defenders to the forthcoming attack — so time for extra defence. When at 13.15 hrs the Crocs arrived out of Vughterstraat they flamed the *wrong* bridge! But still 'D' 'A' and 'C' Coys sped across the broken bridge and battered their way into the buildings opposite. Capt Bartle towed or manhandled the anti-tank guns across. In the enemy shelling the CRE of 53rd Division was wounded whilst examining the bridge, Lt Harpers platoon HQ was buried in rubble by an explosion but survived. Prisoners started to pour in — 800 on that day. A scissors bridge over the broken bridge enabled ERY Shermans to cross over. By the evening of the 26th practically the whole of the town was in British hands.

D+6 27 OCTOBER: 'THE FÜHRER'S PHONE CALL'

6 RWF had captured a letter from General Neumann to the hapless Major Riedel, 'The Führer has personally telephoned and ordered your position to be held in all circumstances.' This message may have galvanised a counter-attack at 08.10 hrs on 7 RWF by 150 infantry, five Stugs SP guns and three Jagdpanthrs. Major Barber knocked one out with a Piat, one went to an ERY Sherman, one to a 17-pdr anti-tank gun and a fourth to a M-10 SP A/Tk gun. This battle took place around the station. Fusiliers Green and Bates of 'A' Coy had distinguished themselves by skilfully infiltrating across lockgates and bridges and 'B' Coy captured Major Riedel.

The factory area north-west of the station was cleared by 6 RWF and the East Lancs captured Willem I Barracks, just beyond the station. The battle was over. In six days of fighting 53rd Division had 123 killed in action, 270 wounded and seventy-five missing. Another twenty-one of the supporting arms were also killed.

For three days, 27-29 October Captain D. Lever 'D' Troop 116 LAA Regiment deployed his self propelled Bofors guns in ground attacks on

Div HQ Conference near 's-Hertogenbosch

factories, buildings and pillboxes. He, Sgt Cousins and Gunner Williams and others did enormous damage to the enemy, captured scores of prisoners in half a dozen actions often with 6 RWF. Lever was recommended for the Victoria Cross, Williams received the DCM and Cousins the MM.

The Germans lost 1700 prisoners and at least that amount killed or wounded. Unfortunately the 90,000 shells thrown into the town had caused 200 casualties to the civilian population and literally not a house was left undamaged. Luc van Gent's book *Den Bosch 1944* records the full story with dozens of magnificent photographs taken at the time. The Corps Commander visited Den Bosch and wrote to the GOC, 'tremendously impressed with the fighting qualities displayed by 53rd Welsh Division throughout all the operations that have led to its capture... fine achievements by 160th Brigade in the early stages and by 158th Brigade in their very fine night operations... '

It was a great battle honour.

12

Autumn into Winter on the River Maas

Nearly a thousand casualties had been inflicted on the Division during October. Three days before he was killed in action the popular Lt Col J. H. Hare, CO of the Ox and Bucks Regt wrote: '25th October. I have only reaped where so many for so many long years have sown. Awards so far are — MCs Bob Holden, Rupert Livingstone, David Taylor. DCM Sgt Clark and four MMs. You will have seen that since the advance started we have had little hard fighting, messy fighting against patchy enemy and precious little rest. Yesterday was a sad day. Rowland Hill was shot in the stomach. Jenkins was shot by a German treacherously in the arm and Jim Callingham was slightly wounded in the back and bottom. All three are company commanders and irreplaceable to my mind. Still we shall go on as we always have, always in the stickiest point of the Brigade, or with the 1st East Lancs, of the divisional front. It is painfully obvious that this is so but I suppose we can take it as a compliment. The real tragedy lies of course in the fact that nowadays after your company commanders have gone there is no one to take their places. For instance, Rowland Hill was wounded very early in his company battle and I had to command his Coy to finish it off. A small business admittedly. However morale is very good and if I can put stop-gaps till David Taylor, Tony Jephson & Co come back we shall survive. It is a problem which keeps me awake at night sometimes. However I wouldn't be anywhere else for words at the moment. There is nothing like the day after a successful battle for sheer joy and relief that all has gone well and on the whole cheaply for the results achieved. We always collect our dead and bury them in the Divisional cemetery. And so to bed.' On the evening of 28th Oct. Lt Col James Hare whilst on reconnaissance of a bridge two miles west of Den Bosch was shot in the head and killed. Lt Col R. G. F. Frisby took over command of 4th Welch, as Lt Col Spirling was promoted to Brigadier.

As Den Bosch was taken a massive German counter-attack with two Panzer and one Parachute Division was launched from Venlo as a 'spoiling' attack on the Allied operations for opening the Scheldt Estuary. The initial onslaught fell on the 'green' US 7th Armoured Division in the Meijel area, twelve miles north-west of Roermond. 83 Field Regt RA was in action on 27th, moved to Bree, then Kinroy in support of the Americans. And on 1 November the Recce Regiment moved seventy miles to Kinroy, Maeseyck and Ophoven — just in case! But 15th Scottish and 51st Highland Division helped close off the quite dramatic inroads made by the German counter-attack. By this time 53rd Division had moved about forty miles south-east to take up positions along the Wessem Canal with 71st Brigade at Ittervoort and Kessenich, 158 Brigade plus 4 RWF based on Weert. Two belligerent Luftwaffe battalions were anxious to prove their mettle and sent out fighting patrols into the East Lancs at Ell/Zwartebroek and the Ox and Bucks on the 3rd. The next day Lt Col Burden left the East Lancs command and was succeeded on the 8th by Lt Col F. F. E. Allen, and the Army Commander visited the battalion in Roggel to congratulate them on their high reputation. News came through now of Major Tasker Watkins', 1/5 Welch Regiment, award of the Victoria Cross for his valour in the Balfour operation on 16 August.

Dutch winter landscape

General 'Bobby' Ross was keen on welfare and amenities for his troops. On 10 November Captain David Bolland, Staff Capt RA, secured for his artillery regiments, 'a stack of welfare goods from Jim Cooper: Twenty-six dozen packs of playing cards, 100 pairs football boots, eight torches, ten bottles of champagne etc. Quite a good bag.' Bert Isherwood 13 FDS played centre forward for his unit against Berghem and won 12 goals to one!

But whatever happens army routine must go on. Captain Bolland attended an Admin AQ conference to discuss amendments to Army Form G1098 of the Gunner regiments. Present were Fuller Cox, Bob Melton, Bert Timworth, Peter Alexander, John Stewart, Edgar Lindley, Ken Baker, Peter Lambert, Norman Hunt, Fergus Lysaght and Stuart Shrimpton. Henry Smith Daye, the Divisional Catering adviser, explained two *main* grouses — shortage of fat and porridge.

The British Army now spent two months trying painfully to squeeze out all the enemy pockets west of the river Maas. In very wet weather 8 Corps with 53rd Division on the right/south and 51st Highland on the left/north were ordered to establish bridgeheads over the Wessem Canal which runs in a straight-line north to south from near Weert to Wessem on the river Maas.

Some of 53rd Recce near Ophoven, November 1944 (Bud Abbott)

Operation Mallard started on the right. The approach to the canal was over open flat country and the canal itself flowed between two raised banks about twelve feet higher than ground level. All the slit-trenches were waterlogged and enemy snipers made it virtually impossible to move out of them.

So 'A' and 'D' Coys 4 Welch moved from Haler under the usual divisional artillery barrage and effective artificial moonlight. Tanks were firing across the canal and Crocodiles were belching out flame over it on to the German positions. The boats were very heavy and in the marshy ground men sank in above their ankles. Opposition was negligible. By 22.30 hrs Buffaloes carrying two to three vehicles 'swam' across the narrow canal. Against the 2nd Mons the opposition was greater. 'B' Coy failed to cross under close range fire and mines, but 'C' was successful and all objectives were taken by 04.15 hrs. A neat little operation which cost twenty-two casualties. The REs quickly set to work to build bridges.

6 RWF moved from Steenweg and because of a mix up with the crossing point were delayed, and mines on the far side destroyed vehicles. By mid-day they had widened the bridgehead and 158 Brigade passed through with 7 RWF leading. Kelpen and Gratham were soon occupied, but 7 RWF ran into a large minefield between Baexem and the railway.

Sgt Harry Martin, 7 RWF:

Near Baexum on 16th November a section of my Assault Platoon were on mine clearance. I had to go back to the CO at HQ to check on an area for B Echelon transport. Whilst I was there, I heard an explosion in the area I had just left. On my return there was just a large crater — 4 men were killed, 3 wounded. The next day I searched and found equipment and other items allowed me to identify those killed and were buried in a farmyard and crosses placed with name, rank, No on them. All my mates gone, some had been with me for six years.

Contact was made with 7th Armoured Division to the south at Panheel lock and 51st Highland to the north. Early on the 16th 1HLI entered Horn and 1/5 Welch pushed north to Nunhem and Beggenum. 4th Welch occupied Heel and 2nd Mons, Beegden... Operation Turf was the codename for Brigadier Elrington's 71st Brigade's assault on the small enemy bridgehead covering Roermund on the west side of the river Maas from 16-24 November. On the 22nd with 4 RWF leading from Horn, then south-east, then west towards the villages of Hatenboer and Oolder Huisje, the Ox and Bucks new CO Lt Col E. H. Howard reported:

We have just come out of the line after a very successful battle, against a strongly held position held by a Bn with an A/Tk ditch and elaborate barbed wire. Three bridges were necessary to cross a small tributary over the Oude; a footbridge for infantry, Bailey bridge for vehicles, an Avre bridge over the A/Tk ditch. At night under a very heavy artillery bombardment with Manchester MMGs and heavy mortars — all went well except the Welshmen [4 RWF] failed to get the bridgehead over the A/Tk ditch. The Brigadier then ordered us to go through and destroy the enemy. He afterwards said he hardly liked asking us! In three hours 'A' Coy crossed the ditch with ladders, went in at the double with fixed bayonets reached objective on Xrds opposite bridge to Roemond. 'C' Coy followed up and captured the brickworks. We captured a bag of 4 Germans officers and 120 men PW and killed 20 Germans. Our own casualties were two officers [and] eight ORs wounded.

Mopping up continued whilst four bridges were constructed over the Wessem Canal. Heugde and De Weerd were cleared but on 23 November the river Maas, after heavy rain, overflowed its banks. That night the Ox and Bucks took Hatenboer and Oolder Hulsje with another seventy-five prisoners.

For the next month the Division guarded an extended front of twenty miles along the Maas from Maeseyk-Wessem-Roermond bridge-Baarlo. Every unit sent out patrols, usually to deter the enemy from sending *their* patrols across the Maas. Private R. Reynolds, 4 Welch: 'Our section near Venlo was detailed

Officers, 'B' Coy. Ox and Bucks at Ittervoort (John Roberts)

to go on a mine sweeping operation with Sgt GWR "Maggi" Evans [His wife Maggi of Llanelli was the dominant character, hence his nickname] — a Pioneer from Bn HQ. It was one of the most hair-raising patrols that I had ever been on. He detected a SCHU mine made it safe, then a Teller A/Tk mine. We were all soaked in sweat. We advanced another mile lifting two more mines on the way, thankfully back to our billets.'

1/5 Welch spent thirty days — an unheard of event — in one place at Haelen on the west bank of the Maas opposite the Roermond blown river-railway bridge. Two patrols on 29 and 30 November along the river embankment were not successful, with eleven Welch casualties. A week later twenty-five German soldiers each with white smocks, on which was a large Red Cross, crossed over the river to retrieve two wounded German soldiers, without, of course, a shot being fired. Another patrol on 9 December under Lt Spencer of 'D' Coy lost two men who stepped on Schu mines. The MO, Captain Clarke with stretcher party arrived and evacuated the two wounded men. But a second patrol to relieve Lt Spencer went through the same minefield and lost a further six casualties. The Pioneers later found fifty more mines in the area.

Another unexpected danger was from the hitherto reluctant Luftwaffe who on 16 and 27 November sharply attacked several units in the Division's localities, inflicting casualties.

Lt Pender and 1LHI were in Hern. On 30 November, it was St Andrew's night and 16 Platoon was on duty in the brickworks whilst Battalion HQ held a traditional St Andrew's night in the officers mess. 'We were asked on the field telephone if we could hear the pipe music, despite the wind and the gurgling river. I could so I requested that "Bonny Dundee" be played for 'D' Coy. We heard that too!' A few days later, 'the Dutch family where my PL HQ was billeted, gave us a wonderful St Nicholas dinner. We were each given a St Nicholas card and presents and we gave them all the chocolate, sweets, food and cigarettes we had available. All my three sections enjoyed the same hospitality in other houses. It was an emotional farewell on 8th December.'

*   *   *

'Wednesday, 29th November. A big day for the Division. Monty is presenting ribbons to the 55 officers and men still present who have won decorations in this campaign. Of this number we had 15 awards which was a pretty good average [David Bolland was referring to the Gunner regiments]. Monty announced that leave to the UK is starting on 1 January at the rate of 3000 per day from 21 Army Group.' A few days earlier Capt Bolland had gone to Rear Division to deliver witnesses statements for the recommended VC for Don Lever.

Capt Jim Cooper, the Divisional Entertainments Officer, recalls: 'Each time Gen. Montgomery came to give medals at our HQ, the Concert Party gave a show for recipients and friends after lunch. The first time was in Helmond. "Bobby" Ross sent me off to 51st Highland Div as they had given shows for Montgomery before.' Jim Cooper obtained Leslie Henson's services — LH was well known by then to Montgomery. On Thursday, 30 November the Supreme Commander, General Eisenhower, and General Dempsey visited the Division. 'We were all on parade for him — the first time that Div HQ had appeared together at one place at one time.' David Bolland noted, on the same day he: 'attended the final parade of 116 LAA Regt who were being split up in two days time. Their CO, Lt Col Walter read out a letter received from Monty and then the GOC, General Ross told them how sorry he was to see them go. They were replaced by 25 LAA from the disbanded 50 Tyne Tees Division. Their guns are SPs and their tactics somewhat different.' Lt Col Tedder, CO 4 RWF, was posted to Burma and replaced by Lt Col J. M. Hanmer. The battalion fought a sharp action to take the lock-gates at Heel on 5/6 December. In the first attack with Typhoons and flamethrowers thirty-nine prisoners were taken but 4 RWF lost nineteen casualties. A counter-attack infiltrated with bazookas and Spandaus and the Germans managed to destroy the weir.

Brigadier Friedberger, the CRA, had a 'new' idea to keep both friend and foe busy. He called it Exercise Wind Up, other divisions called it a 'Pepperpot'. At a certain time of the day starting from 11 December *every* gun of every calibre from 17-pdr to borrowed 5.5-inch medium would fire one round into the enemy localities. Unfortunately it *always* brought equivalent retribution!

Many young reinforcements arrived earlier from RHUs or from the disbanded 50 Tyne Tees Division. On 10 December the East Lancs at Rogge received sixty-five including two officers which put the battalion *above* War Establishment strength. Many courses were held, specifically infantry/tank co-operation, and for young NCOs.

Corporal Bert Isherwood, 13 FDS, and George Stout went on 'a sightseeing tour of Brussels, Sainte Gedule, Theatre Royale, Palais de Justice, Mannekin Pis (in Guards uniform), Palais du Roi and Hotel de Ville. We had an excellent lunch at a small restaurant, halibut with sauce tartare, petit pois and scalloped potatoes washed down with a bottle of Chablis. The wine was on the house. The 3 ton Bedford took a party of twenty of our chaps but the driver completely wrecked it giving his passengers a good shaking up.'

With Christmas looming: 'Welfare is becoming such a major task that I [David Bolland] have decided to open a separate welfare department dealing with entertainments, leave and welfare goods and facilities only. Gunner Pilkington, an eccentric clerk is acting as my welfare clerk.' And Jim

Cooper opened three gift shops for the troops, where silk stockings were very popular. Many of the young Welshmen (and others) were 'adopted' by a Dutch family. Bert Isherwood made friends with the Meyers family in Nispenstraat, Nijmegen (Harry, Charles and three sisters and their mother), and with the Steenackers family in Antwerp (Edward, Alice and two young children). St Nikolaas Day in early December is an important Dutch festival:

> We had a children's party in Weert for some 400 of the local school children. Mickey Mouse films in the cinema — a local couple with accordion and a dancing act with community singing [what a noise the children made]. After which [Div HQ] we had the tea party, complete with Christmas tree, toffee-apples, toys etc. The first party they had had for four years. When they saw the food on the tables in front of them they just goggled at it. The senior officers did the washing up in cold water, dried up with paper towels. [David Bolland]

One of the few redeeming features of that long unpleasant winter was the prospect of leave perhaps to Eindhoven, Helmond, Antwerp (risky as the V-Bombs fell with regularity) but the 'plum' was Brussels. Captain David Bolland and John Lloyd went on 48 hr leave in mid-November:

> We stayed at the Hotel Plaza on Blvd Adolph Max, ran by the NAAFI. Room with bathroom attached, which before the war would have cost at least 15/- per night. For 2 nights cost us only 90 Francs. We went to a concert at the Palais des Beaux Arts, and to a good little French variety show, had a first class haircut, went to the Welfare Gift shop, heard Charles Trenet at a café, then to ENSA Music Hall with Leslie Henson in the cast.

But Lt Pender, 1HLI was less fortunate:

> My 48 hours leave to Antwerp, so I proceeded to the officers club, the Gare du Nord railway station hotel. After a proper bath I went to the lounge for tea, when there was a frightful explosion outside. A V-1 flying bomb had arrived. The large front windows of the hotel caved in slowly hitting the assembled company sitting at their tables causing frightful casualties. After helping the wounded I went off to the Rex cinema run by the NAAFI. I had a strange premonition and sat in the stalls *under* the front of the gallery. The heat was marvellous. I was exhausted, desperately tired and went to sleep. A tremendous explosion and a blinding flash, another V-1 bomb had arrived and struck the roof of the cinema above the screen. The whole place dissolved like a pack of cards. Confusion was everywhere, screams and groans came from all sides. There were some hundreds of Belgians and British troops in that cinema.

Somewhat 'bomb happy' Pender woke up in a military hospital but rejoined 1HLI two weeks later. On 17 December the Division was relieved and moved back into Belgium, 71st Brigade to Lierre, 158 Brigade to Merxplas and 160 Brigade to Herenthals. But not for long.

The Ardennes campaign was fought in deep snow and ice by 'poor bloody infantry' [PBI], ill-equipped for the winter conditions

13

The Ardennes

In almost total secrecy the newly re-formed and re-equipped *Fifth Panzer Army* and *Sixth SS Panzer Army* with about 800 Tiger and Panther tanks under Field Marshal von Runstedt had assembled — and struck on a sixty-mile front in the Ardennes. The US 8 Corps of five divisions stationed between Malmedy and the Luxembourg border/Moselle river received a shattering assault on 16 December. Perhaps surprisingly two American Armies, the 1st and 9th stationed north of the German attack were soon placed under Monty's command. In addition he summoned several of his trusty British units to act as 'longstop' just in case the Panzers crossed the Meuse on their way to seize Antwerp. In the event, part of 8 Corps (53rd Welsh and 51st Highland) plus the armoured brigade of 11th Armoured Division, and the 6th Airborne (flown out from England in a hurry) actually were involved in serious fighting. Although the senior 'management' may have put a brave face to the events that followed in the next week, at grass roots every possible rumour circulated — of total American disasters, German troops in American uniforms, hostile paratroops and spies everywhere! From the rest area near Antwerp the Recce Regiment under Lt Col Williams followed by Brigadier Coleman's 160 Brigade moved south-east to Louvain. The GOC's conference on 20 December revealed that initially the Division would hold the line Louvain-Wavre-Genappe east of Brussels along the river Dyle.

The 1HLI were ensconced near the fields of the battle of Waterloo where they had fought with distinction against a different foe. Their CO insisted that 'their' FOO Major Alan Christianson place his OP on the famous Waterloo monument 'just in case the Panzers arrive'.

Four armoured regiments from the 11th Armoured Division held the river Meuse between Liege-Namur-Dinant. By Christmas Eve it was clear that the *main* German thrust had been halted. Nevertheless by 16.00 hrs on Christmas Day 4 RWF were at Givet, 1HLI about Dinant, with the Ox and Bucks in reserve ten miles west of Dinant. It was 71 Brigade's role to help defend the north-south line of the river Meuse, but they were soon relieved by the 6th Airborne Brigade. There were many moves but Brigadier Sugden's 158 Brigade, in reserve on the river Dyle, celebrated Christmas in some style. On Christmas Eve Capt Bolland listened on the wireless to carols and lessons from King's College, Cambridge, and went to Padre Bennett's midnight Mass. Immediately afterwards Divisional HQ was on the move to the Namur region.

Both 6 RWF and 7 RWF in Leefdael and Wavre respectively were fortunate enough to enjoy a traditional army Christmas. Welsh and English carols were sung, services were held, the NAAFI produced excellent fare with beer and a rum issue. The COs visited all companies at dinner to exchange greetings. 'Nadolig Llawen A Blwyddyn Newydd Dda.' Hospitable villagers lent tables, crockery and domestic help. Then on the 27th 6 RWF carried out a twenty mile route march over icy roads. On Boxing Day a Home Leave draw was held.

Capt Tim Dumas, 4 RWF: 'We were in reserve in comfortable billets and late in the evening on Christmas Eve 'C' Coy cooks started cooking Christmas dinner. It was to be eaten some fourteen days later and fifty miles to the South!'

'At mid-day on 28th HQRA did rather well. The food was plentiful, tinned turkey, pork, plum pudding, apples, oranges, cigars and beer, but somehow the Christmas spirit was lacking,' wrote David Bolland.

Major F. O. Cetre, 'A' Coy, East Lancs describes their Christmas Day near Tombeek where, 'an arctic wind howled and lashed around the countryside as the temperature sank hour by hour. The village hall at Ottenbourg although in 'no-man's land' seemed suitable. The hall had been decked out with paper flags and streamers. An incredible amount of Belgian beer was bought from a nearby 'Bistro'. The food was cooked in the local school some 300 yards away and brought over in a 15 cwt truck to the tables. The men lacked nothing and were served by the Coy officers, the CSM and Sgts in the customary manner. Then a toast to the Company and Battalion was drunk, my own bottles of whiskey had already been deftly 'lifted' and passed down the table! The men moved slowly back to foxholes or farms, but some stayed for a lusty sing song until tea-time.' The officers had their mess in the Ferme des Templiers owned by a hospitable Belgian nobleman and his blonde, charming wife. 1/5 Welch had their Christmas at Champles. The cooks were superb and Private T. Rowlands kept the party going until the spread arrived. Everyone had a good feed and felt at peace with the world, much singing of 'He's a Jolly Good Fellow'. On Boxing day the UK leave draw produced a lucky five officers and 130 other ranks.

Sapper Ned Petty: 'Our RE platoon was moving along a road on foot, a single file on each side of the road. Tommy — one of our chaps had lost a sock recently. As we caught up with a Belgian civilian going the same way and smoking a pipe — clouds of smoke billowing up in the frosty air, I shouted to Tommy, 'I know where your sock is. This Belgian is smoking it in his pipe.' In perfect English came the reply. 'It's alright for you, soldier, but for the last five years we have learned to smoke anything, even socks.' He had been a Tommy in WWI and had married a Belgian girl.'

Philip Cowburn, the Recce historian, noted:

> The Belgians construed our move south in the most pessimistic way possible. Almost overcome with nervous excitement they imagined the Germans to be at their gates. Tales which a few hours before had seemed too incredible to be believed now took on the aspect of sober truth. We caught the words 'à bas les Boches' and 'les sals Boches' uttered with the appropriate gestures, phrases not heard since Normandy. When we stopped we gladly accepted the gravely proffered cakes, fruit and cognac.

But for all units moving south it was a long, tedious, complicated journey which frustrated and annoyed everyone. The moves and countermoves continued but finally on New Year's Eve 160 Brigade relieved 84 US Division in the Marche area and 158 Brigade 2 US Armoured Division on the river Lesse about Houyet and Ciergnon. Eventually a thirteen-mile front was held between Houyet to Aye, with snow on the ground and icy dangerous roads. The HLI Regimental band about forty strong from Maryhill under Band Master Judd came out for a jolly visit over Hogmanay, and soon found themselves in a defensive position where they could see *live* Germans within 200 yards!

On 30 December the Divisional artillery was in action. 83rd Field at Fromville and 133rd at Rochfort. Along the roads lay wrecks of German vehicles of all sorts, abandoned, burnt and shattered, but also many American anti-tank guns over-run by the enemy and shot up at close quarters. 2nd US Armoured Division had given a good account of themselves, but there were many unfavourable comments about our Allies.

Pte R. Reynolds, 4 Welch, near Rochfort: 'We later went to Rochfort to relieve a battalion of Americans in the front line. When we got near to their positions they shouted something like, "you can have it", and then they were gone. There was no official handover and they had not dug a single slit-trench.' And CSM Cullen:

> We were moving across a long viaduct with a concrete balustrade along each side when we saw tanks coming down the road towards us. They were American and in a real state of panic. Crewmen were standing with their heads visible in the turrets and were shouting that the Krauts were behind them. The tanks were moving faster than they should have been on the icy road surface. Suddenly one of them slewed across the road and crashing into a file of our men pinned one of them to the side wall. Only his head and shoulders could be seen and his screams were dreadful. The tank driver went into reverse, stopped and slid

back. Fortunately the trapped soldier had fainted. His bottom half was smeared across the wall and he mercifully died within a few minutes. I thought our men were going to go for the driver and tank crew, but before that could happen they rapidly drove off. Later we found that the tanks were supposed to be there to provide us with support in establishing new positions.

The US VII Corps were to start on 3 January a substantial counter-attack on the north-centre of the huge salient bridge created by Von Runstedt's panzer armies. Lt General Brian Horrocks' 8 Corps were to be responsible for closing out a triangular front of ten miles between Hotton-Menil-Marche-Hargimont with the objectives of reaching Rendieux-Le-Bas, Waharday, Grimbiement and the line of the river Hedrée. 6th Airborne with 53rd Recce under command were on the right/southern flank and US VII Corps on the left/north-east flank. The main opposition was the remnant of *116 Panzer Division* now composed of six infantry battalions each about 300 strong plus some tanks, SP guns and mortars. Elements of 9 *Panzer Division* were in the south-west sector opposite Marche.

The plan of attack was for 158 Brigade with 144 RAC tanks in support on the left flank to advance and take Rendieux-Le-Bas and Waharday. 71st Brigade with Northants Yeomanry tanks under command, would tackle the right flank advance towards Grimbiemont and the line of the river Hedrée. 160 Brigade with the remainder of 33rd Armoured Brigade were in reserve around Baillonville five miles north of Marche.

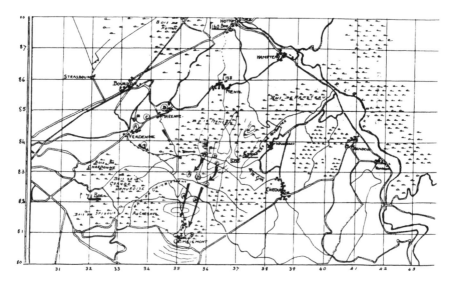

The Ardennes – Grimbiemont

The battle was going to be fought in appalling conditions of heavy snow and icy winds, last four days and take a lot of lives. The white camouflage smocks were not issued until the Ardennes campaign *was over*!

D-DAY 4 JANUARY: 'THE FROZEN MILL-RACE BATTLE'

At 08.00 hrs 1/5 Welch attacked in the left centre and East Lancashires on their right. Waharday was the 1/5 Welch objective and the supporting arms could not get forward. The Manchesters and the mortar platoon had to manhandle their weapons in very cold weather over deeply rutted tracks. Two hours later their CO, Lt Col Nelson Smith and the IO, Capt Bill Owen were both wounded on mines. For the third time Major Jack Morrison Jones, the 2 i/c took over. And Bill Owen relates: 'I felt like a jinx as this was the third CO who had been wounded by my side.' The enemy in Waharday could command with fire and vision all approaches and the khaki uniforms on a snowy background made easy targets. By 11.15 hrs 'C' Coy had fought their way into the village but were driven out by two tanks and a scout car.

It was appropriate that 1st Battalion East Lancs should be supported by 144 RAC, once the 8th Battalion East Lancs. Their objectives were the high ground and forest ahead, Bois Monseu, and ridge 3683. A blizzard set in but at least the enemy were also blinded. All went well for 1000 yards with Lt Langham's platoon knocking out a SP and Lt Tuffnell's destroying four Spandau nests. Lt

Ardennes landscape

Col Allen and Major Lake went off on a stealthy recce and were pinned down by an enemy tank. Enemy SPs knocked out a 144 RAC tank but by dusk for a cost of forty-four casualties, they took forty-nine prisoners and gained their objectives. During the afternoon Brigadier G. B. Sugden had been killed when his scout car overturned in a ditch. Lt Col Hudson, CO 83 Field Regt RA, assumed command.

On the far left of 158 Brigade were 2 Mons, under Lt Col F. H. Brooke. They started off at 10.15 hrs along the road near the river Ourthe towards Rendieux-le-Bas. Held up by a roadblock Corporal Hulton, 11 Platoon, wounded with a broken leg, lay in the river water for nine hours putting harassing fire into the village and Pte Warren earned the MM for using his Bren gun to great effect.

But 'B' Coy lost two entire sections due to the combination of extreme cold, no food, mines hidden in the snow, unlocated tanks and Spandaus. The roadblock under a crest proved almost impossible to take out or bypass, try as they could. The casualties were heavy, ten killed in action, twenty-four wounded and three taken prisoner. Major Jourdain was awarded the MC and Corporals Hutton and Fitzhugh the coveted DCM. During the action 'B' Coy occupied a mill building which was an enemy strongpoint in the partly frozen river mill-race. Major Hughes, their FOO with 497 Bty wrote: 'With the enemy completely alert and firing at every movement the situation was a deadlock. The angle of descent of our shells would not hit the Hun who was too far down in his ravine.' But General 'Bobby' Ross now intervened. An order came from Division *direct* to OC 2 Mons that the attack was to proceed again by night with maximum artillery fire to be used. It was very unusual for orders issued by the General to be sent to a battalion, so plan 'April' involving four Field, six Medium Regts with three Heavy Batteries was fired at 06.00 hrs, a total of 5820 shells. Tragically the rifle companies had moved up; it had got much colder suddenly, and the change in fall of shot caused some medium shells to fall into our own troops and did little damage to the enemy. 160 Brigade in reserve now concentrated in and around Hotton.

Philip Cowburn, Recce Regt: 'Our position on the snow ridges above overlooked the valley of the river Ourthe and the road to Laroche. We dug into the snow. On the hilltop away from most of the vehicles, icy cold, static, and the anti-tank battery covered the road in the valley below.' And, 'Bud' Abbot: 'The 4 January was my 21st birthday, some party! Freezing cold, very little food, rumours of another move and German "Schu" mines scattered about hidden under the snow so you had to tread very carefully.'

On the southern flank 71 Brigade attacked with 1HLI on the left from Marche towards the river Hedrée and the Ox and Bucks on their right. Lt Pender had just rejoined the Highlanders after the Antwerp cinema bombing: 'I caught an American supply column at the hospital gate and rejoined the battalion at Marche. The cold was frightful, we were not clothed for such wintry conditions. The only thing good was the Dan Bonars rum ration. A few days later I was blown up by a shrapnel mine. It didn't do me any good. My platoon and I were subjected to hours of heavy shelling by *one's own* guns. A number of us were hit by shrapnel including "Piggy" Houston — and my platoon shrank again.'

The HLI were heavily shelled during their advance and minefields under the snow gave much trouble. The Ox and Bucks were directed on the Bois de la Rochette and Bois des Spiroux, across fields six inches deep with snow and into dense woods. 'A' Coy had difficulty with snipers and 'D' had two carriers hit by enemy mortars, but between them took twenty prisoners. A strong counter-attack from Battlegruppe Schaeber on 'D' Coy was repulsed with heavy casualties but their OC, Major E. C. Vickers was killed. The Ox and Bucks had suffered heavily but took eighty prisoners and the artillery barrage had accounted for as many again. By 17.30 hrs both battalions had reached their objectives.

Lt Col Dickson led 7 RWF from Menic village to clear part of the forest of Hampteau. Sgt Anstey of No. 12 Platoon 'B' Coy stalked enemy outposts using a Piat; but maps were inaccurate and the enemy outposts hidden behind minefields, so progress was slow. Capt Llywelyn-Williams, 'D' Coy: 'We went into the forest battle from Bourdon and the following three days are not likely to be forgotten by anyone who experienced them. Conditions were appalling — intense cold, deep snow and the eerie darkness of the forest. Any woodland tracks were rigidly glazed with ice, impossible to maintain supplies of food and ammo.'

D+1 5 JANUARY: 'VERY COLD STEW WAS PALATABLE'

The gallant 2 Mons kept up their attacks against the strongpost in the river defile and despite a Typhoon attack made little progress. The German *116 Division* known as the *Windhund* (Greyhound) were a seasoned unit and repulsed further attacks by 'C' and 'D' Coys and even mounted a small counter-attack themselves. Corporal Jones, a stretcher-bearer, and Corp Fitzhughs showed great bravery during those two awful days. There were cases of frostbite and trenchfoot and men collapsed from exposure and exhaustion. Pte Bosley drove one of the twenty-five Weasels allocated to the Division backwards and forward for thirty-six hours taking up supplies and bringing back wounded men.

The East Lancs had received their meal at 03.00 hrs. It had been cooked in Verdenne at 06.00 hrs, but the very cold stew was palatable. The QM, John Moore, had struggled up to the rifle companies with a warming cargo of rum, like some great St Bernard dog. On the 5th, Weasels appeared for the first time and their broad tracks helped them over snow and ice. The line of attack now changed from south-east to south-west to bring them within striking distance of Grimbiemont. The snow stopped for a little and good progress was made but long-range shelling caused twenty-three casualties. For 7 RWF it was a difficult day. 'B', 'D' and 'C' Coys were heavily shelled forming up, the Battalion HQ was hit by artillery fire and at 17.30 hrs a heavy counter-attack with 400 infantry and several tanks over-ran 'D' Coy leaving only eighteen survivors. 'C' Coy in the centre was heavily involved and forced to withdraw after running out of ammunition. Eventually the battalion regrouped. CSM L. Stiff rallied the survivors of 'D' Coy and picked off a number of the enemy with a rifle. Major Barber was wounded and all the officers of his Coy, so Sgt Anstey took over command, later being awarded the DCM. Major Tomlinson called for a heavy artillery DF programme on his original forward positions. Capt Holme FOO, 460 Battery brought down the DF fire almost on top of his OP and saved a dangerous breakthrough. The left flank of the battalion was dangerously weak but 7 RWF survived — at a cost. In their three days of fighting in the snow and black forests near Waharday they lost seven killed in action, seventeen missing and ninety-four battle casualties. They were relieved at 16.30 hrs on the 6th, and returned to hot meals, blankets and billets at Bourdon.

D+2 6 JANUARY

4 Welch were loaned to 158 Brigade, 6 RWF came up to Marche and 53 Recce moved to Bourdon and then relieved the beleaguered 2 Mons in front of the Rendieux-le-Bas defile. 4 RWF were also relieved by 6th Airborne Division units. Brigadier J. O. Wilsey arrived to take command of 158 Brigade but the major attack on Grimbiemont was delayed for 24 hours.

D+3 7 JANUARY

General 'Bobby' Ross now mounted in effect, a divisional attack, despite the appalling weather conditions, and consequent lack of armoured support, south past Waharday (bypassing the Rendieux/river Ourthe roadblocks) towards Grimbiemont and the river Hedrée objectives. From north to south the attack would be mounted by 4 Welch, East Lancs, 1 HLI and Ox and Bucks.

4 Welch were to capture Authiers de Tailles whilst 1/5 Welch secured the flank to the south-west of Waharday. Major A. J. Lewis, OC 'D' Coy:

The Ardennes – a tank battle

The rough mountains would have made the going hard in any case, but snow, ice and the cold made the going even worse. There was no cover and the icy cold wind seemed to whip right through our bodies. The attack was made in the face of heavy machine gun and artillery fire and many were the deeds of outstanding heroism. One private soldier [Pte J A Strawbridge] after being hit was seen to carry back wounded on five occasions before being inevitably being hit again and mortally wounded. A Lance Corporal with his lower arm blown off continued to lead his section in attack until the objective was gained. How could the enemy withstand such courage! Neither soldier received any award for gallantry.

Supported by 144 RAC tanks, the attack, which started at 09.00 hrs and despite considerable opposition, was completed by 11.30 hrs. The attack by the East Lancs then started from the Rau de Grimbiemont on the edge of a wood as Major F. O. Cetre recounts:

The crest was 1500 yds ahead, on the other side was the village of Grimbiemont. The plan was simple. 'A' Coy on the right, 'D' Coy on the left with a black hedge down the middle. The two rear Coys supported by tanks would pass through and clear the village. The attack was supported by two medium and two field regiments [Major D H Macindoe, the FOO, played a key role]. Heavy shelling fell on the start line killing the Adjutant, Capt. Wildgoose, the Intelligence Sgt and wounding seven others. The wireless set was completely degutted. The supporting tanks couldn't get across the stream and casualties mounted steeply. Behind the crest could be seen the antennae of German tanks in hull-down positions. Major

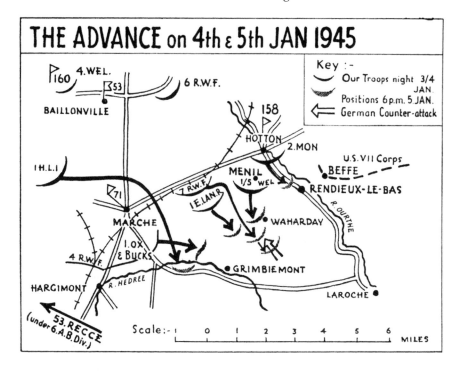

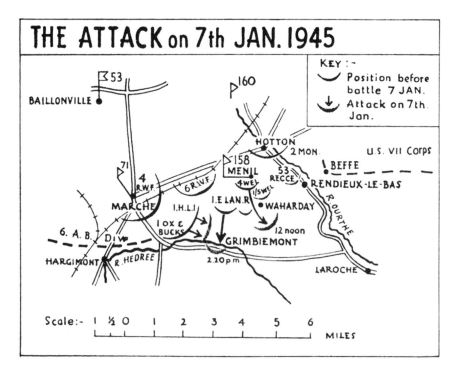

Macindoe's powerful wireless set provided the *only* communications with the outside world. The two leading companies battled their way to the crest, now much reduced in numbers. A troop of our supporting tanks found a way round to a flank and joined the fray.

'A' Coy on the right had all junior officers killed or wounded [except for Major Cetre], the CSM and 25 men, a third of the original strength. 'D' Coy fared little better. 'B' and 'C' Coys with tank support now battled into the village. The Germans fought hard and tenaciously and only some 30 PW were taken. A blizzard sprang up covering dead and wounded with a mantle of snow.

It was a brave operation and cost the battalion during the Ardennes battles eleven officers and 232 ORs killed, wounded or succumbed to exposure. 'It had been a hard fight against a tenacious and determined enemy and against the forces of nature. By 14.20 hrs the village had been captured.'

71 Brigade attacked to the south-east with 1HLI on the left and the Ox and Bucks on the right towards the little river, backed by Wasp flame-throwers and Weasels. Both key woods were captured and the 3" mortar platoon rained down 1000 bombs in half an hour. On the way a chateau and mill were stormed. L/Sgt Crump won the DCM, Major Jephson a bar to his MC, Corporal 'Darkie' Day and Corporal Eric Talbot won MMs. In the village of Champlon Famenne mortar fire continued during the day. The Ox and Bucks took eighty-eight prisoners and killed thirty-forty Germans, all from *116 Panzer Division*.

Major Crozier, 2 i/c of the Manchesters was promoted to be CO on 13 December. His diary entries for the Ardennes battle:

Jan 1. 71 Brigade at Marche taking over from the Americans. 'C' Coy move with 158 Bde and takeover on the left. Jan 2. All Coys had a dreadful day trying to get their carriers up, some only making one mile in eight hours, roads covered in ice. Temperature dropped. Very cold. Jan 3. Moved HQ to Sinsin-Granite, 8 miles NW of Marche. Jan 4. Attack today went well in spite of considerable enemy opposition and very bad weather conditions. Several enemy counter-attacks inc Tiger tanks. Snowing all day about three inches on ground. Going very bad. 'C' Coy abandoned their carriers and carried their guns and ammo up two miles of hillside. Jan 5. 2 Mons after several attacks failed to take their objective on the left and this pm the General decided to switch the attack to the right and centre. Nothing gained all day and enemy counter-attack this evening against 7 RWF met with some success. Heavy snow in the hills and frosts south of Marche and Hotton. Jan 6. Last night's counter-attack postponed our own attack. Jan 7. Very successful battle today, all objectives taken. Division is now on high ground N of Marche — Rendieux road. Our infantry casualties fairly heavy.

And three individual impressions of part of the two week ordeal: 'On the morning that we did eat our Christmas dinner [7th Jan] I got the CSM [wrote Capt Tim Dumas of 4 RWF] to march all ranks 500 yds down the road to a field, grounded arms, fell out officers and NCOs and we had a glorious snowball fight with the men. This was a marvellous tension reliever and many old scores could be, and were, settled in very good spirits.'

Gunner Eric Morgan, 330 Bty RA recalls: 'the awful journey up into the hills near Teuvuren and having to dig in the [25 pdr] guns and find a dry warm spot in about 20 degrees *below* zero, was a very unhappy experience. Christmas morning found us near Mettet pounding a concentration of German tanks just over the snow capped hills. Eventually we got our Christmas Dinner, turkey, pudding, all the trimmings (in our mess tins) washed down by a few bottles of 'special' saved for the occasion.'

Gunner Wally Brereton of 81st Welch Field Regt RA had his Christmas dinner of a cheese sandwich near Marche: 'The gun position was in deep snow, but some of us found a warm barn half a mile away. George who was on duty one night drank all the sections rum ration, fell asleep in the snow, sent back with the casualties suffering from exposure.'

During the final day of the Ardennes battle the Division had taken 155 prisoners and killed about 70 of the enemy. Night patrolling continued but by the morning of the 8th 2 Mons occupied Waharday and 53 Recce finally cleared the well-defended roadblocks on the road to Rendieux-le-Bas.

51st Highland Division now took over the pursuit and by 11 January the Division was out of the line around Liege for a welcome week's rest. Little did they know that their next operation — in Germany — was going to be even more of an ordeal. But the 'Battle of the Bulge' was over.

14

Operation Veritable: through the Reichswald Forest

For the next three weeks the Division was out of the line concentrating round Eindhoven and Helmond absorbing reinforcements and training. Philip Cowburn, the Recce historian: ' "A" Sqn was in farms near Mierlo, 'B' and HQ in Hout and 'C' in Eeinde. Throughout our stay round Helmond it had been obvious that a big attack was coming off somewhere. Supplies and bridging materials were being massed and long columns of troop-transporters and tanks were continually passing our billets. Was there going to be another Arnhem? Or an assault crossing of the Maas near Venlo and push on to turn the Siegfried line beyond? Plenty of rumours.'

On 23 January the three Field Regiments RA went down to Lommel artillery range for calibration and course shooting, and Lt Col Crozier, commanding 1 Manchesters wrote: 'sorry to be back in this dull Dutch country after the Ardennes. The Dutch people are very kind but stodgy and unimaginative.'

Desmond Milligan was an eighteen-year-old reinforcement for the carrier platoon of the Ox and Bucks in St Oedenrode. His OC was Capt Dick Flower and his carrier crew consisted of L/Sgt 'Granny' Smith and the driver, Pte Justice:

> My No 2 on the Bren gun was Pte Cox. I was billeted with several others in the roof loft of this Dutch house. Two of the young sons were thrilled to have British soldiers there and insisted we play 'Monopoly' with them in the evenings by the wood fuelled iron stove. Playing monopoly in Dutch translated by 10 year olds is not easy. Then I was sent on a Weasel driving course in Eindhoven, a small soft skinned amphibian with wide tracks that could traverse any kind of terrain, soft sand, mud or snow and float or propel itself through water.

Training, route marches in severe cold weather, so cold that every man had to spend two hours a day in the 'rest area' with hot meals, hot water, dry socks, so morale was high.

The Ox and Bucks pioneers built twenty sledges for the rifle sections to haul their heavier equipment along over snow and mud. The East Lancs had 284

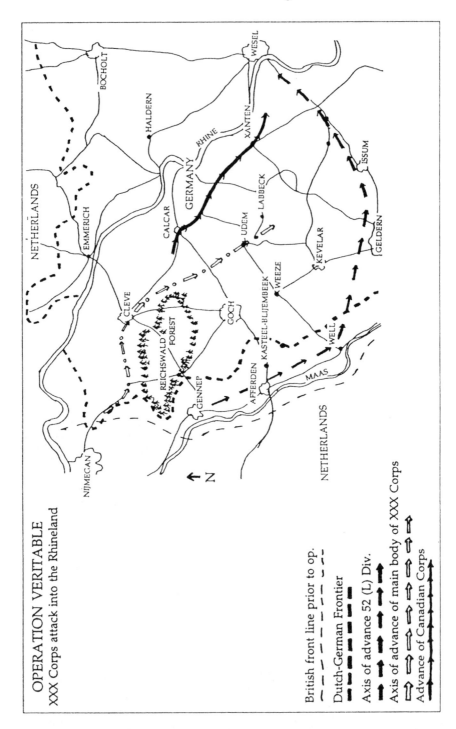

OPERATION VERITABLE
XXX Corps attack into the Rhineland

British front line prior to op.

Dutch-German Frontier

Axis of advance 52 (L) Div.

Axis of advance of main body of XXX Corps

Advance of Canadian Corps

new other ranks reinforcements to absorb and train, plus thirty-five earlier casualties who had rejoined. By 17 January their strength was thirty-two officers and 876 other ranks. Their Battalion HQ was in St Joseph Gaarde, and the school gym was the dining hall. Evening entertainment included dances, variety shows, clubs and cinemas. Capt David Bolland and Capt Monier-Williams of HQ RA put on an amusing play in Neunen called '48 hours' and in one day packed in 320 gunners to see it. Every battalion commander organised extensive training courses. All Brens and rifles were zeroed. Field firing exercises were held, more reading courses, compass work, night patrol practice, weapon training, pillbox assaults and cloth model exercises. The East Lancs carried out a full-scale night exercise in forest fighting in Stippelbeg wood in a howling gale with a fifteen-mile march back to Helmond. Sgt J. Machin, the Intelligence Sgt with 1/5 Welch, wrote, after the briefing to all Divisional officers of the forthcoming operation, codenamed Veritable:

> The Bn command studied in detail the Reichwald Forest, its tracks, density of trees, position of enemy trenches, topography. Each Coy CO learned by heart the way to his Coy objective. Characteristic of Monty the prelude to the offensive was to be a huge artillery barrage. When our CO Lt Col Morrison Jones saw the artillery programme he said. 'It is nice to know that they are on *our* side!'

Reichswald scene

82 Assault Sqdn. RE 'Entry into Reichswald.' (Birkin Hayward)

6 RWF in Aarle-Rixtel were joined by 9 RTR to practise infantry/tank co-operation in the local woods. AVRE Petards were fired at buildings and the battalion Wasps carried out flame throwing tactics. Loading trials in carriers and Weasels were held to try and make the battalion *track*-borne during Veritable. The Corps Commander, Lt General Brian Horrocks, known as Jorrocks, visited the Division and described the forthcoming operation as 'Cracking the Siegfried line'.

Major R. N. Deane, 2nd Mons wrote after the Ardennes battle, of:

> The atmosphere of tension and the feeling of being about to make history. The whole war machine seemed to turn over and we, to be a vital part of its mechanism. This was the attack which was to break through the northernmost Siegfried defence and roll down between the Maas and the Rhine. We felt that now we were going to end the war, or the war would end us.

Major Deane looked at the enemy defences plotted on the maps available: 'If we had known that the entry into the dark, dirty, noisy forest was to be the start of a month's solid fighting, ending in complete but glorious exhaustion, we would have felt ever grimmer.' Behind the scenes the medical services were also preparing. Corporal Bert Isherwood, 13 FDS, collected from Helmond on 23 January, three boxes of condoms for use by surgical nursing sections. 'The military usage was to fix dressings and bandages on damaged fingers to save

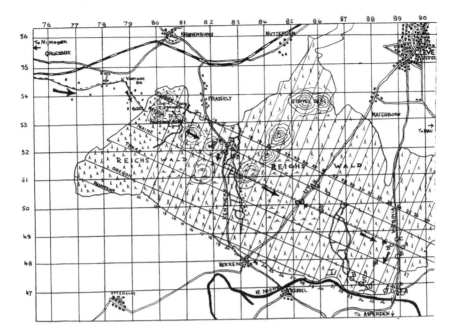

The Reichswald Forest

time, tying off or taping the bandages. Four of these on one damaged hand resembles a cow's udder!'

The enemy had three principal zones of defence between the Maas and the Rhine — the outpost zone west of the Reichwald forests, the Siegfried line itself and the Hochwald rear defences. The Germans had had plenty of time to build extensive defensive 'webs' around the main towns of Cleve, Goch, Weeze, Kevelaer, Geldern and Issum. Minefields, anti-tank obstacles and ditches, deep trenches, concrete pillboxes, bunkers were manned, in the Reichwald area, by *84 Infantry Division, Battlegroup Katzmann,* the *2nd Paratroop Regiment* and part of *180 Infantry Division.*

Monty had deployed five infantry divisions into Veritable, two Canadians of II Corps in the north, 15th Scottish going in just north of the Reichwald, 53rd Welsh through the forest itself and 51st Highland along the southern edge towards Goch. Two more divisions were in reserve to exploit towards the Hochwald, 43rd Wessex and Guards Armoured. And 11th Armoured were ready to help out!

The sinister Reichwald, some nine miles deep by five miles wide was a forest of densely packed, dark pine trees known to conceal the northern end of the original Siegfried line defence. The defence over-print map showed a maze of gun positions and field works inside the forest and recent diggings and new trench systems had been identified. Two other problems were that most of the forest tracks and rides ran across, not with, the line of attack. And on 20 January a heavy thaw set in and all the fields were soon waterlogged. The plan of attack was for 71st Brigade to lead with 4 RWF ahead to smash the German frontier positions west of the Reichwald (Brandenburg) and for 160 Brigade to pass through into the forest and capture the Siegfried line positions (Stoppelberg) by a night attack supported by tanks and flame-throwers. The methodical Germans had made their tracks within the Reichwald into blocks of 800 yards by 400 yards with narrow rides between them. The three roads and tracks running north-south were given American codenames: Kentucky, Utah and Virginia.

The British Army has superb staff planning to back up major operations. Codeword for Goch was Bangor; for Cleve Wigan; the Reichwald Forest was Repton and Nuttterden, Ratby. The various report lines were Vindictive, Ramilles, Malaya, Lion, Resolution, Repulse, Temeraire, Valiant and Howe. Possibly the staff were planning a nautical operation? The official passwords which everybody forgot were D-1 Father-Thames: D-Day Virgin-Snow, D+1 Silver-Ring; D+2 Jolly-Farmer; D+3 Mother-Superior; D+4 Sour-Grapes and D+5 Simple-Simon. Just in case Veritable was extended the 'spares' were Plum-Duff and Short-Odds. Busy little bees the G-staff!

The Reichswald mud was knee-deep

D-DAY 09.30 HRS 8 FEBRUARY: 'MUD WAS KNEE-DEEP'

No less than 1034 guns would be firing in support of Veritable — the biggest concentration of the campaign. The divisional programme started at 05.15 hrs with counter-battery shoots on twenty different targets. Then followed a barrage for four hours at the end of which a further barrage supported 71 Brigade. Lt Col Crozier, 1 Manchesters: 'I am to command the divisional Pepperpot — my Bn plus a Sqn of tanks, a Bty of 17 pdrs and three troops of 40mms. Quite a party!' The 34th Armoured Brigade tanks were also in support, and at 09.30 hrs 4 RWF led the advance of the entire Division. Platoon commanders had made their final reconnaissance from the Groesbeek windmill. Churchill tanks went first, then the Flails and Crocodiles with 'A' Coy (Major Charles Davies) on the left, 'C' (Major Tim Dumas) in the centre and 'B' (Major H Roberts) on the right. Just before the attack, Tim and Charles picked up their mail: 'I received a cake sent by my mother and father from home, we tried it at once. We finished it then and there and we laughed about it. In a month Charles was dead leading 'A' Coy in the attack on Weeze. Then we started clearing Germans from between the Maas and the Rhine in bitter, cold wet weather. The mud was knee deep in places in the forest. Only Weasels could bring up rations and hot drinks.' (Tim Dumas)

Reichswald Forest & Siegfried Line. Top left, British medium 5.5 in gun in action

The CO, Lt Col Hanmer, decided to have three companies forward, close to the barrage and clear thoroughly all farm houses and buildings. The bombardment had shaken the enemy and soon Höst, an outpost in the Siegfried line 1000 yds away, was reached. Sappers opened up the road but the Crocs were all bogged down. One farmhouse yielded twenty-three prisoners and six Spandaus and Provost Sgt Tomlinson rescued some of 'C' Coy *and* the enemy from a minefield. By 12.15 hrs 4 RWF had reached the anti-tank ditch, the bridge not blown, so the Churchill tanks got across quickly. In all 4 RWF captured 180 prisoners, mostly from cellars sheltering from the barrage. Now the Ox and Bucks on the left and 1 HLI on the right passed through into the main forest.

'B' Coy Ox and Bucks against little opposition seized a corner of the Reichwald and became the first British troops of 53rd Division to cross into Germany. 'C' and 'D' Coys then took the high ground of Brandenberg and captured 115 prisoners. But RHQ was badly shelled by 88 mm guns causing many casualties, included the MO, 'I' Section and signallers. Desmond Milligan's book *View from a Forgotten Hedgerow* gives a vivid account. He was a Weasel driver with Major Walker's 'B' Coy. His thin-skinned, wide-tracked vehicle contained boxes of 2-inch mortar bombs, .303 ammunition, .36 Mills grenades, phosphorous grenades, LMG magazines and Piat anti-tank bombs: 'I saw a railway line about 400 yards on my left with infantrymen moving along it. A short way in front a line of Churchill tanks had started

Reichswald Forest & Siegfried Line

to advance. The plain was nearly 4-5 miles wide, nothing was growing on the fields, flat, brown and muddy. This bleak view was broken by one small farmhouse and three haystacks — all soon alight. A terrifying hissing rushing noise was our own rocket blanket.' The Ox and Bucks soon reached the forest, 'the Brandenburg feature a commanding hill and few hundred yards inside the tree line. It was about 13.30 hrs and not a shot had been fired by the enemy at this point. A young German lay dead on the road, face down like a rag doll all awry as if without bones. His skin was wax-like with a yellow tinge. He was the first dead German that I had seen.' Later, 'through the mist came the wail of a bagpipe playing a lament for the dead. The reed-like sounds gave a poignant end to the day's events.' Lt G. C. R. Pender:

> I was promoted Captain, transferred to 'B' Coy [1 HLI], then commanded by Canloan Major Joe Hamelryke. On our right we had 1 Black Watch of 51st Highland Div. Amidst the barrage, tanks, flack, line upon line of infantry. We could hear the sound of the pipes, reminiscent of the 1914-18 war. The battle was hard and the cost was high. By evening of 8th February we had taken our firm objectives, the cold and snow was intense, but we were in Germany at last.

By mid afternoon 71 Brigade had achieved its objectives and 1 HLI pushed on to the Hekkens-Kranenburg road. The follow-up by 160 Brigade was badly

Reichswald scene after the barrage

held up by the disintegration of the roads by usage, by gunfire and by the thaw. So it was six hours later than planned — at midnight — that under artificial moonlight the East Lancs on the right and 6 RWF on the left moved further into the forest.

D+1 9 FEBRUARY: 'SOME SAID TIGERS'

When they went into the Reichwald the East Lancs were *over* strength with thirty-one officers and 914 other ranks — a very rare state indeed. They were shelled on their FUP and the 147 RAC Churchills had to detour round the collapsed Vortsche bridge. Once in the forest the track gave out completely and the forest was so dense that the battalion moved on without its tanks or transport. The artillery barrage had uprooted whole pine trees leaving huge craters. The battalion on a compass bearing followed in file led by Capt Cheesbrough. Rain fell throughout the night. Major Duxbury, 'D' Coy:

> We reached Kentucky but 'A' Coy overshot. A mysterious chugging noise of some IC engine was heard in the woods to our front. Some said 'SP guns', some said 'Tiger Tank', others said 'Motor-Bike'. The mysterious chugger came into view with sidelights on, and was met by a hail of fire. It was an ancient farm tractor of the Fordson type loaded with 122mm shells. Later our own A/Tk guns arrived and we were firm on the ground by 02.00 hrs.

But Major Bain's 'B' Coy now well into the first line of the Siegfried defences was involved in fierce hand-to-hand fighting with bayonets and hand grenades. Lt Kay and CSM Potts held on tenaciously as 10 and 11 Platoons were counter-attacked.

From Driehuizen 6 RWF 'married up' with 9 RTR and moved through the ruined Groesbeek village, past the wrecked American gliders of the Market Garden droppings. At their FUP mortar fire forced the Fusiliers off their 'friendly' Churchills, and Capt Evans, OC HQ Coy was killed. The CO, Lt Col Exham on top of a 9 RTR tank was bogged down three times. It took five hours for 6 RWF to reach their start line. Despite wireless failures the combined attack went ahead and was successful.

The hills leading up to the Stoppel Berg on the northern part of the Reichwald were the next objectives, for the 4 Welch and then 2nd Mons. Major A. J. Lewis, OC 'D' Coy gives a graphic description of the appalling conditions as 4 Welch moved past burning buildings over the last stretch of open ground to the west of the forest:

The single third class road was blocked by bogged transport. Gangs of men worked feverishly to clear it. Any vehicle that could not move under its own power was abandoned and pushed into the swamp alongside. It was vital that no troops should be caught in this open ground at first light next morning [9 Feb]. It was raining hard and everyone was soaked to the skin. It was only with the greatest difficulty that weapons were kept dry and serviceable. At each halt men just lay down in the mud with the rain beating down on them trying to snatch a few moments of sleep. If they were near a burning building they crowded round it, regardless of text-book precepts about dispersion, to get some of the heat. Through a pitch black night of driving rain, the column moved on fifty or a hundred yards at a time. The tanks in support had to take a different route and then try to find their proper place in the column. They were getting hopelessly stuck blocking the track. It was a tremendous struggle to keep any transport at all — yet it meant food, water and ammo. Inside the forest no track was distinguishable in the darkness. The start line for the attack — a lateral track in the forest — was reached at dawn.

On 9 February 4 Welch advanced 2000 yards through dense forest to reach their objectives by 09.30 hrs. Major Lewis:

The strain on the infantryman was terrific. After forcing his way through undergrowth or trudging in the pelting rain along tracks and paths ankle deep in mud, soaked through, tired out, he still had to be alert, never knowing from one moment to another when he was going to meet his enemy. Whenever an objective was reached he had first to dig in, then spend four hours of the night on guard. Then he might, if lucky, get to doze in a waterlogged trench.

The 2 Mons following 4 Welch arrived on the north edge of the forest at Frasselt with supporting Churchills of 'B' Sqn 9 RTR. By 10.30 hrs they had occupied the Stopfelberg feature and dug in. On their left was 15th Scottish fighting near Wolfsburg. Major R. N. Deane: 'The night was so full of thuds, bangs and whistles as a night could be. Tanks and other vehicles fell foul of the mud, but the sweated, heavy feet of the infantry trudged steadily on into the Reichwald.' The 2 Mons tried to move out of the forest near Schottheide, were frustrated by SP guns, but nevertheless captured seventy prisoners without a fight. 7 RWF relieved 6 RWF and reached the north-west corner of the forest, riding on the supporting tanks of 9 RTR, took fifty prisoners and cleared an important track for 43rd Wessex Division to use. 9 RTR had some spectacular shooting up of enemy MT, staff cars and tanks on the Matterborn road.

At 02.00 hrs on the 9th Lt Col Morrison-Jones, the fifth CO of 1/5 Welch in twelve months, led 158 Brigade (the East Lancs were temporarily with 160

Brigade) from Groesbeek and *eight* hours later started their attack towards the Gelden Berg high ground. Despite 88 mm, mortar and Spandau fire, supported by 147 RAC, they took their objectives and by nightfall had acquired thirty-nine prisoners. By the evening of 9 February the Division had captured all its objectives with a good haul of prisoners and mopping up continued.

D+2 10 FEBRUARY: 'MUD, MUD, MUD!'

Early in the morning of 10 February 'B' Coy RWF had a hard fought action against the newly arrived troops of 2nd German Parachute Division in which Lt Shirlow won the MC, Fusilier Besley the MM, but young 2/Lt Garrod and L/Cpl Condick (who won the MM) were killed. Brigadier Coleman made one of his frequent visits to 6 RWF to congratulate them on their progress. Sgt J. Machin, 1/5 Welch:

> We must mention the work of the Signal platoon in the snow and rain, wading at times through knee-deep mud, they dragged that heavy reel of cables. Communications. How important they were. Those same signallers will remember a blow lamp in a carrier shrouded by a tarpaulin. We nicknamed it 'The Hot-Pot'.

The East Lancs sent out their patrols to contact the enemy at Oregon/Kentucky and Kentucky/Maine but the Germans had obviously pulled out to avoid being cut off in the south. All supplies of food, ammo and casualties back had to use the Nijmegen-Cleve main road along the north of the forest which was flooded to two, even four feet of water. The QM, John Moore recorded: 'The water was over our mudguards, going back to "A" Echelon no roads could be *seen*. It was just like a lake and the DUKWs were being used for wounded and ammo.'

The Recce Regt supplied nine Traffic Control points equipped with wireless for the Division and nine more for 30 Corps to assist in the horrendous traffic problems round Groesbeek and the approaches to the forest. 'B' and 'C' Sqns also sent carriers up with explosives and other RE supplies.

The 2 Mons put in an attack to clear the area east of the main Cleve-Gennep road but were counter-attacked by SP guns and a Tiger tank which were gallantly driven off by 56 Anti-Tank Battery of Royal Canadian Artillery. And 4 Welch moved through 2 Mons, every man now carrying a small amount of *dry* tea and Oxo cubes! They too were impeded by enemy tanks and SP guns but by 16.30 hrs had advanced 2400 yards, reached and cleared a network of enemy trenches. One Coy commander captured a German goose. It was held by his batman and was decapitated while German snipers took pot shots at him. Counter-attacks on 'A' Coy were presumably to rescue the headless goose.

Lt Col Crozier's, 1 Manchesters, diary:

> Feb 8th. Attack going very well. 71 Bde have got all their objectives and 160 Bde have passed through. They are all now in the Reichwald Forest. Our [Manchesters] MMGs no good in the forest. 51[H] and 15 [S] Divs also doing well on our right and left. Feb 9th. Everything going fine 15 [S] and ourselves on final objective. So far over 2000 PW taken. The ground is just one vast sea of mud. Heavily shelled at 160 Bde, most unpleasant place. A poor sort of welcome to Germany. Feb.10th. Mud, mud, mud! And getting worse. Sappers building a log road [224 Field Coy]. Rain, sleet and snow.

But 'B' Coy 4 RWF solved one problem — for a short time. They occupied former German dug-outs fitted with stoves, beds and other amenities, whilst the rest of the battalion had to spend the night on road maintenance work.

The three regiments of 25-pdrs had problems every time they had to move forward. Each gun had to be winched out of its pit and into its platform at the new position. After taking part in the enormous fireplan early on the 8th, all regiments had to move up several thousand yards to be in position by 09.00 hrs on 9th Feb. The CRA sent them a nice message. 'Tell troops shooting on 8th was absolutely excellent.' Captain David Bolland, HQRA:

> 10 Feb. The weather has been vile ever since the thaw set in so thoroughly. The mud is ten times worse than anything we have met before. In the last four nights I have been up all through the night without a moments sleep trying to get the guns into action and to dump ammo along the roads and in fields which are nothing short of quagmires. The Hun has an unhappy habit of digging his funk holes *underneath* the roads so if a tank goes over them, they just give way.

No major actions were fought on the 10th, but a firm front was established along the Hekkens-Cleve road, but all the other divisions including 43rd Division and the two Canadians were heavily involved.

D+3 11 FEBRUARY: 'REACHING VIRGINIA'

At this stage about half the Reichwald had been captured and the opposition ahead was now *16th Para Regt*; *20th Para Regt* and *2nd Para Regt* from north-south. After a day of consolidation 160 Brigade were to continue the advance eastwards and 158 Brigade to the south-east. Then 71 Brigade would take over the northern sector and 160 Brigade would come into the fray alongside

158 Brigade. 6 RWF in pouring rain made their third successive attack with 9 RTR, found no opposition and took prisoners and stragglers. On their right, 2 Mons reached the eastern edge of the forest facing Cleve Wald. Sgt G. D. Williams led a two-man patrol to investigate a farmhouse. When challenged by a sentry who gave a bird call the patrol imitated it, rudely battered the sentry into silence, threw grenades through the farmhouse windows and fired into the cellars. Thirty fully armed German parachutists surrendered in panic and Sgt Williams later received the MM. In two days the Mons took ninety-nine prisoners but in five days fighting had fifty-nine casualties themselves. A German *jet*-propelled fighter then bombed the battalion. At 13.30 hours 4 Welch pushed towards Dammershof and gained another two thousand yards, reaching a group of farms where 'C' Coy captured a German tank. During the night they pushed 3000 yards to the eastern edge of the forest.

Brigadier Wilsey, 158 Brigade, kept up the pressure south-east with the East Lancashires on the left, 1/5 Welch on the right. By mid-day the East Lancs had captured the Utah/Maine line despite much opposition. Corporals Monkhouse and Oram did well. The former demolished a Spandau crew of five and the latter when Capt Wilson was wounded, took over command of 18 Platoon. Brigade urgently wanted a bridgehead over the third main road Asperden-Cleve, i.e. Virginia. A hasty plan was hatched with Churchill tank support and smokescreen to get across 1500 yards of open ground between the forest and the next major wood to the east.

'D' Coy leading were temporarily isolated but the FOO of 330 Battery broke up several enemy counter-attacks. Major Morrison 'C' Coy assisted by CSM Linton led a brilliant charge across the open ground, although Capt Mackie was killed. A key crossroads called 'Dead Horse Corner' was taken, as well as sixty-three prisoners during the day. By nightfall the East Lancs were the only battalion to reach Virginia and they stayed isolated for nearly twenty-four hours. But John Moore, the QM managed the impossible, to slip through the enemy at 02.00 hrs on 12 February with the battalion's supper of *cold* stew.

1/5 Welch spent the whole day from 08.30 hrs wood clearing but by the evening as Sgt Machin put it: 'The enemy did not intend to allow us to gain control of the main road. It was now 1900 hrs and clear that no further advance could be made that night.' 7 RWF had also sent patrols south-east to discover the enemy's strength in front of the Materborn-Hekkens road. 'C' Coy met heavy opposition from a strongpoint and could make no further progress. At 20.00 hrs the GOC gave orders for both brigades to halt, dig in and resume the advance in the morning.

D+4 12 FEBRUARY: 'IT WAS BLOODY'

158 Brigade's objective was the capture of the river Niers bridge north of Asperden, with 160 Brigade on the northern flanks getting and keeping control of the Cleve-Asperden road.

7 RWF in early morning ground mist eventually eliminated the strongpoint holding them up, but a Spandau killed Lts Jones and Brooker. Shortly afterwards a heavy counter-attack came in supported by SP guns but by the end of the day the battalion had reached their objectives. 1/5 Welch had to deal with Spandau teams and SP guns and eventually reached the Cleve-Asperden road. Sgt Machin describes the counter-attack: 'The enemy made a real blunder in deciding to counter-attack "B" Coy [at 16.15 hrs]. It was a gunners dream, as they came on in extended order and exposed their left flank to "D" Coy some 300 yards to the south. Both companies opened up with Brens, Vickers and Besas. It was too much for the Bosch who broke ranks, leaving some thirty casualties behind. During the night the gunners went to work on the Bosch with a vengeance firing a total of 12,000 shells.' During their battles in the Reichwald 1/5 Welch had 125 casualties and took 130 prisoners.

The East Lancs with their bridgehead across the key Virginia road were under siege all day. By mid-day the W/T communications to Brigade having failed and the consequent lack of artillery support, things looked ominous. The mortar platoon and all rifle companies were having to conserve ammunition. Enemy shelling became heavier and 200 enemy infantry of *15 Panzer Grenadier Division* (a new formation on the Reichwald front) advanced into the plantation *between* 'A' and 'C' Coys, but 'B' Coy and supporting tanks launched *their* own counter-attack. Lt Smith of 'A' Coy twice went back to Rear Battalion HQ to give fire targets to the Battery Commander's No 22 set — still functioning. In the late afternoon the Panzer Grenadiers came in again into a V-shaped 'killing ground' arranged by 'A' and 'C' Coys. During the evening the rest of the Brigade came up to Virginia. Captain Gerald Lester, the FOO with 'A' Coy, Corporal O'Brien who commanded a platoon in 'A' Coy, Lt Connolly's mortar platoon and the supporting tanks were the heroes of the day. During Veritable the East Lancs suffered 142 casualties. The war correspondent of the *Yorkshire Post* later interviewed Lt Col Allen:

We had to shoulder forward what we could — our mortars and mortar bombs — and feel our way forward on a compass bearing. There were mines, there was always the mud. Often we were without food, often it came up late. We ate our breakfast at 4pm and our evening meal at 3am. We were cold. We were wet. We were hungry and we kept on fighting. It was bloody. Observation was from one tree to the next. We were behind one tree and the Bosch was behind the next.

A terribly wearing business for the men. Psychologically and mentally. It was nearly all bayonet, Sten and grenade fighting. The Bosch reserves fought very well, stubborn and had to be dug out with the bayonet.

Further north 160 Brigade made progress, 2 Mons passed through 4 Welch and cleared the north-east of the forest, but 6 RWF were attacked by *15 Panzer Grenadier* troops supported by SP guns who had also launched a major attack on 1/5 Welch and the East Lancs. The main attack fell on 'D' Coy and infiltration occurred before 'A' Coy and 'friendly' tanks counter-attacked. Major Williams of 'D' Coy was severely wounded and Capt Ross, the MO dealt with the many casualties under heavy fire. The enemy were identified as *115 Panzer Grenadier* Regt in the north, *104 Panzer Grenadier Regt* in the south. All in all the Division had done well to resist such a strong determined attack by these fresh reserve troops. That evening 2 Mons on the left of 4 Welch were astride the road facing Niederdamm.

4 Welch also had a difficult day. 'C' Coy were held up by SPs and infantry but pushed some 800 yards ahead. An enemy attack on the right flank was dealt with by 'D' Coy but a Red Cross flag was needed to bring wounded out. 'B' Coy in front had several killed including their company commander and many wounded. When the enemy attacked round the badly cut up 'B' Coy flanks, the situation became critical, with a real risk of the battalion being cut off. The gunners brought down DF targets and 'D' Coy came to the rescue. At 15.00 hrs the battalion consolidated and at top speed dug in. Piles of cut logs stacked nearby were used as overhead cover, just in time before a terrific 'stonk' came down. In four days 4 Welch had advanced over ten miles, six through thick forest and taken part in four full-scale attacks. From 7-21 February the battalion had 61 killed in action and 250 wounded or missing — probably the worst casualties in the Division.

D+5 13 FEBRUARY: 'SMELL OF CORDITE'

Orders were given for the final clearance of the forest with the whole Division in action. 160 Brigade in the north would continue to mop up, whilst 71 Brigade plus 1/5 Welch under command would clear the sector between Wilhelminenhof and the south-east corner of the forest. Meanwhile 158 Brigade would try to link up with 51st Highland Division near Grafenthal and capture the Asperden bridge.

The 71 Brigade attack started at 10.00 hrs with 4 RWF on the left and 1 HLI on the right. 'B' Coy 4 RWF distinguished themselves, advanced 1500 yards and took 62 prisoners but lost twelve casualties. They stayed on their final objectives for two more days, under fire most of the time. 1 HLI were equally successful and by noon had reached their objectives. Captain Pender 'B' Coy:

For ten days we fought continuously in the forest in snow and rain. An advance of a few hundred yards was often a full day's work. Casualties from the airburst amongst the tree tops were very heavy. We were soaked right through to the skin and covered in mud. The Germans on our front had brought up a colossal gun which fired vast shells making craters on landing, big enough to penetrate Churchill tanks into with ease. They played havoc with our slit trenches. An eerie, much knocked about Schloss amongst the trees, with a WWI monument in it, became a military cemetery. We carried back our dead for burial there at night.

After these attacks the Ox and Bucks came up to relieve 1/5 Welch. The Recce Regiment formed a composite Sqn, mainly 'C', to join 158 Brigade in their drive, with 7 RWF, for the Asperden bridge. Corporal David Henderson's diary noted: 'We were doing flank protection [for 1 HLI] in the pouring rain. They put in an attack, held what they gained, dug and slept in trenches and had nothing to eat or drink. Up at dawn doing guard, a slice of bread and "Bully" and off into the attack again.'

Corporal Bert Isherwood took supplies for 13 FDS from Nijmegen, towards the end of 'Veritable':

Taking the lateral road through the dark and menacing woods of the Reichswald. Even a week after the last German had fired a shot nobody moved with impunity in the rubble of Goch where the smell of cordite still lingered mixed with the stench of putrefying flesh of men. Here our flame throwing Crocodiles had left a trail of war, delineated by the roasted bodies of men in tanks, in pill boxes, in cellars, charred cadavers rigid and ghastly.

Men of the Field Ambulances *carried* the wounded back. The only available track was known as 'Chewing Gum Alley' a clinging morass that everyone loathed. Lt A. Cowan recalled the problems for the Sappers:

In one stretch of two miles Jerry had blown the road in seven places. The craters were huge and there were more prepared charges which had failed to explode and which we had gingerly to remove. Under a layer of mines was a layer of shells and beneath them, six feet underground were charges of hundreds of pounds of TNT. Still we managed to keep the road open and working.

Gunner Wally Brereton, 81st Field Regt RA had just returned from UK leave:

I was soon carrying boxes of shells to feed the hungry guns. Many of the attacks were at night. Searchlights raked the skies to create artificial moonlight. Tracer shells fired from horizontal LAA guns added to the display. F Tp position was near a poultry farm. The gunners chased chickens and boiled them on Benghazi cookers well into the night. I made my bed in a pigsty to get away from the smell. Special tanks [AVREs] that threw bombs the size of dustbins were used to break the concrete emplacements. Other tanks carried folding bridges [Scissors] to span ditches and trenches whilst some projected tongues of flame [Crocodiles] at MG rests. Ahead the [51st] Highlanders were nearing Goch whilst the artillery were already reducing the town to rubble.

Major John Lloyd, 2 i/c 83rd Field Regt RA, was 'given' a Churchill tank for the Reichwald, for added protection during the advance. It was called 'Gibraltar', stuck like all the others in the mud, leaked very badly during the heavy rain. John Lloyd passed it over to the QM in B Echelon and told him to 'lose' it: 'He did his best but it always turned up "like a faithful dog", a grinding noise in the middle of the night announcing its arrival. Fuller Cocks, the Capt. QM, one of the nicest people I met, had been a staff Sgt Instructor at the Army School of Equitation, taught many WW2 Generals how to ride'.

Lt Gen Brian Horrocks wrote in *Corps Commander:*

On their [15th Scottish] right were the 53rd Welsh Division who disappeared into the Reichwald itself, where they were to spend one of the most unpleasant weeks of the whole war owing to the difficulty of movement up the narrow boggy rides. They fought their way steadily forward against increasing German opposition. This was the Division which, in my opinion, suffered most. For nine days without ceasing they edged their way steadily forward. The narrow rides made tank support almost impossible and they were constantly being faced by fresh German reserves. They never faltered and on 18th February they reached their objective, the east edge of the forest having suffered 5000 casualties — 50 percent of the total lost by this Division during all their operations in Europe. The 18th of February is a day of which Wales has every right to be proud. One day when visiting 53rd Welsh Division in the Reichwald I almost stumbled over two young soldiers crouching in a very muddy trench. They were all alone and could see none of their comrades, who were also concealed in foxholes nearby. Here, I thought, is the cutting edge of this vast military machine. These two young men were desperately lonely... Now owing to the power of modern weapons more and more fighting takes place at night yet nothing in their previous life had prepared these young soldiers for their loneliness and the darkness...

So some 50 square miles of pine trees had been captured and initial inroads made into the Siegfried line and over 3000 prisoners taken. Four Panther and several MK IV tanks, plus eight 88 mm guns had been captured or destroyed.

The battle honour of the Reichswald Forest had been gained at a great cost. As usual the gunners had been magnificent and the Churchills of 34th Armoured Brigade had given their all in appalling conditions. 9 RTR had lost thirty-eight tanks and was ordered back to refit as an anti-tank unit. 147 RAC could only muster two very weak squadrons. The 'unsung' heroes were the Sappers who strove desperately to keep tracks open and the regimental quartermasters who came 'hell or high water' got their food, tea and rum up to the rifle companies at the sharp end.

Into Germany at last – a shattered landscape

15

Operation 'Veritable': Battle for the Rhineland

Major General 'Bobby' Ross left the Division on 16 February on sick leave and returned on 10 March. In his absence Brigadier Elrington, 71st Brigade, took over command, and Lt Col T. McLeod, 1 HLI succeeded him.

'We, [Pte Alistair Carmichael and the Command half track crew] met the new [acting] Brigadier, Lt Col McLeod from our HLI Bn. I got along alright with the Col; like him belonging to Scotland may have made a difference. He liked my cooking. He was indeed a front line soldier and at no time showed any love for the Germans. He did enjoy his whiskey. He always carried his own Tommy gun, the times he was with us. I took care of its cleaning.' The half-track crew included Corporal Dick Barker and Signaller Mellor: 'When things got a bit hectic we carried extension aerial poles, 25-30 feet trying to contact the Battalions after dark.'

There was still one key feature to be taken outside the south-east corner of the Reichwald Forest. This was the Asperberg feature, a mile north-east of the river Niers bridge on the Asperden road. 51st Highland Division would move eastwards from Grafenthal towards Hervost and 1 Ox and Bucks and 7 RWF backed by huge barrages would clear the area outside the forest, north-east of the river — on the night of the 16 February. 7 RWF had spent almost two days probing the defences of Asperden and it was now their difficult task to capture the village. Together with the Recce Sqn they cleared to the edge of the wood within 600 yards of the Asperden bridge, which was, predictably, well defended. Capt Llywelyn-Williams 'D' Coy wrote:

The rides and forest paths were mined — the Italian box mines effectively prevented our supporting tanks venturing along the tracks. We had seven Weasels allocated to the Bn but few survived after the strain of ten days combat with the mud. However the forest was eventually cleared. But on the tenth day just outside the forest was a small group of houses [Asperden] astride a stream which commanded the open country to the south. It was occupied by German paratroops effectively blocking [51st Scottish] division on our right.

7 RWF made a series of attacks but were held up. A final attack was laid on for the night of the 16th. A barrage was laid down at 21.00 hrs. The enemy held out stubbornly until the strongpoint was set on fire by flamethrowers. It must have been one of the most fiercely contested actions that the battalion ever waged. All night the battle raged, hand to hand, in and out of the buildings with no quarter asked or given on either side. All the German paratroops were killed or taken prisoners. 7 RWF suffered seventy casualties in this fierce action. Lt V. M. James captured seventeen paratroopers in his first engagement and was awarded the MC. CSM Jones was killed and 'A' Coy strength reduced to thirty. And the key bridge at Aspermuhle was blown.

Mopping up continued on the 17th and a further thirty-three casualties suffered but finally on the night of 16th/17th 152 Brigade of 51st Highland Division actually took Asperden. And on the 19th the battered 7 RWF and 158 Brigade moved back to Nijmegen for four days rest.

The Ox and Bucks were now directed on the farming village of Asperberg to the east of the blown bridge at Aspermuhle. Remnants of *115 Panzer Grenadier Regt* and part of *2nd Parachute Regt* were determined — despite the barrage from seven field and medium regiments — to fight, perhaps to the last man. Major Walker's 'B' Coy quickly captured twenty prisoners, and Major Jephson's 'C' Coy another twenty-two. In ferocious fighting Lt Tony Paget (son of the General) personally killed nine Spandau machine gunners and earned the DSO. But Major Jephson's party was ambushed and he was killed by a panzerfaust, and 'C' Coy lost seventeen killed and twenty-three wounded in the savage house to house fighting. Finally the Ox and Bucks moved across the river Niers, the 2nd Mons and 4 Welch cleared the whole area east of the Reichwald up to the Cleve State Forest. 1 HLI and the Ox and Bucks on the 18th cleared the area between Pfalzdorf and Kaiser Alberdekath capturing 160 prisoners in the process. Finally 4 RWF the next day cleared a factory area on the western edge of Goch with Major Tim Dumas' 'C' Coy and Major Davies' 'A' Coy capturing 168 prisoners of *190 Fusilier Battalion* and *2nd Para Division*.

It was perhaps surprising that despite the savage fighting, so many prisoners were put in the bag.

Although the Division now had a few days rest around Nijmegen, the gunners stayed in action supporting 43 Wessex Wyverns and 15th Scottish in their advance on Goch. On the 19th General Montgomery visited the Division to give us a 'pat on the back' wrote Lt Col Crozier, and the Corps Commander Lt General Brian Horrocks sent a message of congratulation.

Some of 'B' Coy. Ox & Bucks after Asperberg battle (John Roberts)

'We [1/5 Welch] remained in Hau just long enough to mingle with the first German civilians', wrote Sgt Machin. 'The invisible barrier between us was striking. No civilian was allowed in the same building, no one must speak to them unless it was in the line of duty.' 1/5 Welch withdrew into Holland to Helmond for their rest. Over 2000 reinforcements had to be integrated into the Division; 4 RWF needed 365, 7 RWF 359, 6 RWF 276, 4 Welch 281, 1 HLI 239, 2 Mons 243, the East Lancs 148, 1/5 Welch 137 and the Ox and Bucks 203.

Private Fred Shepherd had just come from the Royal Artillery to 'C' Coy, Ox and Bucks as a new reinforcement. He had tried to convince the Medical Officer that as he had flat feet he could avoid a transfer to the PBI. 'Your job is to shoot the buggers, not kick them to death', he was told.

Operation Veritable was the massive operation to clear the entire west bank of the Rhine. Although 53rd Welsh Division had achieved first class results, in the Reichwald, they and the rest of the British and Canadian Armies still had many days ahead of ferocious fighting. Der Fuehrer had ordered that the main defences to the German heartland would be on the carefully prepared killing-grounds of the main Siegfried Line between the Reichwald and the Rhine.

By 23 February the flood level of the river Roer had subsided enough for the US Ninth Army to commence Operation Grenade, delayed for two weeks following the destruction of a dam by the Germans. But there was little doubt that the Hochwald Layback, the third line of Siegfried defences was held in strength.

OPERATION LEEK: 'HARD FOUGHT AND COSTLY ACTION'

Weeze was the next major objective. As part of the Canadian First Army with 30 Corps under command, 53 Welsh took part in the second phase of Veritable five miles south-east of Goch; on the river Niers, Weeze, then Hees and Wemb were defended by six enemy battalions, from *7th Parachute Division* and the remnants of *15 Panzer Grenadier Division*. Under command was 8th Armoured Brigade, a squadron of Crocodiles and one of Flails. The artillery support was awe-inspiring. Twelve field regiments plus sixty-four medium and six heavy guns would back up Operation Leek, which was to commence on 24 February. 160 Brigade would lead and advance astride the Goch-Weeze railway and secure bridgeheads over the anti-tank ditch defences. 71 Brigade would pass through and capture Weeze, and 158 Brigade would move on to Hees and Wemb.

The massive bombardment started at 01.30 hrs and continued through the day. The church tower of Weeze was a perfect enemy OP. When 2 Mons on the right of the railway, 6 RWF on the left, started the advance at 06.00 hrs, they met the heaviest shelling since Hill 112 in Normandy. The ground was wet and the water table was only one foot down so that digging slits was very difficult. Splendid support was given by 13/18 Hussars under Major Wormald who lost fourteen out of eighteen tanks to mines or anti-tank fire.

'B' Coy 2 Mons started the attack with 120 men and only forty reached their objectives, with the platoons commanded by L/Corporal J H Christian and Corporal J Hills. Christian led a dashing attack on a fortified farmhouse, fought for two hours and killed or captured eighteen enemy, for which he was awarded the DCM. Pte Warren, who already had the MM, was killed stalking the enemy with an LMG. And Lt W T McCall in his first action was wounded in the head, arms and side leading his men. He refused to be moved until all the other wounded were picked up. There were eight counter-attacks by the enemy paratroopers during the day, defeated by the 2 Mons FOO, Capt D Bishop DCM of 497 Field Bty. Major Lythgoe, OC 'D' Coy, wounded on two previous occasions, was killed as was Capt Purvis. But the Mons stuck at it and by 1230 hrs had killed sixty of *7 Para Division*, captured another 140 prisoners and eventually 4 Welch took over.

The historian of the 6 RWF wrote: 'The battle of Weeze was probably the most hard fought and costly action of the campaign. The flat ground devoid of cover bounded on the right by the main Goch-Weeze road and on the left by the small river Niers. Enemy OPs were on the high ground behind Weeze and in the woods across the river. We encountered heaviest, most accurate artillery fire met since Normandy.' 'B' Coy captured part of the hamlet of Hohendorf and 'C' the second part led by Lt K. E. G. Reid's dashing example.

In hand-to-hand fighting 'C' took 100 prisoners, much arms and equipment. The 13/18 Hussars lost many tanks helping 'D' Coy into the hamlet of Höst. Lt Rowlands was killed in his first action. Major Sharp was wounded by mine blast as was CSM Proctor, but try as they could, the paratroops still held Höst as the attack petered out.

The acting Divisional GOC, Brigadier Elrington ordered up 71 Brigade under the huge barrage to tackle the Höst strongpoint, then Rottum and the first anti-tank ditch. 1 HLI with Crocodiles in support took Höst and gained their objectives, whilst 'C' and 'D' Coys of 6 RWF mopped up in Höst taking seventy-two prisoners, though the last of the defenders held out until daylight.

> In the fierce fighting near Weeze we advanced for 1500 yards by night over open ground, under the beam of searchlights and a heavy artillery barrage. Enemy resistance was extremely well co-ordinated. There was very heavy Spandau, mortar and DF fire with, in addition, dive bombers and an enemy tank. The latter roared about in the darkness on the main road which was the centre line of advance, causing casualties and confusion till it was chased off by some Jock with a Piat. 'B' Coy fought its way through the earthworks and trenches of two small villages which were really large farms and cottages. We took the first set of buildings, re-organised, placed about 20 wounded in a room to the rear and pressed on to the second village. About 0300hrs my Coy CO Major Joe Hamelryke told me to go back and see how the wounded were being evacuated. [Capt Pender, `B' Coy, 1HLI]

Pender found that the cottage with the HLI wounded in it, had been reoccupied by the Germans. In fact six fully armed Germans passed him at arm's distance:

> One of the rear companies later took some 60 prisoners who had gone to ground in the cellar when we initially took the farm in the darkness. They re-appeared, found our wounded, took them down into the cellar where they were well attended by the German orderlies.

The HLI did well. After Höst, they pushed on to Rottum which they captured by 21.00 hrs but could not reach the first of the anti-tank defence ditches. 4 RWF then took over from the HLI in Höst and Rottum.

4 Welch were now given as their objective a star shaped wood between Goch and Weeze. Passing through 2 Mons, 'D' Coy led and by 18.00 hrs had seized the wood. Extremely heavy German DF fire fell on them. They dug and dug for survival but with a one foot water table, they had to stand in water. There were many casualties. Major A. J. Lewis, OC 'D'

Coy had to tie up the defences both within his own company and with his neighbours:

> To get to the second platoon I had to wade through the swamp and I couldn't find the third platoon at all in the dark. Four mortar bombs Landed close to me, one only two yards away. The Bren gun carrier and my jeep had already gone back to the RAP loaded with wounded, as also had the stretcher bearers. Every spare man was helping our own wounded.

At about midnight 'B' Coy were attacked by infantry supported by flamethrowers — not the Germans, but 'one of our own Brigade'. For two days and two nights 4 Welch stayed under fire in their star shaped wood.

By 08.00 hrs on the 25th, 71st Brigade despite heavy casualties had fought their way to within a mile of Weeze. The Ox and Bucks were ordered to take 'the' wood beyond Rottum. In the darkness, there was great confusion and the *wrong* wood was captured. So a new plan was made to capture the correct wood. Heavy DF shellfire caused forty-two casualties including Lt Paget who had just been awarded the DSO for his Asperberg action a week earlier. Private Desmond Milligan recalled: 'One night we put in an attack on another wood. This time we were fired in by two Churchill tanks, their big Besa MGs pouring streams of orange-yellow tracer fire into the trees ahead of us. I was placed on killing ground duty. As they emerged you got them.'

Throughout the 25th the Division made little progress but remained under constant counter-attacks.

After a day and night of non-stop fighting two diminished battalions of *15 Panzer Grenadier Regt* and a company of parachutists had been killed or captured. But their resistance was incredible, as Captain Pender 1 HLI recounts:

> To add to the general confusion, a large party of Germans attempted to attack 'B' Coy in the flank [at Rottum]. They climbed into assault boats and were halfway across to our side of the river Niere, when they were spotted and engaged by the company Bren gunners. Their boats were sunk and numerous casualties inflicted on them. The survivors made the eastern bank while the casualties were swept away in the swollen river before first light.

But 300 prisoners were in the bag in the first twenty-four hours of Operation Leek.

Corporal Bert Isherwood of 13 FDS commented in his diary on the severity of the fighting:

Saturday, 24th February. Div in action again, the thunder of the guns rising as we near the Goch supply point. The grapevine at supply say that the battle is to take Weeze and advance to Kevelaer. Traffic is heavy, ammo, equipment, troops and supplies going up and wounded soldiers coming back. The medical units are busy. Sunday, 25th. The battle rages forward, 53 Div is having a hard time, large numbers of casualties are coming back, the FAs and FDSs are busy. The way forward and the way back is littered with dead and the debris of war. A shambles of destruction, the near distance thick with smoke and shot through with the flashes of the guns and the blasts of incessant explosions. An infantry supply NCO tells me that the Div has about fought itself to a standstill before Weeze and that the Ox and Bucks have suffered badly, many of their wounded in 13 FDS.

The plan to attack Weeze from the north was now given to the 71st Brigade, which was to take over the whole divisional front. 1 HLI took over Rottum from 4 RWF and the wood where the Ox and Bucks had lost so many company commanders. 8th Armoured Brigade lent their 12 KRRC motorised-infantry battalion to take over from 4 RWF and 2 Mons. So Operation Daffodil came into being. It was of course very complicated. 160 Brigade would take over the 3rd British Division bridgehead (one and-a-half miles north-east of Weeze) over the Muhlen Fleuth stream about one mile north-east of Weeze. On the night of 28 February/1 March 158 Brigade would pass through this bridgehead area, cross the river Niers *south* of Weeze — and then capture Weeze! Sgt Machin, Intelligence Sgt 1/5 Welch: 'The 71 Brigade were concerned solely with a direct attack on the north of Weeze. An anti-tank ditch formed a major obstacle. Our 160 Brigade was deployed to make an assault-crossing of the River Niers and attack Weeze from the east. 7 RWF and 1st East Lancs were committed to the assault, ourselves in reserve.'

6 RWF sent a recce party into the very exposed 3rd Division bridgehead at the moment when the enemy counter-attacked and five key officers were killed or wounded. Major Hughes, Capt Owen, Capt Griffith, Capt Brodrick and Lt Bodenham. At a stroke they were written off — a disaster. Nevertheless, 'A', 'D' and 'C' Coys secured the Muhlen Fleuth bridgehead — an area about the size of a football pitch. 'B' Coy made a gallant effort to enlarge the bridgehead but were virtually cut off until 4 Welch came up on their right to help.

The second phase of the attack on Weeze from the east was made by 7 RWF and 4 Welch supported by Sherman tanks of the Sherwood Rangers, out of the bridgehead. They reached within a few hundred yards of the river Niers but were held up. Captain J. D. Cuthbertson, 7 RWF: 'Forward companies on St David's Day with leeks being bravely worn on every helmet, now in exposed positions, were heavily shelled and mortared. Bn

HQ was accurately registered by SP guns. Lt Col Dickson with unbelievable composure continued to lead and encourage the Bn.'

Corporal David Henderson and 'Bud' Abbot, 'C' Sqn, Recce Regt were part of Robinforce:

> We were flank protection to 158 Brigade, crossed the Muhlen Fleuth. The small bridge was under fire so we waited for an opportune moment between salvoes. The bodies of men felled in previous action were still lying where they had fallen. We finally reached a small copse and 'dug-in'. It was an edgy nervous night peering into the blackness. The ten of us felt extremely vulnerable. At dawn a hail of 'airburst' shells fell directly on our copse. We were unable to get any grub — all we could do was to grovel in our holes, not even able to retaliate and wait for relief.

The Manchesters played their part as Lt Col Crozier reported: 'March 1st. I put 1000 phosphorous bombs into Weeze today and set it well alight. I hope the Bosch found it hot. Our attack came to a stop about 10.00 hrs. 158 Bde on first objective but 71 Bde only partly successful and had very heavy casualties. March 2nd. Division is just about dead beat.'

71 Brigade's attack on the northern flank between the railway track, the main road and the river Niers was held up short of Weeze by flooding, heavy DF fire and anti-tank ditches. The Ox and Bucks were astride the Goch-Weeze railway and 4 RWF east of the railway supported by 4/7th Royal Dragoon Guards tanks. The Fusiliers had a very difficult time and only just succeeded in taking and holding a vital canal to the north of Weeze at Graf. During the battle for Weeze, 82 Assault Sqn RE made two vital 'crossings' of the anti-tank ditches with an 'Assault' bridge and a 'skid' Bailey bridge both essential for the 8th Armoured Brigade tanks to get across. Lt Birkin Haward's dramatic sketches show his AVREs hard at work under fire by 'Monty's Moonlight'. The various phase lines of Operation Daffodil were named Radnor, Clyde and Lancs after the formation entrusted with each.

For the fighting on St David's Day all the Royal Welch Fusilier battalions wore leeks in their hats/steel helmets — a miracle of QM supply. 4 RWF had two anti-tank ditches to bridge and clear. The leading platoons of 'A' and 'B' Coys each carried 30 feet of Kapok bridging for the first ditch. With the brilliant moon, burning houses and artificial moonlight by searchlights, the scene was as bright as day. The leading platoons of 'B' Coy struggled across flat open ploughed fields under heavy fire. Sgt Parry led 12 Platoon across the first Kapok bridge and Major Humphreys Roberts set up his Coy HQ in a cellar. 'C' and 'D' Coys also crossed at 02.30 hrs and AVREs laid a scissors bridge for supporting tanks. Major Davis commanding 'A' Coy was

Above left: Fusilier Fred Smerdon, 4 RWF

Above right: Lt Col Hanmer & Major Gaade, 4 RWF (Fred Smerdon)

killed leading his men but Major Gaade, 'D' Coy with two tanks reached the second anti-tank ditch. 'C' Coy pushed two platoons across as Major Tim Dumas relates:

> I led 'C' through 'B'. When we got to the first ditch there was a lot of resistance and heavy fire coming at us. I remember thinking that if we lay down, I would never get the men upon their feet again, so we moved straight through 'B' towards the second ditch. There was a cottage 60 yards outside of the ditch which the bulk of the Coy reached. I was told there was an undug track or bridge across it. With my batman Fusilier Harry we climbed down and groping around found the instantaneous fuse set to blow it up. We broke all we could find. I moved Coy HQ back to the cottage, with radio reported the situation to Bn HQ. At about first light the Germans put in a counter-attack with tanks on the unblown crossing. I saw a tank coming straight for our cottage HQ, infantry with them. We called for SOS fire. At that point our cottage was full of Germans. Some ten of us were marched back through *our* SOS fire to a large castle, Div, even Corps HQ with roof and walls covered in Red Crosses.

Tim Dumas spent the next three weeks in a prison camp near Hanover, but on
23rd March: 'Our own guards became our prisoners.' The formidable counter-
attack with three Royal Tiger tanks and 100 infantry was eventually driven back
by DF fire and Major Gaade and Major de Brett's gallant defences. Although
over 100 German prisoners were taken, 4 RWF lost 28 killed, 93 wounded and
39 missing. It had been a hard drawn-out fight.

The enemy, almost encircled by the swift progress on the north-east by
160 and 158 Brigades (and the small composite 'Robinforce' of Recce and
Sherwood Ranger tanks), was now withdrawing rapidly. So the East Lancs
and Robinforce were sent to make a left flanking hook to try to cut off
the Weeze garrison about two miles south of the town. Throughout the 1-2
March the East Lancs struggled through woods, losing sixty-nine casualties
on the way to reach the river Niers. The bridge of course was down but three
companies forded the river, having dealt with the hamlets of Kambeckshof,
Rahmenhof and Tilshof. During the capture of Bussenhof, Major 'shorty'
Bain died of wounds, Lt Wignall was killed and Corporal King, though
wounded on three occasions continued to take part in close-quarter fighting.
During the night of 1/2 March 1 HLI patrol found Weeze clear of the enemy.
'The end of the battle for Weeze was an anti-climax, as the enemy pulled
out in the mist. We advanced [Capt. Pender 'B' Coy] into the ghost town of
mines, boobytraps, utter destruction and desolation.' And the East Lancs in

An AVRE Skid Bailey bridge being launched in the attack on Weeze: 28 February – 1
March 1945 (Birkin Hayward)

assault boats got across the river to Schloss Neuehaus and Loeskenshof, and there joined up with 1 HLI. 160 Brigade continued to mop up north-east and east of Weeze, but after nearly a week's hard fighting Operations Leek and Daffodil were completed. Weeze, a really difficult stronghold had been taken — with heavy losses.

British Churchill Crocodile tank belching flame

Shattered village of La Roche (Ardennes) – scene of fierce fighting (Harrison Standley)

16

The end of Veritable: in sight of the Rhine

A few miles east, 3rd British Division were moving in parallel through Kervenheim and 52nd Lowland Division were on the right flank. The pressures on the retreating German battle groups were immense. So 53rd Welsh were directed on Kevelaer, then south-east to Geldern, and east to Issum and Alpen. The American Ninth Army were advancing strongly from the south on a converging course.

On 2 March, 'A' Sqn Recce Regt protected 8th Armoured Brigade flank as it advanced to Kevelaer, scouring the woods with foot and mobile patrols. The Ox and Bucks travelling in Kangaroos went through battered Weeze and Neuhaus towards Kevelaer. On the way SPs and an 88 mm gun, minefields and cratered road held things up, in pitch dark and belting rain. Desmond Milligan driving a Weasel skirted a huge cavity in the road and came across two vintage 1939 MK III German tanks. The following morning Kevelaer was found abandoned except for twenty-two Volksturm prisoners, but boobytraps in houses caused four casualties. Corporal Jim Wilsdon, 'D' Coy was one of them: 'stengun under my right arm. I pushed the door open with my left hand. There was a blinding flash and explosion. I was thrown back into the street, unable to see or hear. Two of the other lads were injured by the blast.' Jim lost several fingers, regained his sight, but needed twenty-seven grafting operations. When 1 HLI passed through on Kangaroos to continue the advance, a German SP gun knocked out four, causing heavy casualties.

Lt J. Gardiner's Recce Troop pushed on south a distance of ten miles to reach Geldern and met up with the US 35th Infantry Division at 14.50 hrs. 'A' Sqn, Recce Regt also cleared Wemb, Twisterden and Lullinger on the right/western flank. The East Lancs cleared Veert where Major E. M. Morrison, 'C' Coy also met the Yanks moving north under Operation Grenade. They also captured a surprisingly docile German colonel. The enemy had pulled out of Geldern by early morning of the 4th. Two of the four bridges were intact and the Sappers soon replaced the other two. The mixed force of Recce, Ox and Bucks and 8th Armoured Brigade Shermans reached Issum soon after noon.

The Ox and Bucks Pioneers had plenty of dangerous work clearing minefields and booby-trapped houses. Lt Moore and Sgt Shephard were a very professional clearance team. In Issum the battalion occupied the town whilst Sappers built or rebuilt bridges for the armour to cross the Nennefer Fleuth. Battalion HQ moved into the local brewery. The manager was persuaded to open every door himself. He then produced several crates of his special brew. He must have realised that the Panzer Grenadiers were not coming back. Several bridges over the river Zen were blown and a set-piece attack was needed to force a bridgehead. 'B' and 'D' Coys 4 RWF attacked at 20.30 hrs. But during a night of heavy fighting a counter-attack forced 'B' Coy back causing twelve casualties. 1 HLI were on the right flank and Major R. S. Nisbet, 'A' Coy, was killed and his unit badly mauled. By 07.00 hrs on the 5th the Sappers put a scissors bridge across. Once again the German *21st Parachute Regt* had shown what superb troops they were. At 08.00 hrs the divisional artillery broke up another determined counter-attack. The Acting Divisional Commander, Brigadier Elrington ordered 71 Brigade to push out of the Issum bridgehead towards Alpen, five miles to the east with 158 Brigade to come through to help clear Die Leucht Forest south of Alpen. On the left flank was the Guards Armoured Division, and on the right, 35 US Division. 1/5 Welch attacked through 1 HLI at 16.30 hrs and had soon captured 130 prisoners and reached the south-west corner of the forest when 1 East Lancs continued the advance. One unusual event occurred, when Major C. S. Campbell, FOO of the 83rd Field Regt, taking his duties seriously, joined in the bayonet charge over open ground which put many Germans into the bag. But Capt N. D. Squire, another FOO, dismounted from his carrier to look for a route, when his driver, Bombardier May, struck a mine which wrecked the carrier. The damage was mainly under Squire's seat! When 7 RWF passed through the bridgehead to continue the attack, their CO Lt Col Dickson was fatally wounded. Major M. R. Saunders, the FOO of 460 Battery, took charge of the battalion which continued the attack and took another 200 prisoners. Major Saunders was regarded as 'one of the family' and awarded the DSO and privileged to wear the Royal Welch Fusiliers Flash as a token of the close liaison between battery and battalion. Captain Dick Cuthbertson, 7 RWF, relates:

When Norman Havard was wounded I took over as Adjutant. On 6th March news came through that the CO, Lt Col G F T B Dickson had been killed. At the end of a day's fighting he had gone forward to see if the leading companies were settling down. All four Company Commanders were engaged. There was no 2 i/c at the time so Major Bill Saunders our Gunner Battery Commander took over immediate command. Col Dickson had been a very popular and brave CO and his loss was felt keenly by all ranks. Bill Saunders received an 'immediate' award of the DSO for his timely action.

Beyond the Issum bridgehead the East Lancs moved up the main road at 2000 hrs and in the clearance of Pottershof, SP guns and mines caused thirty-five casualties and many vehicles, including eight carriers were destroyed. But the *21st Fallschirmjaeger Regt* now put up a very determined defence — first of Issum, secondly of Alpen and its neighbouring forest.

For most of the 6 March, 160 Brigade with 13/18th Hussars tanks under command battled on the right flank of 158 Brigade, and on the left flank of the Americans towards the Bonninghardt plateau which was to the west of Alpen. Leading the attack were 2 Mons, who debussed 500 yards east of Issum at dawn and passed through the East Lancs at 08.00 hrs. SP guns and minefields took their toll but five hours later at a cost of fourteen killed and fifty-seven wounded they had killed sixty and taken eighty prisoners. The 13/18th Hussars lost three Shermans in their support. The Alpen feature was a heather and wood covered height overlooking the Rhine to the east. The 4 Welch made a silent attack at 13.45 hrs with artillery on call. The thick woods screened the wireless and SP guns and mortars caused casualties with awful 'stonks'. Every company met desperate resistance from paratroops hidden in the forest. 'C' Coy in their final assault on the ridge suffered very heavily and Majors Clements and Jones were wounded. The OC, CSM and all except one of the platoon officers and sergeants of 'C' Coy were amongst their forty-five casualties. Both FOOs of 133 Field Regt were wounded, Capt J. S. Mills and Lt D. J. Bibby, but 4 Welch took their objectives and captured sixty-three prisoners. CSM Pat Cullen relates a curious incident near Alpen:

We were being shelled from behind our own lines, but knew of no British battery in that area. My Company Commander took his jeep to investigate and I went with him. We went well behind our lines along a compass bearing which had been taken as the shells came over. We eventually arrived in an American area where we heard gunfire ahead. On receiving permission to move on we found a battery of heavy guns deployed near woods with some tents nearby with officers in them. My officer asked at the nearest tent for the officer in charge and was shown to the next tent in which a Major sat drinking coffee. My officer introduced himself and asked if he could be shown the co-ordinates on which the guns were firing. The Major looked up and said, 'Why worry, it's all Germany in that direction.' My officer, somewhat annoyed said, 'Are you aware Major that there are British soldiers, my own men getting wounded by your indiscriminate gunfire?' The American, lost for words for a moment, replied, 'Why hasn't it been reported to me before?' What could one say to such a man? But at least we stopped them firing.

At 17.40 hrs 6 RWF passed through the right flank of 4 Welch with 35 US Division only 3000 yards away to the south-east. Peter Utley was a Divisional Liaison Officer and served with various units as contact for Divisional General Staff. At the battle for Geldern on 6-7 March, he wrote: 'Our forward troops had reached a river. The main fire was coming from the other side from US patrols and vehicles. The main bridges were blown. I was instructed to accompany a Staff Colonel (not 53rd Division) to make direct contact.' Although treated with scant courtesy and great suspicion, they arrived at an American tented camp. 'Would the US Army kindly stop shooting at the British Army so we could both get on with the war!'

Against light opposition 6 RWF reached the objective an hour later. They fended off several fighting patrols during the night and the area west of the Alpache Ley was clear of enemy at dawn on the 7th. Fortunately orders came through that 52 Lowland Division were to be responsible for the capture of Alpen, now just a mile away. The relief was complicated and took two days. 71 Brigade moved back to Holt, and by the 10th when Major General 'Bobby' Ross returned from sick leave he found his division between the Goch-Venlo road and the river Maas. 53rd Division had been in continuous action for nearly a month and was the *only* British formation to fight throughout the battle of the Rhineland without relief. No wonder that the news of harbour parties moving off to the *Brussels* area was greeted with enthusiasm. On the 7 March 2 Mons mopped up forty prisoners and when the TCVs arrived plus hot tea and rum everyone began singing 'Lili Marlene', 'Don't Fence Me In' and a score of cheerful wartime songs. During Veritable they had had 300 casualties including a third sick due to the appalling hard, wet conditions.

'On 12th March after the battle died away, we were withdrawn from the front line and went into harbour west of Brussels. Great was the activity in the Bn. A vast consignment of Blanco arrived. Adjutants and RSMs parades became the order of the day,' Capt Pender, 1 HLI, recalled:

> Blue Patrols, Tartan Trews, Kilts and Glengarry were unpacked from long forgotten trunks in 'B' Echelon. Dan Bonar, the QM produced hundreds of *new* battle dresses, Kilmarnock Bonnets and lots of other luxuries. The Pipe Band and Archie Wilson's sitting-down band came to the fore with Retreats and Concerts. Battalion officers and Sergeants Messes reformed. I met people again I hadn't seen for six weeks. A great atmosphere prevailed throughout the unit.

The 'rest' activities included football, other sports, minor training, cinemas, hot baths and showers *and* evening passes to the fleshpots of Brussels. Visits were made to the field of the battle of Waterloo. Belated ceremonies of St David's Day were held. There were Church Parades galore when prayers were said for the 1200 casualties incurred during Veritable. The HLI Pipe Band played and many well-earned decorations were awarded.

Lt Col H. W. Tyler became the new CO of 7 RWF, and Lt Col C. F. Hutchinson of 6 RWF as Lt Col Exham was evacuated through ill health. And hundreds of young 18 and 19 year old 'green' reinforcements poured in, many quite unprepared for the final campaign in the heart of Germany.

The Dragons Teeth – Westwall–Siegfried Line (Harrison Standley)

17

Operation Plunder: Across the Rhine

On 23 March the Division, perhaps a little reluctantly, prised itself away from the fleshpots of Brussels back to their old stamping grounds in the Rhineland, around Kevelaer and Weeze. Monty had decided that his two Scottish divisions were rather good at assault landings, although neither 15th Scottish nor 51st Highland had participated in the D-Day landings. So they were to be the assault divisions for Operation Plunder — the forcing of the Rhine — and eventually seize the heartland of Das Reich. Lt General Ritchie's XII Corps would then exploit the Rhine bridgehead, and 53rd Welsh would breakout across the river Issel, advance east and capture Bocholt, Stadtlohn, Ahaus, Gronau and Borken. A massive airborne lift backed by a large ferocious barrage should subdue the east bank defences and lead to the capture of Wesel.

The Divisional gunners had been in action for thirty-six hours, 83rd Field at Ginderich, 133rd Field at Gest sheltered by the huge smoke screens. They fired targets to help 17 US Airborne Division, as well as 15th Scottish and 1 Commando Brigade. An American Liberator crew baled out and wanted to know the way back to Ipswich which they had left ninety minutes previously.

About 5pm on 26 March, 158 Brigade crossed the Rhine opposite Vynen on a class 12 bridge and the rest of the Division by a class 40 bridge at Xanten. By dawn on the 28th, 71st and 158 Brigades were concentrated north of Wesel and 160 Brigade between Wesel and Bocholt, west of Hamminkeln.

'The Regiment [81 Welch Field] remained on the west bank of the Rhine. All along the river banks were smoke generators providing a screen to hide the preparations and so we [Gunner Wally Brereton & CO] lived in a perpetual fog.' On D-Day minus one, large formations of RAF bombers came over and wiped out the town of Wesel in less than an hour. The bombers were followed by swarms of planes carrying paratroopers or towing gliders. The last waves dropped extra supplies and in true Airborne tradition dropped some in the wrong place. Within a few hours of crossing the Rhine, Wally 'saw a British Paratrooper astride a large farm horse. Brave chaps, these Airborne — you would never get me on a horse. He gave us all a wave and a smile as he passed.

Scenes during Operation Plunder

The fields were littered with discarded parachutes and wrecked gliders.' Wally slept that night in a glider, 'very much askew, but clean and dry'.

160 Brigade now led, crossed the river Issel just west of Ringenberg, advanced north and 6 RWF captured Dingden at midnight on 27th/28th. They had bivouacked the night before in the centre of an airdrop at Hamminkeln littered with hundreds of gliders, some with broken backs, others burnt out, bright with coloured parachutes, so coloured scarves became the order of the day. But from Ringenberg the tanks were bogged down and heavy shelling dropped on 'D' Coy causing casualties. Sgt Roberts led his platoon gallantly and won the MM and despite intense 88 mm airburst Dingden was taken. A very pretty Polish girl was liberated from a German farm in the village and the battalion 2 i/c took a keen personal interest in her!

The attack on Bocholt, an important road centre with many narrow streets, roadblocks and minefields would need a full scale divisional attack. Supported by 4 Armoured Brigade Shermans 158 Brigade would make a left flank move through woods to seize the hamlet of Harks on the Bocholt-Werth road, whilst 2nd Mons on the left, 6 RWF on the right would jointly make a direct assault.

Bombards (AVREs) in Bocholt, 82 Assault Sqdn RE (Birkin Hayward)

The 2 Mons led to clear the outer defences and 6 RWF then pushed through the RAF damaged town to the banks of the river Aa. The leading tanks were blown up on a minefield, but Lt A. Owen 'B' Coy dashed across the partly demolished road bridge at the head of his men and won the MC for it. Under heavy mortar fire a bridgehead was established, two companies of 4 Welch helped and 4 Armoured Brigade tanks passed through the next day. On the left flank the East Lancs and 7 RWF using fire and movement skilfully took all their objectives. But the East Lancs near the town of Bielefield were counter-attacked and Major F. O. Cetre was wounded and CSM Montgomery killed. Pte W. Pickard, a regimental stretcher-bearer, brought many of the forty-three casualties back to relative safety. Sgt C. Hatton then knocked out a Mk IV tank. The opposition was a curious mixture of aggressive SP guns and tanks and elderly Volkssturm (Home Guard). Anyway, the East Lancs took a record score of 133 prisoners during the day.
Major J. E. M. Dugdale, 7 RWF:

> Our left flank protection met some minor interference from Spandaus and mines and a troublesome SP gun. AP shells did some peculiar things round Bn HQ buildings. Norman Havard was wounded and Dick Cuthbertson took over as adjutant. The next day we could see enemy mortars firing just in front of us, which our Gunners quickly liquidated.

To the east of Dingden and Bocholt a mixed force of Recce and 4 RWF had been operating on the flank. They were under the command of 4th Armoured Brigade; 4 RWF mounted in Kangaroos fought four successful actions in three days ending up on the Hohe Heide high ground overlooking Bocholt. A troop of 'B' Sqn, Recce had a spectacular success rushing a bridge, but German resistance in Bocholt in the northern factory area continued until 1 HLI cleared during the night 30/31 March.

The next task was for 71st Brigade to lead towards Gronau thirty miles north-east via Winterswijk (just inside Holland) and Vreden. The Recce patrolled to the west of the main road, reached Bredevoort in Holland some seven miles ahead and 'A' Squadron had two actions including a nice little ambush. 'C' Sqn on the right of the axis had more problems with map reading than with the foe. The HLI moved up the main road with the Ox and Bucks on the right near the railway line. Wally Brereton, 81st Field Regt RA:

> At Bocholt the infantry [HLI] split up combing the town for snipers and rearguard groups… to the east of Bocholt we parted company with the friendly tanks as they took a different route. The long columns of the Highland Light Infantry filed out of the town and into the open countryside. Skirmishes continued all morning. Everybody was firing and ducking. The situation was too fluid for the use of artillery support and we all joined in the shooting. These encounters ended when half the Germans surrendered and the rest ran away to fight another day. If they pinned us down with the odd MG we would call up an armoured car of the Recce Regt. A young German deserter attached himself to us like a stray dog. We let him ride on the back of Roger Fox carrier.

A German SP ambushed Desmond Milligan's Ox and Bucks carrier group. The lead tank was brewed up and the eight Kangaroos following were hit and burned, three still full of troops:

> As we ran to help, flames poured out of these Kangaroos. Men were tumbling out, screaming and burning, others trying to beat out the flames of their burning comrades. It was a terrible sight. Lt Col Howard drove up in his jeep [he was driving] to help in the rescue. He returned with several of the burned soldiers wrapped up in bandages and looking like Egyptian mummies. Casualties amounted to thirty. The SP had successfully delayed us, had pulled out and gone.

SP guns also knocked out three Recce cars. By nightfall 1 HLI and the Ox and Bucks were on the outskirts of Winterswijk, so 4 RWF were sent forward late on the 30th but found the bridge over the Slinger Beek blown. Major

Hocquard led 'C' Coy across the river and by dawn were being given a great Dutch welcome with flags and bunting blossoming in the windows. It was a curious situation. A few hundred yards west of the frontier scenes of genuine liberation, and to the other eastern side, fierce mobile rearguard actions and sullen, dispirited occupants in their smashed German villages. On the far right 2 Mons were part of a regimental group with 44 RTR making good progress on a parallel axis Rhede, Stadtlohn and Oding on the Dutch frontier.

The Sappers repaired the main bridge over the Slinger Beek and the Recce led 1 HLI towards Vreden, found to be free of the enemy, but the river Berkel bridge had been destroyed. By the evening of the 31st the Highlanders had advanced another three miles on the road to Gronau before 88mms and infantry held them up. Capt Pender: 'We had repeated engagements outside each small town, and villages on river lines and canals. The enemy often put up tremendous resistance in endeavours to make the rearguard deploy and waste time. The bravery of some of their individual soldiers and small units were outstanding.' When the Recce entered Vreden they acquired a warehouse full of eggs. Everyone in the regiment had at least one Easter egg.

On Easter Day, 1 April, 4 RWF passed through 1 HLI quickly occupied Alstatte and exploited another four miles, without much opposition and were closely followed by 158 Brigade. Bud Abbot, 'C' Sqn Recce Regt went half left to explore Enschede:

> Rumours of 300-400 Germans making for the village. We took up positions in the dark and heard the sound of marching feet from our rear. We naturally assumed they were our own Division troops catching up. How wrong we were. The enemy had circled round and come in from our rear not knowing we were there. Lower down the road all hell let loose, people were shouting and a German halftrack with an ack-ack type gun mounted on top was firing away over open sights.

Bud nipped smartly into the nearest house, grenade at the ready, to be joined by 'Nev' Thomas from his own troop, blithely whistling a classical music tune. But 'C' Sqn lost Phillips and Waddington in that chaotic night. Corporal David Henderson and Trooper Parish fired rifles, Bren and Piat during the wild encounter.

The 1/5 Welch with 3rd/4th County of London Yeomanry tanks in the lead, intended to thrust north to Gronau and turn east to Ochtrupp.

> After travelling for 1½ miles out of Alstatte we ran into the Bosch and his precious 88mm gun. The ambush was about 1½ miles SW of Gronau and the leading tank was brewed up. 'C' and 'B' companies deployed but, SP guns opened up,

killed Lt Carey and wounded Lt Dawe and five others. When 'B' Coy emerged from the wood, bazooka, shell and flak gun fire caused another eight casualties. Nobody slept that night. As well as 88mms the Bosch pressed 20mm flak guns into service. It was like a fireworks display with the various colours of the small ack-ack shells. [Sgt Machin]

New orders arrived for 1/5 Welch to cross the river Dinkel, secure Kloster-Epe and then turn north towards Gronau. The East Lancs had reached Vreden in Germany and in Kangaroos went through Alstatte back into Holland to liberate Glanerbrug. Battalion HQ was in the police station and the local resistance movement was soon hard at work — forcibly shaving the heads of the local girls too warmly inclined to their recent masters.

Brigadier Wilsey now ordered an attack on Gronau for early on the morning of 2 April. The small garrison was quickly mopped up. The East Lancs were charged by a horse-drawn 88 mm gun. Its crew were quickly dealt with and despite snipers, Gronau was quickly taken. The first of many large hospitals was discovered, that in Gronau containing more than 700 German wounded. Early the next morning 7 RWF led across the river Epe bridge along the main road in the direction of Rheine. Major J. E. M. Dugdale:

> The next move took us through Bocholt into Holland again for a brief stay in the pleasant town of Winterswijk. Soon on the move again for the attack on Ochtrup. The advance was very slow owing to mines and SP guns on the flanks. The enemy pulled out after dark and we occupied the town in the small hours of the morning. We met there the first big circular road blocks. Luckily they had not been rolled into position.

On the same day, 3 April, Lt Col J. S. Morrison-Jones, CO 1/5 Welch, with his IO were out on a recce. Their jeep ran over a mine on the verge and the CO was fatally wounded. Their padre said of him, 'Not until he left us did we realise how much we loved him'. The 2 i/c, Major Bowker took command.

Field Marshall Montgomery visited Divisional HQ at Ochtrup on the next day. 71st Brigade were clearing around Gronau, 158 Brigade around Ochtrup and 160 Brigade (2 Mons, 6 RWF) clearing the airfield west of Rheine. Captain Reynolds, 2 i/c 'B' Sqn Recce Regt, ran into a hornets' nest at Over Dinkel near Gronau. Major Williams, the Sqn Leader, surprised an 88 mm crew and with his pistol and Sgt Bell's Bren took them by surprise: 'We shot up 6 or 7 before things began to settle down to a good battle. Capt Pitts used his double-barrelled shotgun to good effect. The Assault Troop attacked the village school, a strongpoint. They then had a ding-dong struggle against parachutists with Spandaus.' After some hours 'B' Sqn retired with honour, taking thirty prisoners and discovering twenty dead the next day for six non-serious wounded. 'A' Sqn helped 2 Mons to clear the Rheine aerodrome. 2 Mons then went on to take Salzbergen on the river Ems, supported by Royal Scots Greys tanks. Although defended by 20 mm flak guns, twenty-six prisoners were taken and many guns captured.

160 Brigade moved to Neuenkirchen, short of Rheine on the Dortmund-Ems canal. Although the armour was over the river and canal the key airfield, north of the town was the next objective. 6 RWF, helped by the Manchesters, Recce and 5th RDG (the Skins from the Desert Rats), plus the Mons, took out two roadblocks, and despite severe ground opposition, cleared the airfield. In a huge state of alertness, movement was spotted in the extensive woods — a herd of red deer who provided abundant fresh meat (albeit out of season). Many Russian prisoners, and wretched Displaced Persons (in effect slaves on German farms) now started to appear. A hospital yielded thirty Italian wounded and an RAF Sgt Pilot. 160 Brigade temporarily under command of 52 Lowland Division remained near Wettringen.

Away to the right 7th Armoured Division were going ahead fast on a parallel axis, so 158 Brigade moved to protect their flank from Ochtrup towards Wettringen. The East Lancs took Rotenberge and Ohne despite a wide variety of booby-traps. By the 5 April the Division was established on the line Gronau-Ochtrup-Saltzbergen. Their new role was to relieve 7th Armoured Division by putting two brigades into the Ibbenburen sector. And 160 Brigade would operate under 52nd Lowland Division in clearing the Rheine area. The three armoured divisions — 11th (Black Bull) was heading for the Baltic — the Desert Rats for Hamburg, flanked by the Guards Armoured and the indomitable 6th Airborne Division.

Lt Col Burden, historian of the East Lancs, wrote: 'signs of prolonged strain had already begun to appear. Slower reactions in the individual; a marked increase in cases of "battle exhaustion" and a slower standard of battle efficiency. It applied particularly to the more seasoned veterans, whose personal example and steadying influence were so essential.'

In the four weeks up to 7 March the Division had 3,700 casualties of whom a fifth were psychiatric casualties suffering from battle stress. There were not enough battle trained and experienced NCOs in the rifle companies.

The seven battalions of young officer cadets and middle-aged very experienced Hanoverian troops ensconced in the Teutoberger Wald near Ibbenburen had defied the cream of the British Army for five days. The infantry brigade of 11th Armoured had taken a beating on 31 March/1 April when Corporal Chapman of 3 Mons won the Victoria Cross. Eventually their brand new Comet tanks were ordered to bypass the Hannoverians. On the north-west flank the Desert Rats had a go. The RAF bombed. Medium and heavy artillery bombarded the cadets and still they hung on defiantly. 53rd

Division were given the task of mopping up the cadets around Ibbenburen supported by 7 RTR Crocodiles and a heavy barrage. At 21.00 hrs 71 Brigade with 1 HLI on the right, 4 RWF on the left advanced over the canal-bridgehead towards the railway line. Major Leiper's Coy of 1 HLI had a two hour battle for the level crossing. 'A' and 'D' Coys of 4 RWF took their objective, and by first light 'C' Coy Ox and Bucks cleared the town as Desmond Milligan recalls:

> We made a house to house search through this now battered little town, constantly dodging the shells lobbed into the area by artillery supporting the cadets. About eight enormous very tall trees had blocked the road and stopped the tanks the previous night. An armoured bulldozer came up to move them and our carriers were given the job of protection. Two German officers carrying a white flag appeared. Lt Hawley led two of us to take possession of a hospital full of Allied wounded.

When they arrived a ragged cheer went up, 'wounded lay and sat everywhere some so heavily bandaged you could hardly see them'. The Brigade captured 370 prisoners for the loss of only thirty-three casualties.

The East Lancs now led the advances from north of Ibbenburen towards the Ems-Weser Canal east of Steinbeck. During the day they suffered thirty casualties but sent back ninety-two youthful prisoners to the Divisional Cage to cool off. It was an eventful day for Major Duxbury's 'D' Coy. Lt Jack Hirst was mortally wounded by a panzerfaust, Capt Coker did some sniping, the supporting Crocodiles shot up the house occupied by 16 Platoon, but fortunately the liquid failed to ignite. 'In a whirlwind advance across the fields we killed about forty Germans and took 58 PW, plus fifteen wounded picked up later. Private Shackleton had his wounds dressed by a German VAD who mysteriously popped up with a First-Aid box, behaved very courageously in the burning house under the fire of her own countrymen.' But both bridges over the Muhlen stream were blown. On reaching the Munster State Forest, the East Lancs moved towards the canal bridge at Kampen. 1/5 Welch tried to capture the Steinbeck Canal bridge and two other Ems-Weser bridges but all predictably were blown. 7 RWF also reached the canal by the evening of the 6th. Hosts of liberated French, Polish and Russian prisoners were streaming westwards, mostly on foot. They meticulously saluted anyone whom they took to be a British officer. The Recce Regiment were now based on Westerkappeln — as was Division HQ — six miles north-west of Osnabruck. 'C' Sqn guarded a fourteen mile stretch of the canal near Mettingen and Sgt A. Edwards, 'A' Sqn Assault troop, captured four officers and 123 young cadets who foolishly had strayed from their weapons. 71 Brigade moved south of Bramsche to guard the various canal crossings and collect stragglers. The Ox and Bucks were billeted in lovely timber-framed farmhouses in Venne where their CO, Lt Col Henry Howard with his IO and FOO were ambushed and had to make a run for it leaving secret papers behind in the staff car.

On 7 April the East Lancs lost another twelve casualties. Lt Co Burden wrote: 'Only 21 PW taken. The Nazi cadets seemed to prefer death to capture, exposing themselves to the full blast of MGs or flamejets from the Crocodiles, as they chanted Nazi slogans to the last, obstinately determined to die for Adolf Hitler. The party propaganda worked on impressionable young minds.' 160 Brigade now took over from a brigade of 52 Lowland Division in the Rheine-Hopsten and Dreirwalde area ten miles north-west of Ibbenburen.

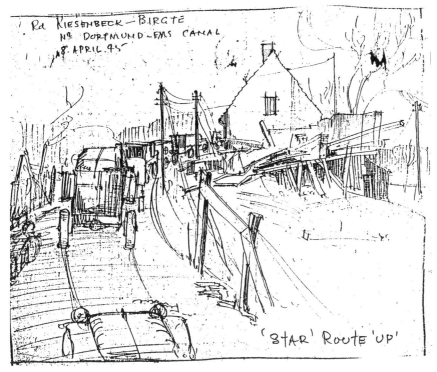

Star Route Up

Churchill AVRE tank with menacing spigot mortar bombard, ideal for destroying enemy strongholds at 100-yards range

Across the river Aller: the savage battle for Rethem

At this stage temporarily halted by the Ems-Weser canal, the two prime targets of Bremen and Hamburg were a mere forty miles north and sixty miles north-east respectively. Soon four divisions would close in around Bremen and three others round Hamburg. But there were still many savage little battles lying ahead. Major General 'Bobby' Ross now ordered Brigadier Coleman's 160 Brigade led by the Recce Regiment to move up towards the river Weser at Hoya. 2nd Mons were directed on the river loop including Stenden, Holtrop and Scheringen. In the centre 6 RWF on the Hoya to Altenbucken stretch with 4 Welch north of Hoya at Hingste, Ubbendorf and Weinbergen. The bridges might be destroyed and 282 Field Coy RE with forty-five assault boats would assist in the crossing of the river Weser. 160 Brigade HQ was at Gehlbergen. 4 Welch sent a patrol over the Weser during the night of the 9th in assault boats and were shot up in midstream. Seventeen men went out; four came back. On

The River Aller

the same day 6 RWF made an assault crossing at Hoya assisted by smoke. The 100 mile peacetime 'swan' made by the battalion from Spelle towards Hoya seemed to indicate the end of hostilities. The Medical Officer's diary said: 'The war is over.' Under cover of deceptive fire Lt Dufty led 'C' and Capt MacHenry 'A' Coy in canvas boats across. It was difficult for two reasons. The high banks on both sides of the river made carrying and launching of the craft almost impossible. And, secondly, the German *2nd Marine Division* were a very difficult lot of young men who seemed to have nothing left to live for and who seemed to enjoy dying. They had obviously taken Der Fuehrer's strictures (from his safe bunker in Berlin) about not surrendering, about not retreating, to heart. Fighting on the far bank was bitter, each house had to be cleared before the next could be taken. No prisoners were taken. The bridging started at noon and a Class 40 Bailey bridge was constructed by midnight. 83rd and 133 Field Artillery Regts plus 72nd Medium Regt were soon in action. 6 RWF lost twenty-one casualties but the river Weser had been crossed with relative ease. So General 'Bobby' Ross ordered 158 Brigade to pass through, and seize a crossing over the river Aller seven miles to the east. The town at Rethem on the west bank was a vital objective.

7 RWF led, crossed the bridge on foot during the night and quickly occupied Hassel on Tuesday, 10 April at 03.00 hrs. 'B' Coy had a brief skirmish with the Hitler Youth who rather surprisingly fled. Soon 4 Welch moved through and by 04.00 hrs had captured Eystrup to the south of Hassel. Next came 1/5 Welch (and the Brigade gunners, 83rd Field Regt) to begin the ten miles advance to

The German counter-attacks 13-14 April 1945, River Aller in foreground

Rethem along sandy tracks, through pine woods across the Hamelheide moor. The battle for Rethem was started by 133rd Field Regt bombarding the Old Town, returned haphazardly by railway Flak guns.

Intelligence reports later showed that the Weser-Aller line was held by *2nd Marine Infantry Division*, up to strength, with three Grenadier Regiments. They were backed by an artillery regiment, an anti-tank regiment, engineers and fusiliers. They were all naval personnel aged seventeen to twenty-three and their GOC, General Hartmann was an ex U-boat commander. Moreover they wanted to demonstrate to the German Army even at this late stage, that the Marines really could fight.

Sgt J. Machin, the Intelligence Sergeant of 1/5th Welch, describes the three battles for Rethem and its bridge over the river Aller:

> The first opposition was met 2000 yards west of Rethem but when 'C' Coy arrived at a cross-tracks heavy small arms and shellfire [from the farm buildings of the Strassengabel strongpoint backed up by a PAK anti-tank gun and crew]. At 1030hrs 'B' Coy moved through the ground mist left flanking to attack the bridge area from the north, passing by a small lake. When they were out in the open, 400 yds north of the village, the mist cleared. Without cover the Bosch opened up with everything he had. The position was hopeless. At 1330hrs a smokescreen was laid down.

Five hours later only twenty-four men out of the complete 'B' Coy returned. But Sgt Moses MM led a section of three carriers and two Wasp flame-throwers into Rethem to try and capture the vital bridge to the west of the village. They destroyed one PAK 40 gun and the crews of two more. 'They thrust deeper into the village, firing flame and machine-guns on both sides of the road, but eventually held up by a road-block at the crosssroads.' On the way back they got lost, but burned up another anti-tank gun. 'Brigadier Wilsey now ordered a direct attack with three regiments of backing guns to start at 1745hrs but "A" and "C" Companies were pinned down on the start line by shellfire from both flanks.' Major Bowker, the CO abandoned the attack. During the day seventy to eighty prisoners had been taken. It was clear that experienced SS were in Rethem to make sure the Marines fought well, despite 24 RAF rocket-firing Typhoons who strafed them!

During the afternoon 7 RWF had attacked on the left and captured Wohlendorf and reached Hulsen north of Rethem and the East Lancs, Hamelhausen halfway to Rethem. Major Lemon, DAA and QMG of 158 Brigade was ambushed by a Marine patrol and killed, cutting for a time the 1/5 Welch axis. On the far right flank 2 Mons, 160 Brigade, were sent off in TCVs and trucks helter-skelter to 'seize' Nienburg which had already been captured by 3 RTR of 11th Armoured Division. [The author was FOO with the 3 RTR/4 KSLI Battlegroup in the Weser and Aller battles]. And on the far left flank 4 Welch moved from Hassel, and took Stedorf and Westen, four miles north of Rethem.

Meanwhile 6 RWF were sent south-east towards the village of Anderton, south of the line Eystrup-Rethem supported by two troops of 5 RTR Cromwells. No recce was thought necessary and the advance through thick pine forests was halted when after three miles the leading platoon ran into a well laid ambush. Several tanks were knocked out and twenty-three Fusiliers were killed, wounded or taken prisoner. Lt Castles was wounded in three places. The Fusilier prisoners were marched to Rethem — still in the midst of an appalling battle — thence to Stalag XIB. Lt Col Hutchinson ordered 'A' Coy to push briskly into Anderton, a mile ahead, captured at 22.15 hrs. But a patrol found Stocken, two miles north-east still held by the enemy. At dawn under a barrage 6 RWF stormed Stocken, most of the houses were burning fiercely, and with 5 RTR exploited south to Rethem Moor, capturing fifty prisoners. Philip Cowburn, the Recce Regiment historian: 'We moved up to the river Weser, a long slow trek of 85 miles in peaceful but very foggy conditions. We arrived at Vilsen at 0800 on 10 April and crossed the Weser at Hoya on the 12th.'

'The last few weeks of the campaign', wrote Capt J D Cuthbertson, Adjutant 7 RWF, 'a number of our new reinforcements were very young and all quickly became exhausted. It was the only time that I observed soldiers asleep standing up, leaning on their rifles.'

7 RWF had a pitched battle to take Hulsen, backed by three regiments of guns which fired a barrage of fifty rounds per gun. House to house fighting went on and finally the village was captured by 03.00 hrs on 22 April with twenty-eight prisoners taken. Another forty Germans were killed in the village or trying to escape swimming the Aller.

The Divisional Intelligence summary showed that even at this late stage in the campaign, enemy reinforcements were being poured into the defence of the river Aller between Verden in the north and Rethem. *Battlegroup Hornemann* was formed to link up with *5th Marine Regiment* defending Rethem.

The wretched 1/5 Welch, now feeling the strains of battle acutely, having been in constant action and without sleep for two days were ordered to make a third attack on Rethem. At 03.45 hrs on 11 April 'A' and 'C' Coys moved towards the start line. An hour later on the outskirts they were pinned down, despite the huge barrage, by very heavy Spandau fire. Their frontal attacks over open ground were doomed to failure. As dawn was breaking the recently promoted Lt Col Bowker ordered both companies to withdraw. To stay where they were during daylight, their losses would have been appalling. Despite a smoke screen the casualties were very heavy. In forty-eight hours 1/5 Welch lost 7 officers and 186 other ranks, most of these despite a strong rumour to the contrary, were made prisoners. 'A' and 'C' Companies, that awful dawn, lost twenty wounded and sixty missing, all made prisoners. The depleted battalion was re-formed into three companies. Rethem still held out, despite attacks by infantry, tanks, mortars, field and medium guns and RAF Typhoons. The bridge was considered to be vital to the Corps axis so 2 Mons under Lt Col Brooke were ordered, with 'B' Sqn 5 RTR, to make on yet another attack on 11 April against the Marines and SS still holding out. Three smokescreens covered the approach over open ground towards the enemy dug into slit trenches between a key farm and the railway embankment. Mines and snipers took their toll. The Marine defenders had numerous PAK 40 anti-tank guns plus five heavy guns mounted on railway flats firing high explosive. Lt MacKenzie of 'B' Coy received six wounds but continued to encourage his men. The armour were deterred by Panzerfaust firers and stood off 800 yards. Both 'B' and 'C' Coys had to withdraw under cover of a smokescreen. Major General 'Bobby' Ross was at 160 Brigade HQ and gave the order for the 2 Mons to break off. He said the town would not be re-attacked until a major air effort bombardment plus Crocodiles (who had been sent off to 52 Lowland Division) were available.

The town was well alight, sixty-five houses were destroyed another sixty-four badly damaged. The 2 Mons lost eighteen killed, twenty-two wounded; Lt MacKenzie was awarded the DSO, Corporal Dawson and Pte Wild, MMs. During the Typhoon attacks the demolition charges on the Aller bridge had blown up, possibly unintentionally, since many Marines were injured in the explosion. During the night of 11/12 April 100 Marines crossed the Aller in small boats and others used a ferryboat which was scuttled afterwards. Another 200 survivors of *Battalion 11/5* took to the woods.

When 5 RTR put some Recce tanks into Rethem on the 13th, resistance was overcome and 2 Mons moved in, found 42 German dead and eventually collected 150 prisoners. The ruined bridge was secured and the gallant U-boat commander of the garrison admitted that only 60 of his 500 Marines had escaped. In fact many more had fled.

4 Welch on the 11th also had a sharp action in Barnstedt, another riverside village where 5 RTR saved the 4 Welch carrier platoon which had been cut off. CSM Roy Finch, 'C' Coy 4 Welch was recommended for the VC. He personally demolished two Spandau posts with their teams, was wounded in the arm and again by a grenade which broke a leg, blowing off fingers of one hand. He continuously shouted encouragement to his men from a barn, twice firing his Sten which was reloaded for him through a slit in the wall. At the end of the battle eighteen Spandaus and twelve bazookas were picked up on the battlefield. He was awarded the DCM for this action.

'B' Coy were in Reida, 'A' Coy in Ahnebergen. Major A. J. (Zonk) Lewis, 'D' Coy, captured Geestefeld supported by tanks:

After the enemy had lost a dozen killed they made a hasty retreat. Our strength was depleted and we dug all round defensive positions at our HQ in Hoftrue farm for the night. All went well until midnight. A runner came in with the rather shattering news that a number of the enemy had penetrated our position unseen. The enemy had entered these houses after overpowering the sentries and had awakened the occupants with the order to put their hands up. The situation was serious, and by this time my Company HQ was covered by Spandau fire. The enemy started shooting up the transport and Coy HQ with panzerfaust. The explosions were deafening and the whole building shook and burst into flames. I gave instructions to my men to make a dash for it across an open stretch of ground to a building about one hundred yards away from where we could reorganise and attempt to restore the situation in our favour. Just at that moment the reserve ammunition went up with a roar and the building started collapsing around us, and it was difficult to tell which were the enemy and which were our own men. Suddenly my men started a free for all and the enemy found themselves being attacked by unarmed men sailing in with fists and feet. There is no etiquette in War! It was a display of guts and courage. Simultaneously, all those who had been taken prisoner turned on their captors and before long the enemy dead included two of their officers, neither of whom had a bullet wound on them. The enemy learned by experience what a British soldier could do to them with his fists and hands. Unarmed combat instruction had not been in vain. The enemy melted away leaving their dead. They had failed to take a single prisoner. I will not belittle them. They were German Marines and had fought with real guts and determination.

The *2nd Marine Division* had concentrated its defences mainly around Verden to the north and Rethem to the south guarding vital bridges. An outflanking operation with an assault crossing of the river Aller was now a possibility. 4 Welch held a site at Westen five miles downstream (north) from Rethem, so the East Lancs marched and drove through woods over heathland on a moonless night to assemble in Westen for H-Hour, 03.00 hrs on 12 April. The Hungarian *Battalion Kolotay* were dug in on the far side. The river Aller was about 100 yards wide with a very strong current. Major Whiteside led 'A' Coy, 'B' and 'C' followed and the East Lancs were 1000 yards inland before they bumped into serious opposition. Behind them Lt Kershaw and two sections of 'D' Coy were swept away by the current and lost. Nevertheless by 12.00 hrs the East Lancs had reached Otersen and captured sixty-five Hungarians. Brigadier Wilsey ordered 7 RWF to cross the river and take Wittlohe whilst 555 Field Coy RE built a Class 9 folding boat bridge.

Major J. E. M. Dugdale, 7 RWF:

In the last phase of active operations the battalion crossed two rivers — the Weser by a repaired bridge after a particularly good job of work by the REs.

We made for the river Aller. Little sleep for anyone. Friday, 13th lived up to all
the superstitions. By the afternoon 'C' Coy were surrounded in the woods near
Hohenaverbergen. At last light 'A' and 'B' launched an attack and simultaneously
the enemy counter-attacked from the right through 'D' Coy. By first light some
very good work by the Gunners restored the position, but 'B' Coy had a very
sticky time of it. During the day [14th] 'A' Coy were pulled back for a fullscale
attack on the village. The main attack went in through 'C' Coy with flame
throwers. The village was completely destroyed.

Lt Graham Povey had arrived in Normandy in a 25-pdr regiment but after
five months of fighting was 'converted' on a six week course on the Isle of
Man into the PBI:

I found my platoon dug in, in scrubby woodland. After a quick briefing by 'C'
Coy CO I settled in staying close to my experienced Platoon Sgt At dark we went
on 50% stand-to. In the middle of the night someone said 'Halte' about five
yards in front of me. The next second the proverbial 'hell was let loose'. Things
got rather confused with lots of flashes and bangs from all around us. A lot of
screaming and shouting, mainly bad language! Things steadied down. Rather
unsportingly the Germans [Hungarians] used rifle dischargers to fire showers of
grenades at us killing Fusilier Bolland. At first light we got support from another
Pl, dug in on the high ground on the right. And later Lt Ronnie Forsythe's carrier
section got through to us. We learned that our platoon was cut of from 'C' Coy
and 'C' Coy itself had been surrounded. Since then I have treated Friday 13th
with respect.

The enemy had almost recaptured Wittloe, had over-run 'D' Coy and
encircled 'C' Coy, and later pushed back 'B' and 'D' Coys who regrouped as a
composite force. The Hungarians resisted fiercely with small arms, Spandaus
and bazookas and 7 RWF finally took Hohenaverbergen on the 14th.
   The Recce Regiment also had a ferociously exciting night of the 13th/14th.
'A', 'B' Sqadrons and RHQ were around Otersen, but 'C' Sqn found that the
village of Stemmen was strongly held, so harboured for the night a mile and
a half away in a group of farm buildings. Just before midnight the first of
four counter-attacks began. 'The night seemed to erupt and the air was filled
with the rattle of Spandau fire and exploding bazookas,' recalls 'Bud' Abbot.
A bazooka blast draped him over the bonnet of a vehicle. He heard: 'a voice
saying, "Bud's had it!" The enemy were shouting in English, "Give up, the war
is over for you", or words to that effect.' Corporal David Henderson:

The next time we were ready and waiting for them. They set the farmhouse
on fire. There seemed to be hundreds of them by the row they made. All the

time Besas were firing endless belts. Terry fired bolt-fed Bazookas back... In the morning we were congratulated by the CO and GOC. Major Harry Goldsmid was badly wounded in the face, arms and legs. He organised the defence with the Humbers [armoured cars] firing all they had outwards over the heads of the carrier crews in their slit-trenches.

There were thirteen casualties and many vehicles and stores destroyed. Major Goldsmid was awarded the DSO. Later German or Hungarian prisoners confirmed that seven companies had been sent out to destroy the bridge over the Aller. During the day 331 prisoners, mainly Hungarians had been taken. They protested emphatically 'we always shoot *high*'. Nevertheless the Hungarians caused thirty-five casualties to the East Lancs and many more to the 7 RWF. They also attacked East Lancs in Wittlohe. Lt Kay did well with 10 Platoon and Sgt Oram MM threw a phosphorous grenade into 'B' Coy cookhouse!

A captured enemy Intelligence digest entitled 'Regrouping of the Defences of Verden and the Aller Sector' started:

> From now on and all through the night the enemy will be attacked in his positions by small assault forces (20-30 men). The object is to deprive the English of *the pleasure of sleeping at night with honourless German women* and to ensure that they live in a constant state of danger and uncertainty in the villages they have occupied. No assault troops without A/Tank weapons. Vehicles, guns etc are to be blown sky-high.

Battlegroup Neintzel, Commander *7th Marine Regiment* and *Battlegroup Jordan*, Commander *5th Marine Regiment* did order attacks of the kind described on Wittlohe and Otersen with much noise in pitch darkness with limited success.

Bridging operations had started at Rethem at dark on 12 April when 244 Field Coy offloaded bridging equipment. By 14.30 hrs on 13 April half of the 110-boat Bailey pontoon had been assembled but well directed artillery and mortar fire caused much delay. Four flights of Typhoons attacked the area where the fire came from. Only on the 15th did Recce cars move across the river. The German Marines had carried out a fine delaying action at Rethem. The GOC then ordered 71 Brigade to pass through Otersen towards Walsrode about ten miles to the east. Philip Cowburn, the Recce Regiment historian, wrote: 'Very secret maps at Division HQ which a few of us had seen showed our old friends 'star' and 'sun' routes leading for Hamburg. It seemed that it might be our last conquest.'

The countryside east of the Aller was mostly heathland with woods of pine and birch and small undulating hills. Poor roads and tracks linked the small villages, often surrounded by thick woods. The Recce leading troops fought, or passed through, Neddenarverbergen, Visselhovede and Jeddingen. Sgt 'Sandy' Vallender, the 3-inch mortar section commander and Corporal Wells, distinguished themselves and 'even' the Provost Sergeant and Signals Officer led wood-clearing patrols.

The Ox and Bucks led 71st Brigade and captured Gross Hauslingen but dozens of isolated defence posts caused casualties. Lt Eric Hawley's carrier with his driver Cyril Gray were ambushed and both killed by a panzerfaust. Casualties amongst 'C' Coy, clearing the higher wooded ground, included Major 'Rollo' Warren, and two 2/Lts Hedges and Norris. Pte Tom King relates: 'The replacement Coy CO was Capt Alan Baxter who by the end of a strenuous day of close combat had lost his voice continually shouting orders above the din of battle. By late evening, enemy resistance came to an end with 90 prisoners taken and many dead all from the 1st and 2nd Marine Divisions.' The next morning the *1st Battalion Marine Regiment* counter-attacked the Ox and Bucks but artillery DF fire and Bren gun fire from 'A' and 'C' Coys demolished the enemy. 4 RWF and 1 HLI also caught part of this attack. 'B' Coy Ox and Bucks captured the CO and HQ staff, fifty prisoners and two field guns. Pte Desmond Milligan wrote: 'The German marines attacked our two companies in a massed wave of men reminiscent of WW1. They charged shoulder to shoulder singing their war songs and shouting encouragement to each other.'

Capt Pender, 1 HLI:

It happened about 0100hrs after the two Companies had done a long 3 mile outflanking movement across country. The two Company Commanders and myself were standing on the road, prior to taking up defensive positions, when we heard marching feet approaching from the east. Major Hemilryke OC 'B' Coy hailed them thinking it was 'C' or 'D' Coy. Immediately heavy firing broke upon us. Major H. was severely wounded and a number of Jocks were killed or wounded along the track to our left rear. Things became particularly unpleasant.

Pender, now OC 'B' Coy, and Major Greenway, OC 'A' Coy, tried to withdraw and extricate themselves:

It was difficult in the dark to find my Company. Some were in a flooded ditch, some under a bridge, some in a scrub plantation. 'A' and 'B' Coy stretcher bearers evacuated some of the wounded but not those who had fallen inside the enemy position, while I got the Jocks to fall back. All the time the Germans were bringing heavy fire to bear on the track. I pulled some of the Jocks out of the ditch physically as I could not make myself heard. Eventually everyone who was on his feet got back to 'A' Coy position. A pretty sorry looking lot we were too. Some had lost their weapons and both Companies 18 set radios were broken.

In the early morning a one-hour truce was arranged to retrieve the wounded on both sides. Lt Jim Hillier held a dialogue with the English speaking German officer: GO; 'I shall like to shake hands with an honourable Englishman.' JH; 'scotsman!' (though he *was* an Englishman in the HLI!). 'You speak very good English.' GO; 'Yes, I was at Oxford University. Firing will start in five minutes time.' Firing commenced on time. A HLI Bren team shot up an ambulance. Pte Buller, a stretcher bearer stayed with the badly wounded Germans:

> All day we were under machinegun, rifle and mortar fire. We could not evacuate our wounded, as we had no transport. Some of them including Major Hemilryke died during the day. There was nothing to eat.

Eventually tank relief came up. 'After having smartened ourselves up we marched back to the Battalion with our Company Pipers playing.'

By 09.00 on the 14th the enemy counter-attack had been halted with 129 killed, 79 wounded and 163 prisoners from *1st* and *2nd Marine Regiments*. In addition the East Lancs had taken 140 prisoners around Neddenaverbergen but had 26 casualties themselves and 1/5 Welch occupied Armsen after a hard fight. Tanks of 3rd/4th CLY and Crocodiles of 7 RTR were now across the Aller, but German resistance north of Rethem was increasing with the arrival of *Battlegroup Schaffer* and *11 Bn, 7th Marine Regiment* from the German *480th Division*. Sgt Machin, 1/5 Welch, wrote: 'At 08.15hrs (between Armsen and Weitzmulen on the way to cut the Verden-Kirchlinteln road), on 15 April 'D' Coy and the tanks again attacked but once again we were forced to withdraw. The situation was becoming critical, *due solely to the exhaustion of the Bn*. Pressure was being brought to bear the whole time for the continuation of the advance.' General 'Bobby' Ross was driving his division very hard even though most attacks now had set-piece battle support, field and medium artillery, the MMG of Lt Col Crozier's Manchesters, tanks of 4th Armoured Brigade, Crocodiles, battalion Wasps and often RAF Typhoon support. At this late stage of the war it seemed absurd to suffer needless casualties, but the Germans and their Hungarian allies put up a superb resistance, in very favourable defence terrain.

The major battle for Rethem, the taking of a score of defended villages, the determined enemy counter-attacks had taken their toll. The Division now was composed in the nine 'teeth' fighting battalions of about 40%, or more, of green recruits. No wonder Lt Col Crozier, whose Manchester mortars and MMGs were scattered around the Division wrote in his diary: 'April 16th. 158

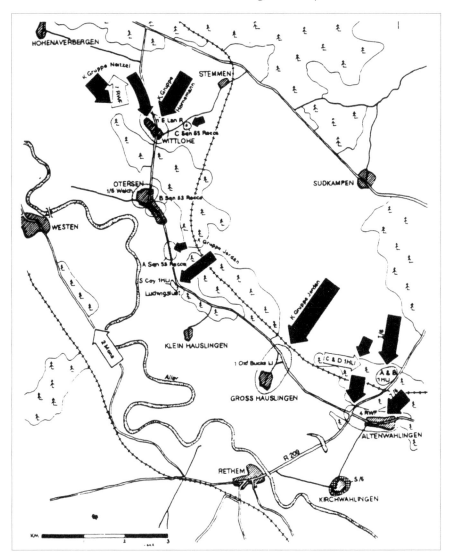

The savage battle for Rethem

and 160 Brigades are played out. Some Bns are less than 200 strong [in the four rifle companies]. And they are very tired.' The tactics to take Rethem can perhaps be criticised. The town could have been attacked from any or all of three sides. Blistering RAF bombing was an option. Although carrier Wasps were available, no Crocodiles were on the spot.

Churchill tank carrying British infantry guarding German PoWs (note their coal-bucket helmets)

19

Swanning with the Greys

Rarely does a battalion of an infantry division get the opportunity of acting as an integral part of an armoured division, or in this case, 4th Armoured Brigade. On 14 April 6 RWF took on this new role to advance three miles over the Aller, to penetrate the enemy lines and on the way to Vreden attack and subdue six well-defended hamlets or villages. The Fusiliers rehearsed climbing in and out of Kangaroos, and learned something about their tactical handling, discussing tactics with the Kangaroo crews and the Royal Scots Greys in their Sherman tanks. Each platoon was allotted three or four Kangaroos, and another to Coy HQ. Battalion HQ needed five and no wheeled vehicles accompanied this marauding expedition. The two COs rode together in a Honey light tank and 4 RHA provided rapid 25-pdr fire support. After 'marrying up' Greys' squadrons with a 6 RWF company, the expedition set off through wrecked Rethem where ten 88s reared their ugly nozzles in the sky. The first assembly point was two miles beyond the river. Despite heavy mortaring from the fanatical 2 *Marine Division*, the advance line ahead started with a tank and Kangaroo alternating and their Besas soon had the dry undergrowth on fire. The column drove down sandy tracks between walls of flame and was almost choked by the smoke. At dawn on 15th, 4 RHA set Kirchboitzen alight and despite a persistent SP gun and determined German infantry the village was cleared with 150 prisoners taken. 6 RWF were greatly impressed by the bold handling of the Greys' tanks and riding almost up to one's objectives in an armoured vehicle was a new and welcome experience for the infantry men. Then a 90 degree change of direction and off a mile and a half to Vethem where the enemy fought so bitterly that the next morning (16th) all that was left of the pretty little village was the smoking remains. Only three houses still stood and five 105 mm and two 75 mm guns were knocked out. Again the Fusiliers admired the way the Greys went right into the enemy regardless of anti-tank fire. At dawn on the 17th the armoured column set off across scrubby and wooded country for Idisgen. The Greys had a drill whereby they fired a few rounds of HE from their 75 mm guns, followed by a burst of Besa, whenever they approached a village. It demoralised the enemy and cheered up the Fusiliers. It was now twenty-four hours since a meal, and ammo and petrol were getting low. On the way to Bendingbostel a stream with swampy ground caused a delay until an RE scissors bridge was thrown across. The village was stubbornly defended and 4 RHA had to 'stonk' two woods some 300 yards square which the enemy held in strength. By dusk there were fifty enemy dead in the woods and an 88 mm, three 105 mm and ten 20 mm guns were taken. 6 RWF then occupied the stricken village where Lts Evans and Mack were wounded. The final objective was the high ground north-east of Verden to link up with 71 Brigade who launched an attack there on the same day. On the way the long armoured column wound its way through the gaps in the woods and overwhelmed several groups of enemy, a battery of horsedrawn 105 mm and some isolated 88 mm guns. Contact was made at Kirchlinten at mid-day with 71 Brigade. Before this successful partnership was broken up, 6 RWF 3-inch mortars and 4 RHA shelled into submission 400 enemy lurking in a wood a mile away. They were so demoralised that they ran out and surrendered to the 4 RHA gunners.

Brigadier Carver, Commander of 4th Armoured Brigade then commented: 'This was a powerful, flexible, and effective organisation. It has proved that a *normal* infantry Bn from an infantry division which had never fought in Kangaroos, had never undertaken a similar operation before, had only just married up with their armoured Regt, which had suffered heavy casualties a few days before — with many new reinforcements — could adapt and function efficiently in this new role.'

When Vreden was reached, 6 RWF Battalion was ordered to revert to 53rd Division. On 17 April Lieutenant-General N. H. Ritchie, Commander of XII Corps, wrote as follows to Major-General Ross, commanding 53d Division:

> Your task in opening up passageways for XII Corps and incidentally also for XXX Corps over the Rivers Weser and Aller is now completed. It has been no easy task, in fact quite the reverse. Yet it has been carried out superbly by you and your Division.
>
> You have responded, as the 53rd (Welsh) Division always does, to every demand made upon you, quite magnificently. It has been hard fighting, made doubly difficult coming as it has done so closely upon your heavy losses in Operation 'Veritable'. To my mind this makes your achievement rank even higher than it otherwise would. Many congratulations will reach you from elsewhere, but I send mine to the 53rd (Welsh) Division for their great fighting qualities and splendid spirit. We in XII Corps are very proud that you have been with us so long.

Major-General Ross, in passing on this message, added:

This is high praise, but it is well deserved. Since making contact after crossing the Rhine on 27th March, the Division has been continuously in action. Not a day nor a night has passed without the enemy being attacked and progress made somewhere. This has imposed a tremendous strain on all ranks of the Division and on all formations and units placed temporarily under command or in support of the Division. It was, however, largely owing to the fact that the enemy was allowed no rest that the final success of the operation was achieved and the gap made through which the armoured divisions are now streaming.

Architects of victory, Field Marshal Bernard Montgomery and Generals Horrocks and Whistler

20

The Last Lap: 'Like Italian washing' – Operation Round-Up

As part of the grim encircling movements round Bremen, 53rd Welsh with 4th Armoured Brigade were to move north to cut Bremen's communications to the east. 71st Brigade had to take the old historic town of Verden, a substantial prize even though on 5 April German engineers had blown up all the bridges, with great blast damage to the cathedral, and on 14 April the RAF had bombed the town rather thoroughly.

Despite enemy threats or promises to fight to the last, the Ox and Bucks who attacked first at 01.30 hrs on 17 April found minimal opposition. 'A' Coy captured the town cemetery, 'D' Coy a small housing estate and for negligible cost the battalion captured 112 prisoners and killed one defender.

Desmond Milligan's Bren gun carrier often led the Ox and Bucks. On the way to Verden:

> We flushed out some young Germans hiding in a shed, their weapons were lying around all over the place. Their womenfolk thought we were going to shoot them and pleaded for their lives. Nazi propaganda had done its work well. On our right we passed one of many PoW camps mainly Russian, men and women, stood outside the gates.

The carrier platoon met French soldiers, prisoners since the fall of France in 1940. They also had to lead into Verden. 'Drive like hell we did, thundering through the narrow streets with our heads down, the streets strangely deserted with white surrender flags hanging like Italian washing out of every window.' The German civilians gazed in horror at Desmond & Co. 'We did look awesome. We were encrusted with dust and grime and had 48 hours growth of beard. We were heavily armed. Hitler's propaganda had told them we would rape and loot and kill all before us. Their fear-ridden faces told us all this.' CSM Corbett 'C' Coy personally acquired dozens of prisoners — claiming he could smell their garlic! RAF Typhoons had a field day. The Ox and Bucks anti-tank platoon had been heavily mortared causing many casualties. Coloured smoke-shells were fired into a wood where the German mortars were hiding. The Tiffies caused explosions, smoke and dust leaving a blue haze over the wood.

Four hours later 1 HLI entered the main town, cleared it and captured an ordnance dump, a field hospital and eight 10.5 cm field guns. 7th Marine Regt had pulled out of Verden to re-appear later at Visselhovede. The DAQMG of *2nd Marine Division* was captured and reported: 'Our Marines have fought so well because they desired to show the Army what the German Navy could do if tested. Our picked crews could be relied upon to give a good account of themselves.' The day before, 1/5 Welch had captured 65 prisoners from *480 Division* (who in two days had lost 1000 prisoners, 60% of its fighting personnel), who wore Luftwaffe uniform having been rushed in from Holland. Nevertheless whether they were young Marine cadets, Wehrmacht, SS, Luftwaffe even Volksturm they could, and did, shoot off Spandaus and panzerfaust inflicting casualties.

General 'Bobby' Ross's command now included 4th Armoured Brigade and 156 Brigade of 52nd Lowland Division. 71 Brigade would clear north of Verden, 158 Brigade to follow 4th Armoured Brigade into and exploit beyond Rotenburg and 160 Brigade to be prepared to move east towards the Soltau pocket. 'The Division's Recce Regt patrolled ahead to places like Hetzwege, ten miles north-east of Bremen and between it and Bremen, a wood encircled aerodrome.' Philip Cowburn wrote: 'All this was tough slogging and there was even some stonking reminiscent of Normandy as well. We had to protect the right flank patrolling to and beyond and cutting the Bremen-Hamburg autobahn.'

On the 18th Lt Col Brooke, CO 2 Mons, left to go to 12 Corps HQ and was succeeded by Lt Col A. J. C. Prickett. On the next day 2 Mons garrisoned the huge Fallingbostel Camp crammed full of thousands of Allied PoW. They then spent a week wood-clearing and mopping up, putting nearly 500 Germans into the bag.

After Verden, the Ox and Bucks prepared to attack Dauelsen to enable 52nd Lowland Division to move through towards Bremen. It was a confused area with converging British columns advancing and remnant columns of German Marines/Luftwaffe troops retreating to the north-east. To Capt 'Dinty' Moore of 'C' Coy just south of Dauelsen, there was the strange sight of 'two distinctly different hordes of ants seemingly going into battle against each other'. There was little opposition but 'D' Coy advancing beyond the village were pinned down by heavy Spandau fire, and RHQ vehicles were 'brewed up' by shelling. The next day 160 Brigade were loaned to the Desert Rats and 158 Brigade took over the area south of Rotenburg. The Marine troops who had left Verden in a great hurry now heavily counter-attacked Guards Armoured Division at Visselhovede, so on the 20th the East Lancs supported by 3rd/4th CLY (of 7th Armoured Division) were directed on Dreessel. Just before tackling Jeddingen an awesome demonstration of firepower was laid on. The 'big bass drums' of Medium and Field Artillery, Manchester 4.2-inch mortars, tank fire and even company 2-inch mortars. Lt T. A. Sutton led 'C' Coy into the town, soon cleared by mopping up operations, taking seventy-seven prisoners for the loss of only eight casualties. From Suderwalsede, 1/5 Welch relieved part of 4th Armoured Brigade and spent two days mopping up. A Recce patrol into Grafel found a lonely 'Master Race' Marine officer who had lost his men and was now in hiding. Another dirty dishevelled downhearted prisoner nicknamed by the Provost Sgt as 'Charley' heartily cursed Hitler for his plight. The 1/5 Welch FOO Major Campbell had plenty of targets for his guns. Soon 158 Brigade linked up with 71st Brigade and on the 21st 700 prisoner stragglers were sent back to the cages, from the triangle Verden-Rotenburg-Visselhovede.

The 6 RWF fought their last battle of the campaign on the 21st and 22nd supported by 'C' Sqn 1 RTR of the Desert Rats. Each village was now treated to a set-piece attack with artillery, Manchester MMGs and mortars. First Oningen and Dittmern where ninety-four prisoners were taken from at least fifteen different units, formed into battlegroups of 60-200 strength. Operation Roundup on the 22nd started with Harber where six rocket projectors, and two anti-tank guns plus sixty prisoners were taken. L/Sgt Derench took over a platoon when Lt Ginnever was killed by a sniper, and won the MM. Next Stubeckshorn where in a large hospital twenty French and two British prisoners were rescued. Then Hotzingen was taken without opposition as were Hambostel and Harmelingen. This Regimental HQ with ammo dump was defended by 88 mm mortar and panzerfaust. The Fusiliers got carried away and fired Piat bombs at 2 Mons nearby in Topingen, without any casualties. During the day 500 prisoners were collected and the spoils included one armoured car, seven half-tracks, three staff cars, several mortars, eight anti-tank guns and two batteries of Nebelwerfers. A horse-drawn column with a ration supply was put in the bag. The Fusiliers had twenty-two casualties during the day. Major General Lyne, GOC the Desert Rats, sent a congratulatory message: 'Thank you 6 RWF.' A RWF Pioneer who was a good stonemason found the words. 'Hitler 1935' on a village monument, so he carefully crafted 'Kaput, 1945!' A few days later almost by mistake on the Elbe bridge they picked up a straggler who turned out to be a major prize. It was Seiss Inquart, the German Governor of Holland, attempting to escape.

Even at this late stage young recruits were pouring in to replace the losses incurred since the Rhine crossing. But two particularly sad events now occurred. Brigadier M. Elrington was directing fire plans near 4 RWF onto woods near Rotenburg when his jeep went up on a mine and he died shortly afterwards. Brigadier C. L. Firbank DSO arrived from 3rd British Division to take command of 71st Brigade. And secondly 7 RWF learned that it was to leave 53rd Welsh Division and join the 56 Brigade of 49 Polar Bear Division.

General 'Bobby' Ross came to say goodbye to 7 RWF which moved off on the 27th to the Arnhem area — with heavy hearts. And 2nd Battalion South Wales Borderers joined the Division from the Polar Bears.

After the Brigadier's death, Desmond Milligan, a carrier driver with the Ox and Bucks noted: 'He died as the result of something we were all terrified of in this advance up untested roads and lanes. The dreaded land mine cunningly placed. How we looked at every verge or every bit of loose earth on the road. We had packed the floors of our carriers with sandbags to deaden the blast should it come. We came across several Recce carriers with neat holes blown through their floors lying on their sides.'

Lt Col Crozier's diary: 'April 23rd. A very bad day, 71 Brigade still leading but made very little progress. Bosch resistance still very tough by 15 PZ Grenadier division.' By the 24th 160 Brigade, mopping up behind the Desert Rats, had brought their tally of prisoners in the Soltau pocket to 5000 with little cost to themselves. The next day 71st Brigade reached the Bremen-Hamburg autobahn with 4 RWF leading and the Ox and Bucks directed on Gyhum and Wehldorf. Private Eddie Priddle rescued two wounded friends, including Pte Ray Powell, under fire and then ordered a German nurse to take care of them. Private Desmond Milligan went into his last action carrying a load of 80 pounds weight: Bren gun, four grenades and a satchel full of Bren magazines. In a ploughed field his mates sank into the ground three inches; 'Yours truly sank *eight* inches'. His platoon were bombarded by a Tiger tank which had a 356 mm mortar throwing a gigantic container of explosive, rather bigger than an AVRE 'bombard'.

The gunner regiments were in action every day with several FOOs being killed or wounded. 330 Bty had Capts Blakelock and Thompson wounded. Lt R. A. Williams, 329 Bty led two guns at night into an ambush, and five were killed, three others wounded and made prisoner. Capt M. H. H. Smith of 332 Bty supporting 6 RWF was killed in a skirmish. After targets were fired on at Kukenmoor, Gohlbeck and Scharnhurst, lorries were seen packed with *captured* Welsh Division prisoners of war mainly taken at Rethem. It seemed the war was nearly over, but still every village was defended and counter-attacks were met. The Third Reich was dying rapidly, but dying hard.

A few days later the Ox and Bucks were issued with 17-pdr anti-tank guns instead of their 6-pdr 'pop guns'. Almost a year too late to be useful. 'C' Coy advanced towards Weldorf against fierce Nebelwerfer and Spandau fire. Capt Jim Moore was hit but the spent bullet was found inside a cake his mother had just sent him: 'somebody produced some gin and lime and four of us grabbed the shattered cake, squeezed it together and ate it.'

The Shermans of 3rd/4th CLY seemed reluctant that day to engage targets. One got stuck in a marsh, had to fight, and much to everyone's surprise destroyed a monster short-barrelled 75 mm SP gun. On the right flank 2 Mons were in action north-west of Rotenburg and 4 Welch from Westerholz cleared the Borchel airfield. German prisoners were sent ahead to point out where they had laid their mines. A large camp of Allied prisoners of war were freed, together with many forced labourers, mostly children and elderly people in deplorable conditions. But Hesedorf, captured late on the 26th was heavily defended. 6 RWF captured Rotenburg airfield and liberated several thousand delighted Russian prisoners of war. Bremen now fell to a combined onslaught without the need for 53rd Welsh to join in the final attack so the Division moved up piecemeal to the river Elbe. 11th Armoured Division was first to reach the Elbe, 51st Highland Division made an assault crossing and on 3 May the Desert Rats moved into Hamburg — now declared an open city. The shores of the Baltic had been reached at Wismar cutting off all enemy troops in Denmark and Schleswig-Holstein.

Soon afterwards the East Lancs marched to Bornsen, some thirteen miles south-east of Hamburg, and on Thursday, May 3rd German emissaries appeared in the person of General-Admiral von Friedeberg and General Kinzel and two staff officers. They were quickly passed along to Field Marshal Montgomery's HQ at Lüneburg.

News of the ignominious death of the Fuehrer in his Berlin bunker was heard on the radio to the sound of Wagner's music. A great quiet descended over the battlefields.

The end of the war. 'Sadness in losing so many dear friends'

Hamburg: Victory in Europe

At dawn on 4 May 53rd Division entered Germany's second city and largest port, to assume responsibility and garrison Hamburg. Philip Cowburn, Recce historian:

> We crossed the pontoon bridge over the Elbe on the evening of 2nd May. A slow crossing, and raining hard. In harbour south of Bergedorf we had our last battle contact with our old friends the 340 A/Tk SP Battery. Some of them had crossed the Elbe in boats and were driving about in civilian cars rounding up droves of willing German troops towards us to be taken to the cages. We were told 'Monty' was meeting von Busch to discuss surrender terms when we learned that it was rumoured that a cease-fire had been ordered, the lads just went on playing football.

Entrance to the city of Hamburg, 5 May 1945

And David Henderson, 'C' Sqn:

> Our last patrol, what a delightful job it was. Picturesque scenery, flowers, lovely houses and the richest market-garden land. We went for 15 miles along the winding dyke road with slave-workers cheering us on. The dialogue with the citizens went, 'Alles Kaput' or 'Hitler tot' or 'SS nix good' and of course 'Me no Nazi'. If we didn't like the look of them we smashed up their firearms and left with the parting words. 'The Ruskies here tomorrow.' We stayed in Hamburg for a month. We boated on the Alster, sent out armoured car patrols picking up civilians out after curfew. We got our vehicles up to scratch, went back to our light-coloured blanco.

Pte Desmond Milligan, Ox and Bucks:

> From Willinghusen and Barsbuttel we entered the city [Hamburg] at 6am. It was deserted, the population had been told to stay indoors. A clear day, calm, no wind. This gave the city the appearance of a vast deserted dusty Hollywood film set, partly in ruins from the bombing. A hospital was full of wounded German soldiers. They crowded the windows to watch us in sullen silence. The whole city had been prepared for a siege. Massive barricades of building rubble built across the roads with tram tracks sticking out to stop tanks.

Temporary Major Pender, 1 HLI:

> We were at Huddingon on 20th April, Wittorf on 21st, attacked Westerhohe on 25th and Mulshem on 26th April. 1st May we were at Honstedt. On 3rd May we heard rumours of peace. We motored into Hamburg on 5th May through miles of rubble, over mountains of bombed buildings till we came to the centre of the city. Bn HQ took up position in a posh hotel beside the Alster lake. We placed a platoon on guard on a German Naval Marine warehouse. In the morning most of the Jocks were unwell. A large naval barge had contained 'Angus Mackay Scotch Whiskey'. I told the CO Lt Col Dick Kindersley DSO MC of our find. Div HQ got onto the racket and sent down 24 TCVs to collect. 'B' Coy officers celebrated VE night at a party at Bn HQ by firing off 2" mortar parachute flares and Verey lights. There were no girls as the order from on high was 'No fraternisation'. A stupid order. Some Jocks ignored it. The Military Police could not enforce it 100%.

Gunner Wally Brereton, 81st Field Regt RA, 'recognised the shells of a theatre, cinema or department store. In the ruin of a small Gothic church we found a most unholy gun emplacement with one of the enemy's famous 88 mm guns intact and ready to fire in the direction we had come.'

Hotel Atlantic – Hamburg Victory Dinner

General 'Bobby' Ross sent Joe Grimond and me into Hamburg the day *before* the troops went in to take over the surrender. Joe went to reserve 'A' Mess and offices at the Hotel Atlantic [which became Div HQ]. I took the Schouspielhaus Opera (2000 seats) for show business. Again a sincere confirmation of Bobby's concern for the welfare of the Division, I was instructed to arrange a Cabaret for the Divisional dinner. [Jim Cooper]

G Staff, Div HQ May 1945
(front row, l-r): Capt J. Paynter, SC 'A'; Capt J. C. Suffolk, Div IO; Capt D. Phelps, GSO3 (Int); Lt Col C. H. Harrington, GSO1; Maj Gen R. K. Ross, GOC; Maj P. (Monty) Meinertzhagen, GSO2; Capt E. L. Williams, GSO3 (Ops); Capt A. I. F. Simpson, GSO3. (second row, l-r): unknown; Camp Commendant; Lt H. C. Kenway, LO; unknown; Lt P. Utley, LO; Lt F. Yates, LO; Lt C. Piggott, LO; Maj E. G. Oldham, OC APIS.

After almost a year in action — the 'bocage' battles, the low country canal actions, the divisional capture of 's-Hertogenbosch, longstop in the Ardennes, the weeks fighting in the dark Reichwald forest, the savage Rhineland battles around Weeze, the many river and canal operations in the heart of Das Reich — what better way to end 'Red Crown and Dragon' by looking at the photographs of that 'bon viveur' Major General 'Bobby' Ross and his superb team, celebrating victory in Europe in the Atlantic Hotel, Hamburg.

THE END

Envoi

As the GOC Major General 'Bobby' Ross said in his Victory Order of the Day. 'Battles cannot be won without paying the cost and we have had heavy casualties. Nearly 10,000 officers and men were killed, wounded and missing, but in turn the Division captured some 35,000 Prisoners of War and probably accounted for the same amount in dead and wounded.'

General Sir Miles Dempsey, Commander of the Second British Army speaking to two thousand men of the 53rd (Welsh) Division at the State Theatre, Hamburg at the end of the campaign, said:

In the early spring of last year, the Second Army consisted of two types of division — some with a great deal of fighting experience in the Mediterranean and others, of which you were one, which clearly had been well trained but had no past experience at all.

Of that latter type it was not at all clear what would happen when they got into battle. The Division came in some days after the assault on Normandy and went straight into tough and difficult fighting on the Odon.

It was there, in the battle on the bridgehead, that the defeat of Germany became quite clear. You began to find your feet on the Odon, where you had a tough start against seasoned German troops. There you began to show what sort of division you were going to be.

As the months went by you proved yourself up to the hilt. You have become well known for toughness in your fighting. You are absolutely reliable.

You have always won what you set out to gain. That is the reputation you have won for yourselves. I shall always think of that start on the Odon, then Falaise, and over the Seine to Antwerp.

Next those difficult battles on the canals in Holland, your brilliant capture of 's-Hertogenbosch, that very difficult and wet fighting on the Meuse, and so up to the Rhine and over the Rhine to Hamburg.

Of the later battles you fought, one, to my mind, was outstanding — the crossing of the Aller at Rethem. You were then up against the best German troops on the whole front.

You fought like tigers, and by winning the battle, as you did, opened the way for the Second Army to get straight to the Elbe, and so to the Baltic.

I have placed that last battle of yours very high. It was a most decisive victory. You must see to it that the victory you have won in war is in no way lost in peace.

Each one of you has a big responsibility, while you are out here, both in the work that you do and by your example in governing this country and its degraded people.

When it is over and you go home, each one of you in the knowledge that you have helped to make the history of a magnificent Division.

Appendix A

SPECIAL ORDER OF THE DAY BY MAJOR GENERAL

R. K. ROSS, CB DSO MC

Tomorrow, 9 May, has officially been declared 'V' day and so ends for 53rd (W) Division a campaign in which the Division played a part second to none.

I attach as an Appendix to this order extracts from a letter I have received from the Corps Commander and my reply on behalf of the Division.

The Corps Commander has paid us a high tribute and all ranks of the Division can feel justly proud that General Ritchie, who knows the Division better than any other higher commander, has felt able to speak so highly of us.

Further, the unbroken line of successes of the Division throughout the whole campaign enables all ranks to feel with quiet confidence that General Ritchie's generous praise is well deserved.

'V' day coming as it does one day short of the completion of the fifth year I have been privileged to serve the Division as Brigadier and Divisional Commander, I am in a better position than most to appreciate the years of hard work and effort by all ranks which has forged that efficient fighting machine which has proved itself consistently on the battlefields of Europe.

General Ritchie is right when he attributes our success largely to the magnificent teamwork which exists throughout the Division, but good team work is born of a thorough knowledge of and confidence in the ability of each member of the team and this cannot exist without a long period of hard work and training. Further it implies complete loyalty to the team and allows no place for petty jealousies or individualism. I would say therefore that General

Ritchie's tribute to our teamwork is the highest compliment he could pay us.

Those of you who can look back to the conditions of May 1940 in Ireland — conditions of complete lack of transport and negligible equipment — will realise, as I do, how far we have gone since those days, and the immense amount of work which has been put into it by everybody to achieve the present team.

Battles cannot be won without paying the cost and we have had heavy casualties through I am thankful to say that the numbers who have made the supreme sacrifice are astonishingly few considering the almost continuous fighting in which the Division has been engaged throughout the campaign. I feel at this moment we should pay tribute to those whose gallantry contributed so much to our successes but who are unable to be with us now at the moment of our supreme triumph.

I would end on a personal note. I have had the honour of commanding 53rd (W) Division *for the last 2½ years*. It has been and will always be a matter of great pride and satisfaction to me that I have been privileged to be in charge of the final preparation of the Division for war and to have seen the campaign through with you all to its successful end. I wish to acknowledge with gratitude the unfailing loyalty, understanding and support I have received at all times from all Commanders of whatever grade, from all Staffs, and, indeed, from all ranks of the Division, which has made my work so simple and at the same time pleasant. I am most grateful to you all.

(Signed) D. K. ROSS
Maj-Gen
Comd, 53 (W) Div.
British Liberation
Army,
8 May 45

Bibliography

Barclay, Brigadier C. N. *History of 53rd Welsh Division (1956)*
Bolland, A. D., OBE, MBE *Team Spirit* (1946)
Booth, P. *The Oxfordshire & Buckinghamshire Light Infantry* (1971)
Brereton, Wallace *Salford Boy Goes to War : 81st Field Reg* (1991)
Brett, Lt Col G.A. *History South Wales Borderers and Monmouthshire Regt* (1953)
Burden, Brigadier G. W. P. N. *History East Lancashire Regt* (1953)
Cowburn, Philip M. *Welsh Spearhead, History 53rd Recce Regt* (1946)
de Courcy, J. / Lomas, Maj Gen C. E. N. *History Welch Regt* (1952)
Davies, Major R. B. S. *The Seventh [Royal Welch Fusiliers]* (1950)
van Gent, Luc *October 1944, Den Bosch* (1990)
Kemp, P. K. / Graves, J. *Red Dragon [Royal Welch Fusiliers]* (1960)
Laugher, Lt Col F. F. / Roberts, Hugh *History 6th Bn Royal Welch Fusiliers* (1946)
Machin, J. *1/5th Bn — the Welch Regt* (1945)
Milligan, Desmond P. B. *View from a Forgotten Hedgerow* (1993)
More, J. N. / Phillips W. L. C. *Monmouthshire Volunteer Yeomanry* (1958)
Neville, J. E. H. *History 43rd Light Infantry* (1954)
Petty, Ned *So many Bridges — One Sappers War*
Roberts, John D. *Enshrined in Stone [Ox & Bucks LI]* (1994)
Roberts, John D. *Archivist 43rd Light Infantry*
Russell, John *No Triumphant Procession (1993)*
Watts, L. B. Proud Heritage [Highland Light Infantry] (1963)
Ward, Major C. H. Dudley *History of 53rd Division 1915-1918* (1927)
Brief History 81st Field Regt RA (1946)

PERSONAL JOURNALS

Abbot, 'Bud', 'C' Sqn 53rd Recce Regt
Bolland, David, OBE, MBE, journal/diary, Division HQ
Carmichael, A. (Mac), Journal Brigade HQ
Crozier, Lt Col H. B. D., Journal 1st Manchester Regt
Cutcliffe, Major Nick P., 4th Bn Royal Welch Fusiliers

Dean, Major R. N., MC, 2nd Monmouthshire Bn
Henderson, David, diary, 53rd Recce Regt
Isherwood, Herbert, Diary, Journal 13 FDS
Ottewell, John A., (and poems) *A Cry from the Heart*
Pender, Lt Col G. C. R. L., CBE, 1st Bn Highland Light Infantry
Thomas, Mostyn W, 1/5 Bn The Welch Regt

Index